MYTHS

AN ILLUSTRATED GUIDE TO THEIR ORIGINS AND MEANINGS

& LEGENDS

METRO BOOKS
New York

MYTHS

AN ILLUSTRATED GUIDE TO THEIR ORIGINS AND MEANINGS

& LEGENDS

PHILIP WILKINSON

METRO BOOKS
New York

METRO BOOKS
New York

An Imprint of Sterling Publishing
387 Park Avenue South
New York, NY 10016

© 2009 by Dorling Kindersley Ltd

DK London
Senior Editors Sam Atkinson, Paula Regan
Editors Patrick Newman, Manisha Thakkar
US Editor Elizabeth Brais
Project Art Editor Anna Hall
Designers Dean Morris, Adam Walker
Jacket Designer Mark Penfound
Managing Editor Debra Wolter
Managing Art Editor Karen Self
Art Director Bryn Walls
Publisher Jonathan Metcalf
Associate Publisher Liz Wheeler
Production Editors Joanna Byrne, Luca Frassinetti
Production Controller Inderjit Bhullar
Picture Researcher Roland Smithies
Illustrations Anshu Bhatnagar and Debajyoti Dutta
DK Delhi
Project Editor Rohan Sinha
Editors Suchismita Banerjee,
Kingshuk Ghoshal
Design Manager Arunesh Talapatra
Project Designer Tannishtha Chakraborty
Designers Mitun Banerjee, Mahua Mandal, Ivy Roy
Illustration co-ordinator Malavika Talukder
DTP co-ordinator Balwant Singh
DTP Jagtar Singh, Preetam Singh
Head of Publishing Aparna Sharma

ISBN 978-1-4351-5199-4
A catalog record for this book is available from
the Library of Congress.

Manufactured in China

2 4 6 8 10 9 7 5 3 1

www.sterlingpublishing.com

CONTENTS

INTRODUCTION

Myths—stories of the gods, of heroes, and of great cosmic events—are told in all of the world's many cultures. They deal with the deepest, most fundamental issues: the creation of the universe and of the human race, the nature of the gods and spirits, what happens to us when we die, and how the world will end. They examine love and jealousy, war and peace, good and evil. Myths explore these crucial issues with intriguing plots, vivid characters, memorable scenes, and concepts that touch our deepest emotions; and so they have become eternally fascinating.

Myths began as tales told around the fire by successive generations, and in places they are still passed on orally. Later, with the invention of writing, people began to write their myths down and adapt them in new ways—turning them into plays, poems, or novels, for example.

Some of the world's greatest literature, from the Greek epics of Homer to the sagas of the early Icelandic writers, are based on much older myths that were originally told orally.

MYRIAD MYTHS

Because of their oral roots, myths are not set in stone. Each one, endlessly retold, has spawned variations. Often, there is no single "correct" version of a myth. The name of a god will change from one tribe to the next; a twist in a tale will be explained in different ways by neighboring groups. Written versions of a myth multiply the retellings still further.

This book can only tell a fraction of the world's myths, and usually only gives one version of each story. But it does contain a generous selection of myths from around the globe, including many from the cultures of

SOME CULTURES HAVE THOUSANDS OF DEITIES, SO THE SCOPE FOR VARIATIONS IN THEIR MYTHS IS ALMOST INFINITE.

Europe that, because they have been written down and widely circulated, have had an enormous influence across the world.

COSMOS AND PEOPLE

Among the seemingly endless variety of myths are common themes. Nearly every mythology starts with the question: "How did the universe begin?" Often, a shadowy creator takes the first step; a god, perhaps, who wills himself into being. Frequently, the creator is faced with a cosmic egg. In one variation of the Chinese creation myth, for instance, the god Pan Gu has to break such an egg to form the land and sky. Sometimes the creator has to fetch land from the depths of a primal ocean—like the

Earth Diver, a common figure in Native American myths. In other myths the world is the offspring of a male and a female creator.

Often, people come much later. Usually they are molded from clay or carved from wood. Like human sculptors, the gods often make several false starts. Myths from Mexico to Greece tell of three versions of people, only the last being right. Sometimes the first people are male, and when they begin to die the gods make women so that the people can reproduce.

GODS AND THEIR POWERS

Most cultures have a large number of gods or spirits—sometimes thousands, because there are spirits everywhere. In places as far apart as

FOR EARLY PEOPLES, THE EXISTENCE OF DEITIES EXPLAINED WHY THE SUN SHONE AND WHERE THE RAINS CAME FROM.

Japan and Africa, every rock, stream, lake, and hill may have its own spirit. Many are local deities, worshipped mainly by the people who live nearby and share their sacred space.

Yet even in cultures that have thousands of deities there are "core" groups of widely known gods with special powers. There are gods of the sun, the rain, the sea, the sky, the mountains, and the rivers. Specific gods look after hunting, farming, love, childbirth, war, and death. The myths involving these gods tend to relate closely to their roles.

Many other myths involve mortals with extraordinary superhuman powers. These heroes accomplish apparently impossible tasks, win battles single-handedly, and even visit the

Underworld. They may also be culture heroes, who teach people important skills such as fire-making. Their achievements are often so great that they become gods when they die.

MYTHS OF THE ELEMENTS

Among the most prominent gods are those of the elements, notably the sun and the rain. They determined whether crops grew, so the sun and weather gods were often the most widely worshipped of all the gods. From the Inca sun god Inti to the Greek sky god Zeus, they were supremely powerful.

Some of the most familiar mythical themes concern the elements. Many cultures have a myth in which the sun disappears, depriving the world of food and warmth and explaining night and day. Other cultures, such as China and parts of Africa, have a myth in which there is too much sunlight, which the gods reduce, or counter with night. Worldwide, wrathful gods send great floods, sometimes wiping out all but one human family before normality is restored. Stories like these explain natural disasters and encourage people to honour the gods, so that they will not unleash their anger; they are also gripping tales of adventure and rescue.

THE IMPORTANCE OF MYTHS

Myths reinforce the cultural identity of the people who tell them. For the Aborigines of Australia, the origin myths of each tribe tell not only of the ancestors, but of the routes they took across the land when they brought each natural feature into being: the land, its people, and their myths are united inextricably. Myths were just as important to the ancient Greeks, who named their greatest city, Athens, after its patron goddess, Athena; to the Incas, who believed their rulers to be descended from the sun god himself; and to the Norse, whose warriors tried to emulate their great god Odin.

The vitality and importance of myths is seen not only in their countless retellings, but in the way their gods, heroes, and creatures have inspired artists. From China to ancient Rome, artists have painted and carved images of the gods, an activity that is sometimes itself an act of worship, sometimes more simply a celebration of the deities and their deeds.

Myths arise from an intimate relationship between people and the natural and spirit worlds—something so many of us have lost. They operate on the borders between reality and fantasy, celebrate oddity and uncertainty, and describe terrifying cosmic forces. But they also deal with great excitement and inspiration. Myths are the most enthralling stories we have, because they touch our hearts and minds and reach to the very core of our being.

EUROPE

▲ **Altar to the goddess Fortuna**
This altar comes from the city of Cerveteri, built by the Etruscans, who were the Italian
forerunners of the Romans. It depicts a sacrifice to Fortuna, a goddess of destiny who
steered the course of people's lives and who was also later worshipped by the Romans.

CLASSICAL EUROPE

The myths of ancient Greece and Rome, with their tales of the great loves, rivalries, and achievements of the Classical deities and heroes, are some of the most familiar stories in all world literature.

The civilization of ancient Greece, which reached its zenith in the 5th century BCE, was founded not by one large nation or empire, but in a series of city-states, each of which had its own traditions, culture, and deities. As a result, many of the gods and goddesses of ancient Greece had local followings. For example, Athena was closely associated with Athens, Zeus with Olympia, and Apollo with Delphi. But ancient Greeks everywhere came to recognize a large group of deities who interacted with one another—and with the world of people—rather in the manner of an extended human family, with its myriad close relatives. Members of this great pantheon of gods and goddesses fell in love and had relationships—even with mere mortals—had immense personal and political rivalries, and frequently went to war.

▲ **Sicilian temple**
Classical temples such as this one in Agrigento in Sicily were rectangular structures enclosed by rows of columns. Inside was a room with a cult statue of the temple deity, where valuable offerings such as gold and silver were left.

THE GREEKS AND THEIR GODS
The ancient Greeks worshipped their deities by leaving offerings to them in temples, and honored them by holding regular festivals. Much is known about this worship because many of their temples, together with ritual objects and cult statues, have survived, and ancient Greek writers described religious rituals such as making offerings of food and wine. In return, worshippers hoped that the deities would look kindly on them, since most gods and goddesses were said to take a keen interest in human affairs. In the mythical great war between Greece and Troy, for example, every stage of the conflict, together with the final outcome, was influenced as much by the actions of the deities as by what the men of the two sides actually achieved on the battlefield.

The myths of Greece also show this interaction between deities and humans in the guise of numerous heroes: figures who are mortal but, because they often have one divine parent, have some of the characteristics of the divine. Stories of heroes like Heracles and Jason, involving great adventures and journeys as far as the Underworld, have been endlessly retold.

AN ENDURING INFLUENCE
When Greek civilization declined, the myths lived on in various ways. As the Romans built up their vast empire, they adopted local deities wherever they went. They found the gods and goddesses of Greece especially appealing, and combined their personalities with their own deities to create figures that were closely related but subtly different. The sky god Jupiter, for example, is the Roman equivalent of the Greek god Zeus, but differs from him in several ways: the Romans linked him with justice, with the keeping of oaths, and with their magistrates, who made sacrifices to him when they took up their office.

The art, architecture, and mythological depictions of the Greeks were also preserved and had a longer-term impact, particularly on artists and writers in Western Europe during the Renaissance (c.1350–c.1550).

▲ **The sacred robe of Athena**
This scene is part of a frieze—a series of carved reliefs—that once decorated the Parthenon, the great temple of Athena on the Acropolis in Athens dating from 438–432 BCE. It depicts temple officials holding up the sacred robe of Athena.

ANCIENT GREEK CREATION

Classical mythology contains several accounts of the creation, telling how creator deities gave the universe shape and form before the first races to inhabit the cosmos were born. These creation stories give the background to the birth of the gods and goddesses who dominate much of Classical mythology and who were believed to dwell on Mount Olympus.

THE MYTH

In the beginning there was nothing but a vast, dark void called Chaos. Out of this emptiness the creative force emerged. The various Greek accounts of creation give this force different names. In some, she was a goddess called Eurynome, who coupled with a primal serpent called Orphion to begin the process of creation, while in others, she was Gaia, Mother Earth.

THE PRIMAL EGG

Eurynome took the form of a dove and laid a great egg, around which Orphion coiled. Warmed by the serpent's coils, the egg hatched, and out of it came all things that exist: Uranus, the sky; Ourea, the mountains; Pontus, the sea; and all the stars and planets. Gaia, the Earth, and her mountains and rivers emerged from the egg at the same time. When all these things were born, Eurynome and Orphion travelled to Mount Olympus and made their home there. But Orphion declared himself sole creator of the cosmos, and Eurynome punished him for this by first kicking him and then, when he persisted, by banishing him to the Underworld forever.

MOTHER EARTH

Others say that the primal creator was Gaia. She and Uranus, the sky, made love, and Uranus sent life-giving water onto her surface. From this union were born not just

▶ **Orphion**
The serpent Orphion coiled itself around the egg laid by Eurynome, which contained the beginnings of all things that exist.

the lakes and seas, but also the earliest races of creatures that inhabited the Earth. The first of these were the Hundred-Handed Giants, each of whom had 50 heads and 100 arms branching out from their shoulders. Then came the Cyclopes, a race of one-eyed giants who were skilled in metalworking. Some say that later they attacked the god Asclepius, so his father, Apollo, killed them. Their ghosts still haunt the caves beneath the volcano Mount Etna.

Others claim that the power and skill of the Cyclopes frightened Uranus, who thought that they might rob him of his power. So Uranus banished them to the Underworld. The most important race produced by Gaia and Uranus were a group of giants known as the Titans. They became the first rulers of Earth and started families with their female counterparts, the Titanesses. Their children became some of the most powerful gods and goddesses, such as Helios, the sun god, and Eos, the goddess of dawn, who were the children of Hyperion. Most influential of all were the children of Cronus, the leader of the Titans, who became the deities of Mount Olympus.

▲ **The dove**
The story of the primal goddess Eurynome taking the form of a dove is a very early one that exists mainly in fragments of ancient Greek writings.

KEY CHARACTERS

The ancient Greek cosmos begins with shadowy characters whose main purpose is to get creation started, but who do not have the highly developed personalities or complex myths associated with the later Olympian deities. Eurynome, for example, is described as the goddess of all things, a figure who can dance across the primal chaos, brood on the water, or take the form of the bird that lays the universal egg. Other characters, such as Cronus, originally a harvest god, preside over natural forces. The Titaness Rhea was a primal goddess like Gaia, a maternal figure strongly identified with the Earth. The Titans also ruled the various heavenly bodies. Phoebe and Atlas ruled the moon, while Rhea and Cronus governed the planet Saturn. Theia and Hyperion were the rulers of the sun.

▲ Gaia, the mother goddess
With her consort Uranus, Gaia was said to be mother of such geographical features as seas, rivers, and streams.

▶ Cronus eating his child
Famous for swallowing the first five of his children, the Titan Cronus lived with his consort Rhea in a rocky citadel on Mount Othrys.

▲ Uranus
Uranus was castrated by his son, Cronus, who was incited by his mother, Gaia, since Uranus had imprisoned her other children.

◀ Rhea tricking Cronus
To save her sixth child from being swallowed by his father, Rhea handed Cronus a stone wrapped in swaddling clothes.

THE GIANTS AND CYCLOPES

Among the first creatures in the universe were races of giants, such as the one-eyed Cyclopes and the Hundred-Handed Giants. These races had superhuman strength and because of this (and their disturbing appearance) the Titans banished them to the Underworld. Later myths, however, tell of a number of Cyclopes who found a route back to Earth, where they lived as shepherds. Most of these Earth-dwelling Cyclopes were gentle, but a few liked to eat human flesh.

▲ Cyclopes
The name Cyclopes means "round-eyes," and these creatures were so called because of the single eye in the middle of their forehead.

◀ Hundred-Handed Giants
The Hundred-Handed Giants lived in Tartarus, the deepest part of the Underworld, guarding those who were condemned to dwell there.

▲ The three Hesperides
The three daughters of the Titan Atlas were called the Hesperides, which means "daughters of the evening." They tended a beautiful garden with a tree bearing golden apples.

▶ The three Fates
The three Fates were the daughters of Night. Clotho was believed to spin the thread of life, and Lachesis measured its length. Atropos, the third daughter, cut it at the moment of death.

THE TRINITIES

The Titans and other primal beings produced a number of children who had the status of lesser deities, but could still have great influence over the lives of others. They often came in groups of three, such as the three Hesperides and the three Fates. The latter were endowed with tremendous power, controlling the lives not only of humans but also of the gods—the Greeks believed that no one could escape the power of fate.

COSMIC WAR

The gods of Mount Olympus, who are the dominant characters in most of the myths of ancient Greece, took control of the universe by fighting a long war with their ancestors and rivals, the Titans. The story of this Cosmic War, which is also known as the Titanomachia, involves many themes—such as oracles, lost children, and revenge—that are prominent in later myths. At the end of the struggle, Zeus emerged as the supreme ruler of the entire cosmos, and the defeated Titans were banished to the Underworld.

THE MYTH

An oracle had told the Titan Cronus that one of his children would kill him. As a result, whenever a child was born to his wife, Rhea, Cronus would swallow it. After Cronus had disposed of five children, Rhea hatched a plan. When their next child, Zeus, was born, she sent him to Crete, where Amalthea, a friendly goat-nymph, brought up the child. Meanwhile, Rhea wrapped a stone in swaddling clothes and gave it to Cronus to swallow.

▲ **Bronze shield and sword**
The Greeks used to make fine bronze weapons. Myths about metalworkers like the Cyclopes show how vital these skills were to them.

THE RETURN OF ZEUS

After Zeus grew up, one day his foster-mother, Amalthea, revealed his true identity to him and narrated how Cronus had swallowed all his siblings. An enraged Zeus then resolved

to take revenge on his father for this crime. When he declared his intention to the Titaness Metis, she told him that he could still rescue his brothers and sisters. She gave him a drug that, when it was

◀ **In battle**
Hurling heavy rocks was one way in which the gods and giants attacked each other. This painting shows a scene from the Gigantomachia, the battle between the gods and Gaia's children, the giants.

administered to Cronus, would make him vomit up all his children. Zeus followed Metis's instructions and rescued his siblings—the gods Poseidon and Hades, and the goddesses Hera, Hestia, and Demeter. Then Zeus freed the Cyclopes, the one-eyed giants whom Uranus had banished to the Underworld. The gods and the Cyclopes led by Zeus declared war on Cronus.

The two sides were equally matched and the conflict seemed destined to last forever. But the Cyclopes were master metalworkers, and they created a number of magical weapons, including a thunderbolt for Zeus, a trident for Poseidon, and a helmet for Hades that made the wearer invisible. These eventually gave the gods the upper hand in the conflict. At the end of the war, the gods controlled the cosmos and the Titans were imprisoned in Tartarus, a region in the Underworld full of fearsome monsters guarded by the Hundred-Handed Giants.

FURTHER BATTLES

Gaia, outraged that her children had been dispatched to Tartarus, began another war against the gods, bringing the Giants, who were also her children, into battle against Zeus and the other gods and goddesses. The gods were finally the victors in this battle, known as the Gigantomachia, and the Giants were buried beneath volcanoes. But even then their rule was not secure. Zeus was challenged one last time by Typhon, yet another of Gaia's offspring. Although Zeus injured Typhon—a huge creature with many heads and countless legs and arms—with his thunderbolt, the monster continued to hurl enormous rocks at him. Zeus retaliated by attacking the rocks with thunderbolts, so that they rebounded on Typhon, knocking the strength out of him. Finally, Zeus hurled him down to Tartarus. His rule was secure at last.

WEAPONS OF THE GODS

The deities of ancient Greece resembled humans in several ways. When the gods fought a war, the Greeks imagined them as beings in human form, fighting with weapons. These weapons were made for them by Hephaestus, the god of metalworking, craftsmanship, and fire, who was a kind of celestial blacksmith. But the weapons of the gods had powers that went far beyond earthly swords and daggers. When Zeus wielded his thunderbolt or Poseidon struck his trident, the entire cosmos shook. Hephaestus sometimes made armor for mortal heroes like Achilles, and when a hero showed special prowess in arms, people said his weaponry must have been made by Hephaestus.

◄ Trident
Poseidon's weapon was the trident, which he used to stir up storms, to shake the ground—thereby causing earthquakes—and even to fork up new islands from the sea bed.

► Thunderbolt
Zeus used a thunderbolt as his weapon. As well as making the whole sky shake with its power, he could aim it with precision, either to kill an opponent or to shatter his opponent's weapon.

▲ Helmet
Hades's helmet made him invisible, so that he could attack his enemies without being detected. Because he ruled the dark realms of the Underworld, Hades was never depicted in ancient Greek art.

ATLAS

Son of the Titan Iapetus and a sea nymph called Clymene, Atlas ruled a large island kingdom called Atlantis. He had many subjects, but they became degenerate, so the gods decided to punish them by destroying the entire race. They sent a great flood that killed all the people and sank the island beneath the sea. Resentful towards the gods at the loss of his kingdom, Atlas led the Titans in the Cosmic War. When the gods won the war, they punished Atlas for his part in it by making him hold the sky on his shoulders forever.

► Bearer of the skies
The celestial globe held by Atlas was sometimes mistaken for the Earth, leading both to the belief that he held the world on his shoulders, and to the use of Atlas's name for books of maps.

DISGUISES OF THE GODS

One enduring theme in Greek mythology is the way in which the gods could disguise themselves. Deities used their shape-changing ability to serve different purposes—from fighting battles to pursuing loved ones. When they were challenged by the monster Typhon, all the deities except the brave Athena fled to Egypt, where they disguised themselves as different creatures and went into hiding. However, Zeus eventually forsook his disguise and came forth to fight the monster.

▲ The crow
While hiding, Apollo took the form of a crow, a rather unassuming disguise considering that he was the god of music.

▲ The ram
The normally brave Zeus disguised himself as a ram, a creature that was aggressive and impressively armed with a pair of horns.

◄ The cat
Artemis, who was a huntress and the goddess of the chase, chose to transform herself into a cat, also a hunting creature.

TYPHON AND THE WINDS

Gaia bore the fire-breathing monster Typhon, who was the god of winds, with the intention of creating a son so powerful that he could defeat the gods. Some accounts say that after Zeus overcame him, he was condemned to the Underworld. Other versions of the story relate how he survived and went to live on Mount Olympus. There he made peace with the gods, occasionally giving birth to mighty storms called typhoons. Certain myths also claim he dwelled in Mount Etna where he spewed out smoke and lava.

► Typhon in hell
In the most widespread retelling of the myth, Typhon was imprisoned in the Underworld after his defeat by Zeus.

THE TWELVE OLYMPIANS

The twelve dominant deities in Greek myth lived on
Mount Olympus and controlled life on Earth: they were
Zeus (king of the gods), Aphrodite, Apollo, Ares, Artemis,
Athena, Demeter, Hephaestus, Hera, Hermes, Hestia, and
Poseidon. This family tree shows their relationships to
each other, as well as to some of the Titans, such as
Cronus and Rhea, and a number of lesser gods.

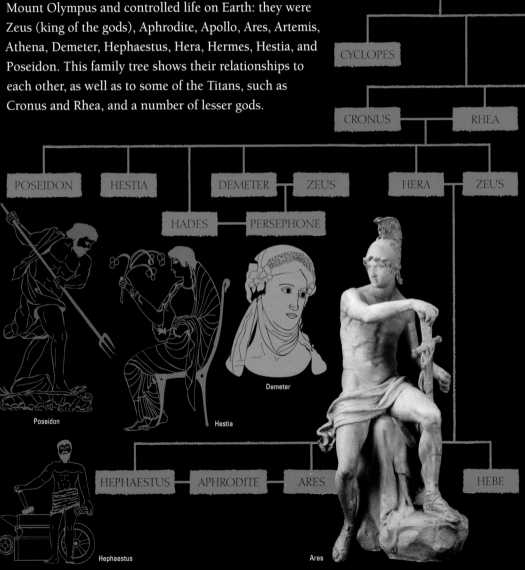

GAIA

CYCLOPES

CRONUS — RHEA

POSEIDON   HESTIA   DEMETER — ZEUS   HERA — ZEUS

HADES — PERSEPHONE

Demeter

Hestia

Poseidon

HEPHAESTUS — APHRODITE — ARES   HEBE

Hephaestus

Ares

Aphrodite

URANUS

APHRODITE

GIANTS

MONSTERS

Zeus and Hera

COEUS

PHOEBE

OCEANUS

TETHYS

ZEUS

LETO

ASTERIA

Artemis

APOLLO

ARTEMIS

CLYMENE

IAPETUS

ZEUS

METIS

PROMETHEUS

EPIMETHEUS

ATHENA

PLEONE

ATLAS

Athena

MAIA

ZEUS

HERMES

Hermes

Apollo

ZEUS

Zeus, son of the Titans Cronus and Rhea, was the god of the sky and thunder. His most feared weapon was his thunderbolt, fashioned by the Cyclopes. He became ruler of the gods when he led them in their defeat of the Titans during the Cosmic War. Though he married the goddess Hera, he was famous for his many other sexual conquests, which included goddesses, nymphs, and mortal women. Some of the numerous children of these liaisons wielded immense power over the people of Earth.

▶ **Zeus the ruler**
Although he was the king of the gods, Zeus generally left the work of influencing the lives of humans to his many children, using his personal power sparingly.

THE DISGUISES OF ZEUS

Zeus's shining body could terrify mortals and his thunderbolt could burn to death anything that came too near. For these reasons, and because many of his sexual partners were unwilling, Zeus adopted various guises when approaching his loves. He charmed Europa by taking the form of a bull, got through Danaë's prison by turning into a shower of gold, became a satyr to rape Antiope, a princess of Thebes, and approached Leda as a swan. He tricked Alcmene by disguising himself as her husband, Amphitryon, and turned into an eagle to carry off Ganymede, a young man he had fallen in love with. Zeus could disguise the objects of his love too, turning Io, a priestess of Hera, into a cow and Callisto, a nymph of Artemis, into a bear to allay the suspicions of his wife.

◀ **Europa and the bull**
Europa, a Phoenician maiden, saw Zeus in the form of a white bull. Just as she stroked it lovingly and climbed on its back, the bull sped away with her.

◀ **Danaë and the shower of gold**
Imprisoned by her father because her child was destined to kill him, Danaë fell prey to Zeus in the form of a golden shower.

▶ **Leda and the swan**
Zeus took the form of a swan to woo the Spartan queen, Leda. Their children included Helen of Troy and the Dioscuri .

ZEUS AND HERA

Zeus took his sister, Hera, the goddess of marriage, as his wife. Hera had been ignored when the great gods Zeus, Poseidon, and Hades divided up the cosmos between them, so marrying Zeus and ruling the sky as his consort gave her the power she had been denied. Most of the stories about Hera recount the jealousy she felt at her husband's affairs and the vendettas she launched against her rivals. When Io was transformed into a cow, Hera sent a fly to sting her perpetually and drive her mad. When the goddess Leto was expecting Zeus's children, Hera banned her from giving birth on the mainland or on any island. She tricked Semele into demanding that Zeus appear to her in all his glory. When he agreed reluctantly, Semele was burned to ashes by his powerful thunderbolt. Hera also persecuted the offspring of Zeus's affairs, including Dionysus and the hero Heracles, whom she drove insane—as a result of which he killed his own wife and children in a fit of madness. However, the effects on Hera's victims were rarely permanent.

▲ **The divine couple**
Although Hera was famously jealous, her worshippers stressed the importance of marriage, and some artists portrayed her and Zeus as a tender, loving couple.

※

▶ **The three Graces**
The three Graces accompanied Aphrodite and Eros. They brought people happiness, especially in love, and their breath helped plants flourish.

THE CHILDREN OF ZEUS

Zeus had dozens of children by his various partners, and some of these offspring had prominent parts in other Greek myths—either as immortals who ruled different aspects of the cosmos, or as heroes whose exploits became famous among mortals. Zeus and his wife, Hera, were the parents of deities such as Ares (the god of war) and Hebe (the handmaiden of the gods). Hermes was the product of his union with Maia, and his affair with Metis resulted in the birth of Athena. With Leto, Zeus fathered the twin deities Apollo and Artemis, while with Eurynome he produced the three Graces. His liaison with the Titaness named Mnemosyne (memory) produced the Muses, and his affair with Ananke produced the Fates. Among his mortal loves, Europa was the mother of Sarpedon (a hero of the Trojan War), Minos (the King of Crete), and Rhadamanthus (who became a judge of the dead). Danaë gave birth to the hero Perseus, while Alcmene was the mother of the famed Heracles.

THE MUSES

The daughters of Zeus and Mnemosyne were the Muses, who presided over the arts and were associated with Apollo in his role as the god of the arts. There were originally said to be many Muses, who together inspired poetry and other arts, but later writers named nine, giving each a specific art. The nine Muses were Calliope (Muse of poetic inspiration), Clio (history), Erato (lyric poetry), Euterpe (instrumental music), Melpomene (tragedy), Polyhymnia (harmony), Terpsichore (dance and choral song), Thalia (comedy), and Urania (scholarship or astronomy). The Muses were said to dwell on mountains, where their singing and dancing charmed and inspired all those who encountered them.

The Muses with Apollo

THE CREATION OF HUMANKIND

Unlike many cultures, ancient Greece did not have a single story narrating the origins of humanity. Greek myths mention several attempts at creating humans, or mortals as they were known. Three of these attempts failed before the current race of humans finally emerged, although it is not clear who is responsible for their creation. However, the origins of key cultural skills, such as fire-making, are firmly attributed to the Titan Prometheus, who is portrayed as a friend of humanity.

THE MYTH

The first attempt at creating a human race took place when the Titans, led by Cronus, ruled the cosmos. The result was the Golden Race, a group of people who lived an ideal existence without work or ageing, and for whom life was one long feast. When the people of the Golden Race finally died, their death was like a peaceful sleep. Nevertheless, it left the Earth unpopulated.

Intent on filling up the void, the Olympians created the Silver Race, who lived for a long time but grew very slowly to maturity. Their children were brought up carefully by their mothers, and spent one hundred years as babies before reaching adulthood. However, they turned out to be dull and unintelligent people, fighting continuously among themselves, and once they became adults they tended to die quickly. These qualities, together with their refusal to worship or even respect the gods, exasperated Zeus, so he banished them to the Underworld. Zeus then crafted a new race out of clay. The people of this race wore bronze armor and used tools made of the same metal, so they were called the Bronze Race. Like the Silver Race, they were aggressive, and destroyed themselves in ruthless battles.

▲ **The forge of Hephaestus**
Prometheus found his fire in the workshop of Hephaestus, where the craftsman god (and, some say, the Cyclopes) forged Zeus's thunderbolts and other powerful weapons.

▶ **Prometheus steals fire**
Prometheus stole a spark from Mount Olympus and wrapped it in a stalk of fennel, where it burned safely as he carried it to humanity.

THE HUMAN RACE

Finally, the current race of humans appeared. Some say that the great Titan craftsman, Prometheus, was its creator. Whether or not he actually created humanity, Prometheus certainly became its protector. He taught humans many important skills, including navigation and medicine, and showed them how to make sacrifices, by keeping some of the meat for themselves and offering the rest to the gods. Once, the people killed a bull but could not agree on which part to offer the gods. Prometheus cleverly wrapped the meat in the bull's skin, and the bones in its fat. Zeus chose the bones covered in fat, and became so angry at the deception that he refused to give fire to the humans.

THE THEFT OF FIRE

Taking the side of humanity, Prometheus stole fire from heaven and carried it to Earth so that the people could cook their food and heat their homes. Zeus punished Prometheus for the theft by having him chained to a rock, where an eagle came to peck at his liver every day.

THE GOLDEN AGE

During the Golden Age, the world was ruled by Cronus (known to the Romans as Saturn). It was a time of peace and tranquillity, as there was no war or injustice, and the Golden Race did not have to work because enough food was readily available from plants and trees. In later eras, the Golden Age became a byword for a time in the distant past when things were much better than the present. The idea of the Golden Age became fashionable in the Renaissance (c.1350–c.1550), when Italian artists and writers rediscovered the culture of ancient Greece, and this Classical era became a favorite subject for painters.

◄ **The Golden Race**
Renaissance artists saw the Golden Age as a time of such peace that humans could live side by side with wild animals without any fear of attack.

► **Cronus**
Despite his violence towards his own children, Cronus is often seen as a gentle, just, and kind ruler of the Golden Age. He was worshipped as a harvest deity.

PROMETHEUS BOUND

As punishment for stealing fire from the gods, Zeus had Prometheus chained to a rock in a place said to be on the borders of Earth and Chaos. Here, he was condemned to suffer while an eagle pecked at his liver, which constantly repaired itself so that the torture could continue. Zeus decreed that Prometheus should remain bound until another creature offered to be bound in his place. After thousands of years, a wounded centaur called Cheiron offered to take Prometheus's place. When he arrived at the rock, Zeus turned Cheiron into a constellation of stars, while the Greek hero Heracles killed the eagle, ending Prometheus's agony.

▲ **Aeschylus**
The Greek dramatist Aeschylus, who lived in the 5th-century BCE, wrote several plays about the myth of Prometheus.

► **Prometheus's punishment**
The eagle came each morning to peck at Prometheus's liver all day long, then left in the evening. By night the liver repaired itself, ready for the next day's torment.

PANDORA

Zeus wanted to punish the humans after Prometheus stole fire for them, so he (or, some say, Hephaestus) created a beautiful mortal woman called Pandora. She married Prometheus's brother, Epimetheus, who took her to Earth. The gods gave her many gifts, which she kept in a jar. When she opened the jar, it contained plagues and disasters, which condemned humanity to a life marred by misery. The only positive thing in the jar was hope, the sole consolation for the human race.

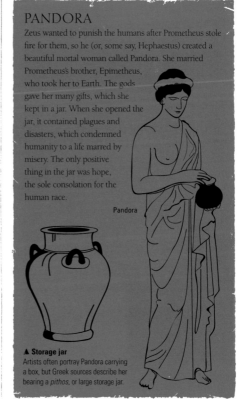

Pandora

▲ **Storage jar**
Artists often portray Pandora carrying a box, but Greek sources describe her bearing a *pithos*, or large storage jar.

APOLLO

Portrayed as a handsome young man, the god Apollo had power over many aspects of life. Patron of archers, his bow brought pain to humans, but he was also a god of healing and father to the mythical physician Asclepius. He was the god of music and the arts, and an accomplished player of the lyre. The son of Zeus and Leto, Apollo was also worshipped as the god of light and the sun.

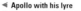

THE LYRE OF APOLLO

Once when Apollo went on a journey in pursuit of one of his lovers, he left his fine herd of cattle untended. Hermes, who had long admired the creatures, saw that they were left alone and decided to steal them and hide them in a cave. But Apollo, who had the gift of prophecy, knew exactly where the cattle were and went to find Hermes and demand his animals back. When Apollo arrived, Hermes began playing an instrument that he had created from the intestines of one of Apollo's cattle. Apollo was enchanted on hearing the music of the lyre, and agreed to exchange it for the cattle.

◀ **Apollo with his lyre**
The lyre of Apollo (also called the *kithara*) was originally made with the strings stretched across the shell of a tortoise.

◀ **Hermes**
Both a trickster and the messenger of the gods, Hermes wore winged sandals to enable him to fly between Olympus, Earth, and the Underworld.

▼ **Eros**
Eros was the son of Aphrodite, from whom he got his beauty, and Ares, from whom he inherited his love for mischief.

APOLLO AND DAPHNE

When Apollo scorned the archery skills of Eros, the god of love, Eros decided to take revenge. He shot Apollo with a gold-headed arrow, to make him fall in love, but shot the object of his desire, Daphne, with an arrow tipped with lead, so that she would reject him. Apollo chased Daphne, but she would not give in to him and, as she ran, she prayed to Zeus to be transformed into something that would save her from Apollo's pursuit. Zeus responded by turning her into a laurel tree.

▶ **Daphne**
When Zeus turned the fleeing Daphne into a laurel tree, Apollo made a wreath from her leaves, which he wore as a crown.

APOLLO AND DELPHI

When Zeus's wife, Hera, found out that her husband had had an affair with Leto, she decided to take revenge on her and sent a great serpent, known as the Python, to attack her. The snake lurked around the great peak of Mount Parnassus and laid waste the area of Delphi. Apollo killed the serpent with a bow and arrows given by Hephaestus, the divine craftsman. Afterwards, Delphi became sacred to Apollo, and his shrine was built there. The Pythian Games were held there every four years to commemorate Apollo's triumph over the Python, and Apollo has been associated with Delphi ever since. The activities at the games included poetry and music competitions, in addition to several athletic events.

▲ **The temple at Delphi**
The Temple of Apollo at Delphi, first built around the 7th-century BCE, stands on a hillside and was originally surrounded by statues of mythical Greek heroes.

▶ **Apollo killing the Python**
The god slew the mighty Python with his poison-tipped arrows. The healing power of Apollo was balanced by the ability to kill with the deadly poison and disease his arrows bore.

THE ORACLE OF DELPHI

Apollo had the power of prophecy, and at Delphi, his priestess, known as the Pythia, delivered oracles as she sat on her tripod seat holding laurel leaves and a bowl of water from the Kassotis spring. She answered people's questions while in a trance-like state. These questions could be on matters of political and religious policy, as well as enquiries about the questioner's future. Since the Pythia's words were hard to understand, priests stood by to interpret them for the listeners. However, these interpretations were also puzzling and difficult to understand—but often they came true in the most unpredictable ways.

The Pythia

▲ **Musical duel with Marsyas**
Marsyas was foolish to tangle with Apollo, who tricked him into losing the musical challenge, then punished him for his impudence in one of the cruelest ways imaginable.

THE FLAYING OF MARSYAS

The satyr Marsyas was just as accomplished a performer on the double flute as Apollo was on the lyre. Marsyas thought that he was the better musician and challenged the god to a contest. Apollo agreed on the condition that the winner could punish the loser in any way he chose. No one could decide who was the better player until Apollo suggested they both play their instruments upside-down. This worked with Apollo's lyre, but not with Marsyas's flute, so Apollo was judged the winner. He punished Marsyas by skinning him alive.

POSEIDON AND THE FLOOD

Many ancient Greeks lived on islands or in settlements close to the coast, so their lives were dominated by the sea. Consequently, the sea god Poseidon, a bringer of violent storms, who also controlled natural forces such as earthquakes, was one of the most powerful gods of Mount Olympus. But he longed for more power, and became involved in a dispute with Athena for the great honor of being the patron deity of the city of Athens.

THE MYTH

Poseidon and Athena both wanted to be the controlling deity of the city of Athens. Rather than declaring war and fighting a battle, the two gods decided that they would settle their dispute by competing to provide the best gift for the city's people. The sea god climbed the Acropolis (the hill overlooking Athens); when he reached the top, he struck the ground hard with his trident and a saltwater spring began to flow. Then Athena came to the Acropolis and offered her gift: the first olive tree to grow in the city.

▶ **Poseidon**
The god of the sea is often shown as a bearded man holding a trident and enthroned in a giant clam shell or aboard a shell-like chariot pulled by dolphins or sea horses.

THE GODS' JUDGEMENT

Zeus summoned the other gods from Mount Olympus to judge the gifts and decide which of the two was greater. The appearance of the spring was impressive, but salt water was of little use to the people. The olive tree, on the other hand, provided a source of olives, and their oil was useful for both cooking and lighting. Olive oil was valuable not just to the

Athenians but also to those with whom they traded—so the tree could both nourish the people of Athens and make them rich. They would be able to use the olive wood, too, to construct things. King Cecrops, the ruler of Greece, confirmed that such a tree had never been seen on the Acropolis. After hearing all the evidence, Zeus declared Athena to be the winner of the contest. She became the city's patron deity, and the place was named after her.

THE COMING OF THE FLOOD

Poseidon was furious when he heard the result of the competition. He took up his trident and smote the sea many times, causing a great storm. The waters rose and the plain of Eleusis, where Athens stood, was flooded. The waters covered the plain for a long time, but finally they subsided, allowing the Athenians to repair their city. They built a temple to their new goddess, Athena, who would bring them prosperity, but also made offerings to Poseidon, to placate the angry god.

▶ **The dispute with Athena**
Poseidon with his trident and Athena with her spear made formidable opponents, although they decided to settle their dispute peacefully.

POSEIDON AND THE BEASTS

Poseidon was linked closely with the vitality and energy of animals. Two creatures especially associated with him were the bull and the stallion. Both were singled out by the Greeks for their sexual potency and violence. During his sexual exploits, Poseidon sometimes took the form of a horse, as on the occasion when he was pursuing the goddess Demeter, who had turned herself into a mare. The destructive bull that rose from the sea in some myths, such as that of Hippolytus, is also a manifestation of Poseidon's power.

▲ **Stallion**
One myth tells how the first horse grew from semen that Poseidon had spilled on a rock.

▲ **Pasiphae and the Cretan Bull**
After a curse from Poseidon, the queen of Crete, Pasiphae, fell in love with, and mated with, a bull sent by the sea god. The offspring of this union was the Minotaur.

OTHER CLASSICAL SEA GODS

The Greeks worshipped several other sea gods, although they were not as powerful as Poseidon. Some of them were linked with particular sea creatures. For example, Glaucus was associated with fish, while Proteus was a herder of seals. Others possessed special abilities. Triton, for example, was famous as a musician who played on the conch shell. Proteus was also known for his great wisdom, although he did not like answering people's questions.

▲ **Glaucus**
Originally a fisherman, Glaucus was made immortal when he ate a herb with magical powers. He became one of the minor gods of the sea.

▶ **Proteus**
Renowned for his wisdom, Proteus was called the "ancient one of the sea." He often changed his shape to avoid being questioned.

◀ **Triton**
Half-fish, half-man, Triton was a familiar deity of the sea. Some myths say there were several Tritons.

POSEIDON AND ODYSSEUS

Homer's *Odyssey* describes the return of the tragic hero Odysseus from Troy to Ithaca as a series of mishaps at sea. Most of these were due to Poseidon and came about because Odysseus had blinded the Cyclopes Polyphemus, who was the sea god's son. The poem describes vividly how the god stirred up storms and tempests, which wrecked Odysseus's ship and drowned his companions. Many of the perils Odysseus faced, such as the whirlpool Charybdis, were the offspring of Poseidon.

▶ **Poseidon stirs the waves**
Sometimes Poseidon smote the sea with his trident to create stormy waves, and sometimes he stirred them up with it.

TEMPLES TO POSEIDON

As a powerful deity, Poseidon was widely revered and some of his temples have survived. He was not always worshipped as a sea god —some temples were dedicated to Poseidon Hippios ("Poseidon of horses"), and many people worshipped a form of Poseidon who was a god of plants. At least one of his temples in Greece, though—the temple at Sounion, in Attica—is sited on a spectacular cliff top overlooking the sea, a clear reminder of the deity's sphere of influence. Boat races were held there in honor of the god.

◀ **Temple at Sounion**
Poseidon's temple at Sounion could be seen by ships far out at sea. Now it survives as an evocative ruin, with two rows of columns set on a stone platform.

DIONYSUS

The god of wine, Dionysus, was an anarchic figure who presided over drunkenness and other irrational or altered states, such as religious ecstasy. A shape-changer, he could take the form of an animal but also appeared as a human, when he was often accompanied by revellers or animals. These qualities made him a patron of actors, and plays were regularly performed at the Athenian festivals held in his name.

THE RESCUE OF DIONYSUS

When Zeus, disguised as a mortal, began an affair with Semele, the daughter of King Cadmus and Queen Harmonia of Thebes, his wife, Hera, grew jealous and plotted her revenge. She took the form of an old woman and persuaded Semele to ask the god to appear before her in all his splendor. When he did so, the heat from his thunderbolt killed Semele, who was a mortal. One of the gods—some say Hermes, others the river goddess Dirce—rescued her unborn child, Dionysus, and took him to Zeus, who cut an opening in his thigh and placed the child safely inside until it was ready to be born. When Dionysus emerged from Zeus's thigh, Hera was so angry that she incited the Titans to tear the baby into pieces. His grandmother, Rhea, took pity on Dionysus, put his body back together, and carried him to foster parents. Again, Hera discovered what had happened, so to protect him Rhea disguised the child as a ram.

▲ **Dionysus**
The god of wine in all its aspects, Dionysus has often been portrayed as a handsome young man carrying a cup, with vine leaves in his hair.

▲ **Hera**
In the story of Dionysus, Hera plays her usual role as jealous wife. She defeats her rival Semele, but not Semele's child.

▶ **Semele**
Flames from Zeus's thunderbolt killed Semele. Her story became a popular subject for painters and for the composer Handel, who wrote an opera about her.

CLASSICAL EUROPE

THE JOURNEY OF DIONYSUS

As he grew up, Dionysus became restless and went on a series of long journeys. Wherever he traveled, he became famous for his drunken excesses, which ended in a kind of insane frenzy. Many said that this frenzy was caused by Hera, who was still resentful that the son of Semele had survived. Dionysus was accompanied on his travels by satyrs, led by their king, Silenus. Also among his companions were a group of female followers called the "Maenads." The Maenads were possessed with a kind of madness, in which they worked themselves into an ecstatic frenzy. As they did this, they danced a wild dance, eventually getting so out of control that they would rip apart any creature they came across. The Maenads drew their strength from Dionysus, so that nothing— neither fire nor the sword— could stop their dance or bring them to harm.

▶ **Satyrs**
The offspring of a mountain nymph and a goat, a satyr was half-man, half-goat. Satyrs were famous for getting drunk and for being lewd.

◀ **Maenads**
The Maenads wore sheer dresses and danced to the music of the double flute and tambourine. They had power over wild beasts and were sometimes shown riding panthers.

▶ **Silenus**
A wise old satyr, Silenus led Dionysus's followers. Some myths say he was one of those who brought up the god when he was a child.

THE WINE-DARK SEA

As he travelled around the Mediterranean, Dionysus told those who met and followed him how to harvest the grapes, press them, and turn their juice into wine. When people tasted the results, he became very popular. Once the god was on his travels when he was captured by pirates, who thought he was a wealthy young man. When the pirates tried to tie him up, however, the knots kept untying of their own accord. Dionysus then made the mast and rigging turn into grape vines, and transformed the sea around the ship into wine. The pirates were so frightened by the sight of this that they jumped into the sea.

▶ **Pirate porpoises**
When the terrified pirates jumped into the sea, Dionysus turned them all into porpoises, as depicted in this painting on the inside of a cup from around 530 BCE.

THE TRAGEDY OF PENTHEUS

The dancing journey of Dionysus and the Maenads brought them to Thebes, which was ruled by Pentheus. The young king's mother, Agave, was attracted to Dionysus and became a Maenad, getting drunk and joining the frenzied dance. Pentheus was horrified to see his mother's behavior and decided to try to stop the dance. He turned for advice to Dionysus, who told the king to hide and watch secretly before doing anything. However, the Maenads discovered Pentheus and tore him to pieces.

◀ **Death of Pentheus**
Among the Maenads who attacked Pentheus was his own mother, Agave. In her frenzy, she at first thought she was killing a lion, before realizing it was her son.

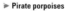

ATHENA

A powerful war goddess, Athena was usually depicted with her shield or protective cloak, known as the aegis. She was also a patron of crafts, especially pottery, weaving, and shipbuilding, and the goddess of the city of Athens. She inherited the wisdom of her mother, Metis, an attribute that made her favor Odysseus, the wisest and most cunning of the Greek heroes. In all these roles she was especially valued because she was always accessible, unlike many gods who kept their distance from humans.

THE BIRTH OF ATHENA

One of the first loves of the god Zeus was Metis, daughter of the Titans Oceanus and Tethys. Metis was known not only for her beauty but also for her brains—her name means "cunning intelligence." She was especially dear to Zeus, but when she became pregnant, Gaia and Uranus told Zeus that after she had given birth to a daughter, Metis would then have a son, also by Zeus, who would take away all his power. They advised Zeus to act at once to prevent this. Gaia told Zeus that the best way to stop this chain of events was to swallow Metis whole before she gave birth. Zeus did this, but when it was time for Metis's daughter to be born, Hephaestus intervened, splitting open Zeus's head with an axe and enabling the child to step forth. Miraculously, Athena emerged from Zeus's skull fully armed, uttering a war cry. According to several accounts, Athena was her father's favorite child, and the only one allowed to use his aegis.

► **Athena armed for war**
Athena's favored weapon was her spear, which she held upright when at rest, and brandished aloft when in battle. She also wore a helmet to protect her head.

GODDESS OF ATHENS

Athena won the right to be venerated as the goddess of Athens when, in a competition with Poseidon, she gave the citizens of Athens the valuable gift of the olive tree. The people acknowledged her importance by putting images of her and her sacred bird, the owl, on their coins. To worship her, they built the Parthenon on the Acropolis above the city, where the contest between Athena and Poseidon was depicted in a sculpture. This temple also housed a massive ivory and gold statue of Athena, created by the noted sculptor Phidias. Unfortunately, the statue no longer exists, though many miniature reproductions of it have been found. The temple's name comes from the title Parthenos (virgin), given to the goddess because she guarded her chastity so carefully.

◄ **Athena's birth**
Early depictions of the birth of Athena, such as this vase painting, show the goddess emerging from her father's head, already equipped with arms and armor.

The Parthenon

Athenian coin

▼ **Arachne turning into a spider**
Athena took pity on Arachne and turned her into
a spider, so that she could go on spinning and
weaving forever while hanging by a thread.

THE WEAVING CONTEST

One of Athena's roles was as the goddess of weavers and embroiderers. When someone was good at weaving, people said their gift came from Athena. But Arachne, a mortal girl and a fine weaver, insisted that her gift was her own, and had nothing to do with the goddess. This angered Athena, so she challenged Arachne to a weaving and embroidery contest. Athena saw that Arachne's weaving was at least as good as her own work, which showed the gods victorious over the mortals. However, she was offended by the subject of Arachne's tapestry, which depicted the various infidelities of her father, Zeus. In her jealousy and rage she tore up Arachne's work. A humiliated Arachne resolved to hang herself. But Athena decided that this was too harsh a punishment and transformed Arachne into a spider instead, so that she could continue weaving.

▼ **Arachne weaving**
Athena was spellbound by the beauty and quality of Arachne's work. Some say she was so jealous that in a fit of anger she struck the girl with her own weaving shuttle.

TO THE GODDESS YIELD, AND HUMBLY MEEK A PARDON FOR YOUR BOLD PRESUMPTION SEEK.

Ovid, *Metamorphoses*

ATHENA AND HEPHAESTUS

The craftsman god Hephaestus, who rescued Athena from her father's skull, had a lasting interest in the goddess. As she grew up, Hephaestus fell in love with her and asked Zeus for permission to marry her. Zeus agreed, provided that his daughter was willing. But Athena valued her virginity and did not want to marry, so she turned Hephaestus down. Hephaestus then tried to rape Athena, but the powerful goddess pushed him away and Hephaestus spilled his seed onto the ground. The seed fertilized Gaia (Mother Earth) and Erichthonius was created. Athena agreed to rear the child, and he grew up to later become the ruler of Athens.

▲ **Athena the foster mother**
Gaia hands over her newborn son Erichthonius to the waiting Athena while Hephaestus looks on.

THE BATHING OF ATHENA

Athena, who was a modest goddess, did not like others to watch when she bathed at the sacred spring called Hippocrene on Mount Helicon. But Tiresias, a man from Thebes, was so entranced by the beauty of the goddess that he followed her and her attendant nymphs, and spied on the goddess as she took off her clothes and bathed. When Athena realized she was being watched, she climbed out and in her anger hit Tiresias across the eyes, making him go blind. One of the nymphs was sorry for Tiresias and begged Athena to give him something in compensation for the loss of his sight. So Athena gave Tiresias the gift of prophecy.

▶ **Tiresias**
The seer Tiresias predicted many events, using his gift of prophecy to intervene in numerous myths, including those about Oedipus and the city of Thebes.

ATHENA

31

THE LOVES
OF APHRODITE

The name of Aphrodite, the goddess of love, means "born from the foam." She was born in the frothing sea and was famous both for her exquisite beauty and for her many lovers, who included both gods and mortals. Her partners found it impossible to resist her charms, and this magnetic attraction made her one of the most powerful of all the deities. Yet some accounts describe her as vain, ill-tempered, and easily offended. Her children included the Trojan prince, Aeneas, and Priapus, the god of fertility.

THE MYTH

Aphrodite was married to Hephaestus, the divine blacksmith. He adored her and crafted beautiful gifts for her. Among them was a golden chariot drawn by doves, which were sacred to her. However, she was frequently unfaithful to him. Of her many affairs, the most famous of all was with Ares, the god of war. This affair produced four children, the first two of whom took after their father, while the second two inherited their mother's character. They were Deimos (Terror), Phobos (Fear), Harmonia (Harmony), and, according to some accounts of the story, Eros (Sexual Love).

THE LOVERS TRAPPED

It was some time before Hephaestus found out about his wife's liaison with his brother, Ares, but when he did, he decided to take revenge by ridiculing the couple. He used his skill in metalworking to make a large net out of bronze wire, and secretly suspended this above the lovers' bed. When the pair were in bed together, Hephaestus tugged the net so that it fell on to the couple, trapping them. Then he called the gods to witness the ludicrous sight.

MORTAL LOVES

Another of Aphrodite's loves was a mortal called Adonis. Unfortunately, Persephone, wife of Hades, the god of the Underworld, also fell in love with him. Of the two, Adonis preferred Aphrodite, and a jealous Persephone told Ares about the affair. Enraged, Ares unleashed a wild boar, which attacked Adonis and killed him. When he died, Adonis arrived in the Underworld, where he was immediately pursued by Persephone. Aphrodite appealed to Zeus, and the king of the gods decided on a compromise. Adonis would spend half the year in the Underworld with Persephone, and the other half with Aphrodite.

Dove, symbol of Aphrodite

The death of Adonis shows how dangerous it was for a mere mortal to fall in love with Aphrodite. Another mortal who fell for her charms, Anchises, also paid dearly. Anchises was a shepherd, whose liaison with Aphrodite produced the hero Aeneas, ancestor of the Romans. Aphrodite disguised herself as a mortal to sleep with Anchises, but he glimpsed her in her true form. Aphrodite made him promise not to reveal the affair—an alliance with a mere shepherd would damage her reputation. But once, when Anchises was drunk, he revealed the secret and was blinded (or, some say, lamed) by Zeus as punishment.

◀ **The goddess of love**
Usually depicted as a beautiful young woman, Aphrodite is often shown naked. Because she represented physical perfection, she was a favorite subject for sculptors.

APHRODITE'S BIRTH

Aphrodite is said to be the daughter of the Titan Uranus. Gaia and Uranus had many children, including the Cyclopes and the Hundred-Handed Giants. Aghast at their monstrous appearance, Uranus decided to imprison all of them in Tartarus. Gaia did not want any more children and pleaded with her offspring to protect her from Uranus's advances. Finally, Cronus borrowed a sickle from his mother and cut off his father's genitals, which he threw into the sea. Their seed fertilized the water, and Aphrodite rose fully grown from the foaming waves.

▶ Aphrodite
The birth of Aphrodite is often depicted in paintings where the goddess is shown rising from the waves on a shell.

APHRODITE'S LOVERS

Aphrodite's power to make others fall in love with her came from her great physical beauty. She also had an aphrodisiac girdle, ironically gifted to her by Hephaestus, which she wore next to her breasts. This girdle was the envy of other goddesses who wanted Aphrodite's allure. Homer's *Iliad*, for example, tells how the goddess Hera borrowed it to distract Zeus with her charms during the Trojan War so that the Greeks could win. Although Aphrodite was married to Hephaestus and was in love with Ares, she also used her charms to attract many other lovers.

◀ Adonis
The mortal Adonis was a passionate hunter. He disregarded Aphrodite's warning about hunting an animal that knows no fear, and paid the price when he was killed by a wild boar sent by Ares.

▲ Hermes
The messenger of the gods was attracted to Aphrodite when he saw her under the net with Ares. His affair with her produced the child Hermaphroditus.

◀ Ares and Aphrodite
The sun god Helios, from whom nothing was hidden, spied Ares and Aphrodite together and informed Hephaestus, who then planned his revenge.

HEPHAESTUS

The god of fire and metalworking, Hephaestus was also the deity who controlled volcanoes, which were said to be his workshops. He was lame, as the result of an injury that came about when he had an argument with Zeus, who then threw him off Mount Olympus. This infirmity gave Hephaestus a comic quality for the Greeks, who revered physical perfection. In spite of this, he was admired for his ingenuity and skill in making things, from the net that captured Aphrodite and Ares, to a magical throne on which he could imprison his enemies.

▼ Hephaestus's net
The gods looked down from Mount Olympus and laughed at the sight of the adulterous couple ensnared in Hephaestus's net.

PYGMALION

Pygmalion was a remarkable sculptor who poured all his energy into his work. He was so skilled that once he carved a statue of a beautiful woman that was incredibly lifelike. He fell in love with it and prayed to Aphrodite to let him make love to his creation. Aphrodite took pity on him and transformed the statue into a real woman named Galatea, whom Pygmalion later married.

Pygmalion and Galatea

THE UNDERWORLD

The Underworld is usually seen as a parallel world to our own, with its own deities. In most cultures it is populated by the souls of the dead, and fenced off by rivers, walls, or flames, making it impossible for living mortals to enter. Souls pass through on their way to a new life—or spend an eternity among the demons of this dark realm.

RULERS OF THE UNDERWORLD

The ruler of the Underworld has supreme power there, acting with all the authority of an earthly ruler, and as such is one of the most feared beings in the cosmos. He or she is also often a judge, hearing each newly arrived soul's account of its life in the world of the living before passing sentence. Underworld rulers vary greatly in their appearance—some look like decaying corpses, while others are so dark that they are barely visible.

▲ **Mictlantecuhtli**
The Aztec Underworld has nine layers, the deepest of which is Mictlan, ruled over by the terrifying Mictlantecuhtli.

▲ **Hades**
The ruler of the gloomy Greek Underworld bears the same name as his kingdom and is usually invisible in his dark domain.

▲ **Hel**
The Norse ruler of the dead, Hel is said to recline on a bed called Disease, where her lower body rots while her face remains beautiful.

▶ **Yama**
In Tibetan and Chinese Buddhism, Yama is the king of hell and judge of the dead. He is said to be directly answerable to the supreme ruler of heaven.

CHTHONIC CREATURES

The Underworld would be frightening enough if it was populated solely by a ruler and the souls of the dead. But mythologies add to its terrors by imagining all kinds of hellish demons and monsters—creatures that exist either to terrify the souls or inflict agony on them. In addition, the gates of the Underworld are usually guarded, to prevent mortals intruding and souls attempting to escape. Cerberus, the guard dog of Hades, is one of the most famous of these chthonic, or Underworld, creatures. Some accounts give him three heads, others 50.

Cerberus

GUIDING THE DEAD

A dark and remote place, the Underworld is not easy to reach or find, so some cultures tell of figures called psychopomps, who lead the souls of the dead on their way. Images of these guides are often found on coffins or on the walls of tombs, to ensure that the dead person's soul has a safe passage. Psychopomps can take many different forms, although a number of them have wings or inhabit the bodies of birds, for swift flight to and from the Underworld.

▲ Hermes
The Greek god Hermes escorted souls to Hades. Some sources say that as he was a trickster deity, he could not be fooled into neglecting this task.

▲ Baron Samedi
The spirit Baron Samedi is a key figure in Haitian voodoo. He is said to wait at crossroads, where dead souls will pass, ready to guide them to the Underworld.

▲ Charon
The Classical Underworld Hades was surrounded by the dark waters of the River Styx. For the fee of a single coin placed on the dead person's tongue, the ferryman Charon took his or her soul across in his boat.

◀ Ankou
In the folklore of the Breton people of Western Europe, Ankou gathered up the souls of the dead in an old cart.

▶ Xolotl
In some stories this dog-shaped Aztec god created the human race, but so hated his handiwork that he took on the job of leading the dead to the Underworld.

UNDERWORLD GODDESSES

Many goddesses of darkness are associated with the Underworld. Some act as queens there, alongside male rulers; others have a less clear, but equally terrifying, role—some even visiting Earth. Because of the contrast between the light Earth and the dark Underworld, many are also linked with the sun, rain, and fertility.

▶ Hecate
A Greek moon goddess and queen of the ghosts of Hades, Hecate led her troop of howling, dancing spirits on terrifying visits to Earth.

◀ Izanami
This Japanese creator goddess was so badly burned when she gave birth to the fire spirit Kagutsuchi that she went down to rule Yomi, the Underworld.

◀ Mari
In the Basque region of Spain, Mari was a rain-bringing fertility goddess who came out of her Underworld realm by way of mountain caves.

▲ Persephone
When this beautiful Greek goddess of fertility was kidnapped by Hades, Zeus decreed that she should spend half the year in his world, and half on Earth, where she could make crops grow.

THE LABORS OF HERACLES

The hero Heracles, renowned for his great strength, was the son of Zeus and the mortal woman Alcmene. Zeus's wife, Hera, was jealous of the affair and resentful towards Heracles, and she persecuted him throughout his life. The hero married Megara, daughter of King Creon of Thebes, but Hera made him go mad and kill his wife and children. To punish Heracles, King Eurystheus of Mycenae set him 12 apparently impossible tasks to accomplish.

THE MYTH

The labors imposed on Heracles by King Eurystheus involved slaying horrific monsters, bringing back trophies for the king, and other tasks, each of which was more difficult and sent the hero on a longer journey than the preceding one. The first labor was to kill the lion of Nemaea, not far from Mycenae. Heracles throttled the beast and skinned it, taking the creature's pelt as his cloak. The second labor was to slay the Hydra, a water monster with many heads that lived at Lerna. Heracles found that each time he cut off one of the creature's heads, two new ones grew. So he asked his helper, Iolaos, to cauterize the stumps, to stop the new heads growing. The third labor was to capture and bring back the Keryneian hind, a golden-horned deer consecrated to the goddess Artemis. This involved the hero in a long chase, but eventually he succeeded. The fourth task was to seize the Erymanthian boar, a fierce creature that posed little problem for Heracles.

WITH ATHENA'S HELP

Next, Heracles undertook two tasks that required more ingenuity. He was helped in these by Athena, the goddess

◄ **Heracles and the bull**
The powerful bull of Crete was the target of Heracles's seventh labor. The hero needed all his strength to subdue the beast.

▶ **The Stymphalian birds**
This vase shows Heracles shooting the Stymphalian birds with a sling, a more effective weapon than his club or bow.

of wisdom. For the fifth labor, he was told to go to Elis and clean the stables of King Augeas, which were fouled with great heaps of horse dung. Heracles ingeniously cleared out the stables by diverting two rivers so that they washed the mess away. Then, for his sixth labor, Heracles had to visit Lake Stymphalis, northwest of Mycenae, to rid it of a plague of birds. He frightened the birds with castanets that Athena had lent him, then shot them as they flew into the air.

FARTHER AFIELD

For his subsequent labors, Heracles had to travel farther, leaving mainland Greece. His seventh labor was to capture a monstrous bull belonging to King Minos of Crete. After that he was sent north to Thrace, where he caught some man-eating mares that belonged to King Diomedes. The ninth, tenth, and eleventh labors required Heracles to steal items of great value. First he took the belt of Hippolyta, queen of the Amazons, who lived to the south of the Black Sea. Next he led away the cattle of the giant Geryon, who dwelled in the far west. After this, he managed to obtain the golden apples of the Hesperides. But even these labors were straightforward compared with the twelfth: to go to the Underworld and bring back its guard dog, Cerberus. To the amazement of Eurystheus, Heracles succeeded in this seemingly impossible feat too.

THE MONSTERS OF GREECE

Like other Greek heroes, such as Perseus, Heracles was tested during confrontations with numerous creatures, many of whom were monsters that would terrify most people. These creatures ranged from the Nemaean lion, an animal of supreme strength, to monstrous creatures—such as the three-headed dog, Cerberus—which seemed to come from the world of horror and nightmare. By overcoming them, Heracles was able to demonstrate both his superhuman strength and his exceptional bravery. He also gained from some of these combats by adopting the attributes of his adversaries—for example, he took the lion's skin as his cloak and the Hydra's gall to poison his arrowheads.

◄ The Nemaean lion
Wrestling the Nemaean lion brought Heracles into danger from the animal's claws and jaws, but he finally prevailed.

▼ The Hydra
Heracles dispatched the multi-headed Hydra with the help of Iolaos. As Heracles cut off each head, Iolaos cauterized the stumps.

▼ The Erymanthian boar
When Heracles brought the vicious boar to Eurystheus, the frightened king hid from the beast by climbing into a large storage jar.

▼ Cerberus
After showing the terrifying guard dog of the Underworld to Eurystheus, Heracles returned the creature to Hades, its master.

THE HERO'S CLUB

King Thespius, ruler of a kingdom called Thespiae, was troubled by a lion that attacked his cattle. Thespius's men had failed in killing the lion, so Heracles volunteered to try. He made himself an enormous club by tearing up an olive tree. He clubbed the lion to death and was allowed to sleep with all but one of Thespius's fifty daughters as a reward.

► A formidable weapon
The legendary club of Heracles, with which he overcame many opponents, was so heavy that only he could pick it up and wield it with ease.

HERACLES AND NESSUS

Heracles was travelling with his third wife, Deianira, when they met a centaur, called Nessus, who offered to carry Deianira across a river. When they were across the water and a safe distance from Heracles, Nessus raped Deianira, but Heracles saw what was happening and shot the centaur with one of his deadly arrows. As he died, Nessus told Deianira that if she wove Heracles a shirt from the hairs on his back, the wearer would never leave her for another woman. Some time later, Deianira suspected her husband's fidelity, and gave him the shirt to wear. But when Heracles put the shirt on, he discovered it was an evil trick. Its hairs made his skin blister and burn as if attacked by flames. In agony and begging for death, the hero asked to be put on his funeral pyre.

▲ Heracles fighting the centaur
The centaur Nessus had once been defeated in a fight with Heracles, and longed for revenge.

► On his funeral pyre
As the smoke from Heracles's pyre reached the heavens, Zeus saw his agony. He drew him up to Olympus and made him a god.

THE CHARACTER OF HERACLES

First and foremost, Heracles is a hero, a figure of incredible strength and outstanding bravery. But ancient Greek writers treat his character in different ways according to the parts of his story they are narrating. For example, in *The Children of Heracles*, Euripides portrays him as the tragic figure who kills his own children, but in another play, *Alcestis*, he gets comically drunk. Sophocles deals with the hero's relationship with his wife, Deianira, and other writers concentrate on his heroic adventures.

The dramatists Aeschylus, Sophocles, and Euripides

THESEUS AND THE MINOTAUR

The Minotaur was a monstrous flesh-eating creature, half man, half bull. Minos, the King of Crete, kept it imprisoned in a labyrinth near his palace. According to a treaty between Minos and Aegeus, the King of Athens, 14 young people had to be sent every year from Athens to be devoured by it. But the Greek hero Theseus resolved to kill the creature and put an end to the carnage.

THE MYTH

The sea god Poseidon once gave a white bull, known as the Cretan Bull, to King Minos. However, when the king decided to keep the beast rather than sacrificing it, Poseidon was angered. He asked Aphrodite, the goddess of love, to make Minos's wife, Pasiphae, fall in love with the bull as punishment. This union produced a beast called the Minotaur, which had a monstrous appetite for human flesh.

King Minos wanted to avenge the death of his son at the hands of the Athenians. He waged a war on King Aegeus of Athens and won. As compensation, he demanded that 14 young people be sent from Athens each year to feed the Minotaur. Aegeus's son, Theseus, decided to go to Crete as one of the ill-fated people, and kill the beast. The ship carrying Theseus and the other victims set sail from Athens with black sails, and the hero promised his father that he would return with white sails hoisted on his ship if he succeeded in killing the Minotaur.

THESEUS ON CRETE

When the Athenians arrived at Crete, Minos's daughter, Ariadne, saw Theseus and fell in love with him. She knew that Theseus would need help in finding his way out of the impenetrable labyrinth, once he had slain the creature. So Ariadne gave him a spindle wound with woollen thread. As Theseus made his way into the labyrinth, he unwound the thread behind him, so that it would mark his winding path and show him how to exit the labyrinth.

◄ Leaving the labyrinth
The central portion of this vessel from Greece shows Theseus dragging his dead victim out of its prison as he retraces his steps through the labyrinth using Ariadne's thread.

▶ Theseus kills the Minotaur
The Minotaur almost managed to defeat Theseus in battle, but the hero fought courageously and stabbed the monster with his sword.

In the middle of the labyrinth, Theseus confronted the beast and killed it with a blow from his father's golden sword. He then retraced his steps with the body of the Minotaur by following Ariadne's thread, until he finally emerged from the entrance to the maze. His fellow Athenians rejoiced when they saw that Theseus had been victorious and quickly ran to their ship to set sail for home, Theseus taking Ariadne with him. In the excitement, they forgot to hoist the white sails to signal Theseus's success.

TRAGIC ENDINGS

On the way home, they called at the island of Naxos for water. When they returned to the ship, Theseus abandoned Ariadne on the island, sailing away without her. Some say that he did this since he already had a wife at home; others that Dionysus spotted Ariadne on the island, fell in love with her, and put a spell on Theseus, making him forget her. After marrying Ariadne, Dionysus gave her a crown made of seven stars.

As the ship approached Athens, Aegeus was watching anxiously for his son from a cliff top. He saw the black sails from afar and assumed that Theseus had been killed. Overcome with grief, he flung himself into the sea, never to know of his son's success.

THE LABYRINTH

King Minos ordered the building of the labyrinth as a prison for the Minotaur. He entrusted the design of the labyrinth to the master-craftsman Daedalus, who was famous as an inventor—he was said to have invented sailing boats and sharp underwater rams that made the Cretan ships unbeatable in battle. His labyrinth became a byword in the ancient world for complexity and impenetrability. The story of the labyrinth seems to combine two ideas—the real palace at Knossos, Crete, which has hundreds of rooms and appears impenetrable; and drawings of mazes found on ancient carvings and coins.

▲ **Ancient labyrinth**
Unlike the puzzle-mazes seen in European gardens, which have many alternative routes, most ancient labyrinths had only one route, which led to the center.

KEY CHARACTERS

The myth of Theseus and the Minotaur contains a varied cast of characters, most of whom are people who mean well but meet tragic ends. Ariadne's abandonment and Aegeus's suicide come about because they play minor roles in a larger drama— the career of the hero Theseus. The lives of the characters are driven more by destiny than by personal choices or their individual traits.

▶ **Ariadne**
Ariadne had begged Daedalus to help her ensure Theseus's safe return from the labyrinth. He gave her a magical ball of thread, which she handed over to Theseus to find his way back after killing the Minotaur.

IN THE MIDDLE OF THE LABYRINTH, THESEUS KILLED THE BEAST WITH A BLOW OF HIS GOLDEN SWORD.

THE CRETAN BULL CULT

The bull plays a central part in the myths surrounding Crete—the creature that fathered the Minotaur had been sent to Minos by the sea god Poseidon as a confirmation of the king's right to rule on the island. Many ancient images of bulls have been found on Crete, so the animals seem to have been important in the customs and beliefs of the real islanders, too.

▼ **Bull head**
This Cretan Bronze-Age vessel in the form of a bull's head is carved from black stone.

▶ **Double-headed axe**
Two-headed axes are a common feature in Cretan art. Experts believe they are based on weapons used for sacrificing animals, a ritual of the bull cult.

▼ **Bull-leaping**
A fresco from Knossos shows a young man turning a somersault over a bull's back. This feat was perhaps performed as a sport or had some ritual significance.

◀ **Aegeus**
When Aegeus saw the black sails of the returning ship, he was convinced that his son was dead. In despair, he threw himself off the cliff. The sea in which he drowned has been known as the Aegean Sea ever since.

THESEUS

After becoming the King of Athens following the death of his father, Theseus embarked on a long trip to the Underworld with his friend Pirithous. On his return, Theseus's throne was taken away from him, and he spent his last years as a beggar. His life ended at the behest of the goddess Artemis, who had Theseus murdered in revenge for his killing Antiope, her follower.

Theseus

THE EXPLOITS OF PERSEUS

Perseus—one of the greatest Greek heroes— was the son of Zeus and Danaë, the daughter of Acrisius, the King of Argos. An oracle had once predicted that Acrisius would be killed by his daughter's son. To prevent the oracle's warning from coming true, he imprisoned his daughter and grandson, Perseus, in a wooden chest and threw it into the sea. The chest reached the island of Seriphos, where Perseus and his mother were rescued by the king, Polydectes, who brought him up. Many years later, Polydectes would be the one to send Perseus on his most perilous journey— to retrieve the head of the Gorgon Medusa.

THE SLAYING OF MEDUSA

Perseus rashly boasted to Polydectes that he would behead one of the three monstrous Gorgons. When Polydectes held him to his boast, Perseus decided to slay Medusa, a Gorgon who could turn men to stone with her gaze. Divine assistance was needed for Perseus to complete his task, so the deities of Mount Olympus lent Perseus several objects that helped him succeed. He used Hermes's winged sandals to fly to the place where Medusa lived, and Hades's helmet of invisibility to gain access to her dwelling. With Athena's shield, polished like a mirror, he approached the Gorgon, avoiding her direct gaze. And with Hephaestus's diamond sword, he chopped off Medusa's head, thus making good his boast.

▶ **Medusa meets her death**
Medusa's deadly glance only worked when she looked at her victims directly, so Athena helped Perseus use her shield as a mirror as he took aim with his sword.

▼ **Head of Medusa**
Like the other Gorgons, Medusa was a female monster with snakes for hair. However, she was the only mortal among the Gorgons.

▶ **The three Graeae**
Wearing Hades's helmet, Perseus crept past the Graeae, three sisters with one eye and one tooth between them, who guarded the cave of the Gorgons.

THE RESCUE OF ANDROMEDA

Some say the winged horse Pegasus grew from Medusa's blood after Perseus had slain the Gorgon, and he left for home on this magical steed. As he flew, he saw a woman chained to some rocks on the Phoenician coast. She was Andromeda, the daughter of Cepheus, the King of Ethiopia. His wife, Cassiopeia, had boasted that Andromeda was more beautiful than the sea nymphs. Furious at this insult, the god Poseidon had sent a sea monster to terrorize Ethiopia; the beast would only be satisfied with the sacrifice of Cassiopeia's daughter. Perseus swooped down and killed the monster, rescuing Andromeda. He asked for her hand in marriage but when her parents refused, Perseus showed them Medusa's head, turning them to stone, and left with Andromeda.

▲ **Perseus and Andromeda**
This painting of the rescue of Andromeda by Perseus shows the hero still flying on the winged sandals of Hermes. Some versions of the story have him riding across the sky on the winged steed, Pegasus.

▲ **Turned to stone**
Perseus confronted Polydectes with Medusa's head just as the king was about to force Danaë to submit to his demands. The Gorgon's gaze was enough to petrify Polydectes and his men instantly where they stood.

THE PETRIFICATION OF POLYDECTES

After his adventures with the Gorgon and the sea monster, Perseus finally returned home to the island of Seriphos. King Polydectes had fallen in love with Perseus's mother, Danaë, and had been trying to persuade her to marry him. He had sent Perseus away in the first place for this very purpose. Danaë hid herself in the temple of Athena and Polydectes laid siege to the building. Enraged by what he saw on his arrival, Perseus revealed Medusa's head to the king and his soldiers, turning them to stone. Perseus then returned the gifts that the gods had loaned to him, and gave Medusa's head to Athena, who attached it to the front of her shield.

THE DEATH OF ACRISIUS

Perseus was going to return to his homeland of Argos, but he heard about the oracle that had predicted that Danaë's son would kill his own grandfather, and so he decided to stay away. He travelled instead to Pelasgiotis (or according to some accounts, Larissa) in Thessaly, where the local king, Teutamides, was holding funeral games for his recently deceased father. Perseus was keen to compete in the games, especially in the discus, which was his favorite event. But when he took his throw, the discus went astray, hitting and killing one of the men watching. Unfortunately, the victim turned out to be Perseus's grandfather, Acrisius.

▲ **Abandonment of Danaë and Perseus**
Acrisius's death had been foretold in a prophecy, which led him to put his daughter and grandson in a chest and throw it in the sea.

▲ **Discus thrower**
Perseus was fond of discus throwing, which became a very popular sport in the ancient Greek Olympic games.

OEDIPUS

Laius and Jocasta, the King and Queen of the city of Thebes, were told by the oracle at Delphi that their son would kill his father and marry his mother. Terrified by the prophecy, when their son, Oedipus, was born, they abandoned the child on a mountain and left him to die. So began one of the most tragic tales in all Classical mythology. By the end of the story, the entire family was destroyed, victims of fate and the impossibility of avoiding it. Oedipus became the archetypal tragic hero, trying to live well but thwarted by destiny.

THE MYTH

Soon after he was abandoned on the mountainside by Laius and Jocasta, Oedipus was found by a group of shepherds who took him to the city of Corinth, where the king and queen, Polybus and Merope, brought him up as their own son. One day someone told him he was a foundling, so he went to the oracle at Delphi to find out the truth. But rather than enlightening him about his true parentage, the oracle told him he was destined to kill his father and marry his mother. Thinking the oracle had meant Polybus and Merope, Oedipus decided to leave Corinth and set off on a long journey. On the way he came to a crossroads where an old man in a chariot was travelling in the opposite direction. The man ordered Oedipus to get out of his way, offending him with his rudeness. The pair quarrelled and fought, and Oedipus ended up killing the man.

The infant Oedipus
When the shepherds found Oedipus, they took him to their king and queen who were childless and longed for a son.

ANSWERING THE RIDDLE

Oedipus continued his journey and eventually arrived in Thebes, where a monster called the Sphinx was devouring the city's children and the king had mysteriously disappeared. Each day the Sphinx asked a baffling riddle and when nobody could answer it correctly, it grabbed another child and ate it up. Oedipus alone was able to guess the correct answer to the riddle and, when he did so, the Sphinx died, breaking its neck in a fit of rage. A triumphant Oedipus became the most popular man in Thebes, and having caught the attention of Queen Jocasta, a descendant of the founding family of the city, he married her.

THE TRUTH REVEALED

For some years Oedipus and Jocasta enjoyed a happy marriage and had four children—daughters Antigone and Ismene, and sons Eteocles and Polynices. But after this period of contentment, Oedipus discovered the horrifying truth about his life when the prophet Tiresias revealed what had happened. The chariot rider that Oedipus killed at the crossroads was his true father, Laius, and the queen he had married in Thebes was his own mother, Jocasta. The queen killed herself in despair over what had happened, and Oedipus took a pin from her dress to stab his eyes, blinding himself. He left Thebes to spend the rest of his life as a wanderer, comforted only by his daughter Antigone, the one member of his family who had not rejected him for his deeds.

After many years of travelling as a blind beggar, Oedipus reached the city of Colonus, on the edge of Athens, where the oracle had said he would die. Here, the King of Athens, Theseus, welcomed him. However, Oedipus's sons wanted him to return to Thebes, convinced that his return would bring good fortune to the city. Oedipus ignored their demands and walked into the sacred grove at Colonus, disappearing from view and starting his last journey—to the Underworld.

The death of Laius
The fatal meeting of Oedipus and Laius took place at a crossroads not far from Delphi. There, the words of the oracle were partly fulfilled.

THE FAMILY OF OEDIPUS

As a royal dynasty, Oedipus's family were closely involved with the politics of their city, Thebes. When Oedipus blinded himself and left the city, Jocasta's brother, Creon, took over the throne until Oedipus's sons, Eteocles and Polynices, were old enough to rule. But the brothers fought and killed each other, and Creon returned to the throne. He tried to rule for the good of the city but was known for his ruthlessness. He did not even spare Antigone, who was betrothed to his son, Haemon, and confined her in a cave to die for supporting her brother Polynices against his wishes.

▲ **Jocasta**
Queen Jocasta hung herself in anguish on realizing that she had mistakenly married her own son, Oedipus.

▲ **Antigone**
Oedipus's daughter Antigone supported her father and stood up for her brother, Polynices, after his rebellion (see right).

▲ **Creon**
Trying to deal firmly with the rows and tragedies in his family, Creon acted violently and became the archetype of the cruel ruler.

THE RIDDLE OF THE SPHINX

The puzzle posed by the Sphinx to the people of Thebes is now a familiar riddle, but it baffled everyone when they first heard it. In its most famous form, the riddle is: "What goes on four legs in the morning, two legs in the daytime, and three legs at night?"
Oedipus rightly guessed that the answer was a man, who crawls on four limbs as a baby, walks upright on two legs as an adult, and uses a stick, or third leg, in old age.

▶ **The sphinx**
Sphinxes take various forms in the ancient world, but the Greek Sphinx had the head of a woman, the body and legs of a lion, and the wings of a bird.

THEBES

Although it is a family tragedy, the story of Oedipus and his sons is intimately bound with the history of their city, Thebes, in Boeotia, whose ruling family traced its ancestry back to a magical event in the life of the hero Cadmus, the founder of Thebes. Much later, when Polynices was ousted by his brother Eteocles, he fled to Argos seeking help from its king, Adrastus. Together, they started a war with five other rebels, collectively known as the "Seven Against Thebes." Their army was slaughtered, both brothers were killed, and the noble line begun by Cadmus came to an end.

▶ **Cadmus slaying the dragon**
Cadmus killed a dragon that lived on the plains of Thebes and planted its teeth in the ground. From the monster's teeth grew an army of men who became the ancestors of the Thebans.

OEDIPUS AT COLONUS

The oracle had told Oedipus that he would die in a place sacred to the Furies. Colonus was such a place; it was also special because it was the location of one of the entrances to the Underworld. After Oedipus came to Colonus, there was a thunderstorm, which he thought was a sign from Zeus that his life was coming to an end. It was from here that, ignoring the demands of the Thebans, Oedipus passed below the Earth to the next world. The Greek playwright Sophocles (496–406 BCE) was born in the area and described these events in his play *Oedipus at Colonus*.

◀ **Oedipus as a blind beggar**
In his blind wanderings, Oedipus was guided by his daughter Antigone, the only member of his family who remained faithful to him.

FREUD AND OEDIPUS

The pioneering psychoanalyst Sigmund Freud (1856–1939) has been linked with the Oedipus myth ever since he coined the term "Oedipus complex" to describe the sexual obsession of a child (usually male) with the parent of the opposite sex. The phrase is somewhat misleading, as Oedipus did not know that Jocasta was his real mother. It has been widely used in both psychology and literary studies.

Sigmund Freud

THE TROJAN WAR

Homer's great epic poem, the *Iliad,* describes a war between the Greeks and the Trojans that lasted for ten years. The conflict began after Paris, a prince from Troy, eloped with Helen, the wife of the Greek king, Menelaus, and the Greeks mounted an expedition to get her back. On Mount Olympus, the gods and goddesses looked down on the battlefield, taking sides and influencing events as heroes of both sides fell. Finally, the Greeks were victorious and took Helen back home.

THE MYTH

The two sides were well matched. Each had the services of good leaders, like the Trojan prince, Hector, and the Greek general, Agamemnon. Each had other famous soldiers and fighters on their side—Paris for the Trojans and men such as Achilles and the cunning Odysseus for the Greeks. Each side also had the backing of several gods and goddesses—Aphrodite and Poseidon were on the side of Troy; Apollo, Athena, and Hera favored the Greeks. Therefore the stalemate continued, with many minor battles but no overall victory, for years.

▶ **The Trojan horse**
The Trojans were known as skilled tamers of horses, so the booby-trapped wooden horse was an ironic gift from the Greeks, which had disastrous results.

ACHILLES AND PATROCLUS

The war reached a climax when two of the Greek leaders quarreled. Agamemnon, who had been forced to give up one of his concubines, took as his mistress one of the many women of Achilles. In disgust, Achilles withdrew his forces from the fighting and the Trojans began to get the upper hand. To win back the initiative, Patroclus, a close friend of Achilles, asked his comrade for permission to lead his troops and disguise himself in the armor of Achilles. When the Trojan soldiers saw the best of the Greek troops back on the battlefield, apparently led by Achilles himself, they began to lose heart. This gave the Greeks more success, but just as they seemed to be winning, Hector killed Patroclus.

THE GREEKS GAIN GROUND

The death of Patroclus roused Achilles, who returned to the fight, killing Hector and dragging his body around Troy's walls. Next, the gods encouraged the Greeks to bring the great archer Philocretes into the battle, and the bowman killed Paris, a huge psychological blow for the Trojans. The Greeks then stole Athena's statue, which was a sign of good fortune for the Trojans, from her shrine in Troy.

Finally, the gods put into the mind of Odysseus the trick of the hollow wooden horse, in which soldiers could hide. The Greeks left the horse in front of the city and feigned a withdrawal. The Trojans dragged the statue into the city. During the night, Greek soldiers emerged from its belly and opened the city gates. The rest of the Greek army poured in and Troy was destroyed.

▲ **Soldiers in combat**
In this engraving created in the style of Greek vase painting, Trojans attack the Greek ships with fire, while the Greeks defend themselves with their spears.

THE JUDGEMENT OF PARIS

The event that started the war occurred on Mount Ida, where the Trojan prince, Paris, was visited by three goddesses: Hera, Athena, and Aphrodite. Eris, goddess of discord, had given them a golden apple, inscribed, "For the fairest." Each of the three claimed the apple. Zeus commanded Hermes to take them to Paris, who would decide which was the most beautiful. The goddesses tried to influence his decision by offering bribes. Athena pledged to grant him success in war, Hera promised power, and Aphrodite offered the hand of the world's most beautiful woman, Helen. Paris chose Aphrodite's offer—but Helen was already married to Menelaus of Sparta. When she eloped with Paris, hostilities between Greece and Troy began.

▲ **The three goddesses**
After Paris judged Aphrodite to be the fairest among the three goddesses, he earned the wrath of both Athena and Hera.

▶ **Helen of Troy**
Several reasons have been given for Helen's desertion of her husband, such as wickedness, forced abduction, and the influence of Aphrodite.

THE HEROES

The story of the Trojan War is full of heroes who are the epic's main characters. They are generally brave in battle, but Homer's depiction of their characters is particularly interesting. Many are motivated by honor—the dispute between Achilles and Agamemnon over their concubines, for example, ignites because when Agamemnon appropriates the woman of Achilles, the latter's honor is affected. Homer shows that intelligence is essential in battle too: the hero Odysseus is renowned for his cunning.

▶ **Achilles binding Patroclus's wound**
Friendship was an important motivation in the war—when Patroclus died, Achilles returned to the battle with renewed energy.

▲ **Agamemnon returning with Cassandra**
At the end of the war, Troy was captured and sacked. Agamemnon carried off Cassandra, the daughter of King Priam of Troy, as a prize.

▲ **Menelaus pursuing Helen**
Seen here pursuing his wife, Helen, Menelaus is portrayed in the *Iliad* as a noble king who fights bravely for his cause.

▲ **Hector fighting Achilles**
Achilles and Hector's fight was a key moment in the war. With Hector's death, the Trojans were weakened by the loss of one of their greatest fighters.

▲ **Ajax committing suicide**
A great warrior, Ajax survived the war, but went mad after a dispute with Odysseus, and killed himself.

> ATHENE AND HERA THUNDERED, DOING HONOR TO THE KING OF MYCENAE, RICH IN GOLD.
>
> Homer, *Iliad*, Book XI

THE ANCIENT CITY OF MYCENAE

Although the story of the *Iliad* is a myth, all its characters come from real places in ancient Greece. Mycenae, in the northeastern Peloponnese, was said to be the home of Agamemnon. The city state was a strong military power during the Late Bronze Age. This ancient site was excavated in the 19th-century by the German archaeologist Heinrich Schliemann. He discovered stunning jewelry and other artifacts among the ruins, dating back to the 2nd millennium BCE. He claimed these objects belonged to Agamemnon, though there has never been any evidence to support this.

◀ **Gold mask**
Schliemann called this face of beaten gold unearthed from Mycenae "the mask of Agamemnon," but it could have belonged to any early Mycenaean king.

THE ODYSSEY

Homer's second epic, the *Odyssey*, tells the story of the Greek hero Odysseus (Ulysses to the Romans) on his journey home to Ithaca after the Trojan War. He faces many perils, including monstrous creatures and seductive women. Each encounter stretches his intelligence and cunning. But his greatest challenge comes when he arrives home to find his wife besieged by suitors who believe him to be dead.

THE MYTH

After leaving Troy, Odysseus and his sailors first came to the country of the Lotos Eaters. These inhabitants, who lived a lazy life of ease, tempted them with the lotos fruit, which had the power to make them forget the past. Odysseus had to force his reluctant companions back to their ships. Next they encountered the Cyclopes, a race of one-eyed giants. Odysseus and his followers were caught by one of the Cyclopes, Polyphemus, who kept them captive in a cave and ate some of them. When the Greek hero was asked to identify himself, he cleverly said he was called Outis (meaning "no one"). Odysseus plied Polyphemus with wine and then blinded the giant with a heated stake. When Polyphemus shouted, "Outis [no one] is killing me," the other Cyclopes heard him but did not come to his rescue because they thought he was drunk, and the Greeks managed to escape. Polyphemus complained to his father, the sea god Poseidon, who sent terrible storms to hinder Odysseus's journey.

> **Greek ship**
> Greek ships had banks of oars but were also equipped with sails, so Odysseus's ships would have been able to take advantage of the wind.

AT THE MERCY OF THE WINDS

At their next port of call, Aeolus, the god of the winds, gave Odysseus the winds tied up in a bag, allowing him to control his course homewards. But Odysseus's men, filled with curiosity about the contents of the bag, untied it, letting loose all the winds. The ship was blown far off course, first to the land of the giant Laestrygonians, who destroyed most of their ships, and then to an island inhabited by the enchantress Circe, who turned Odysseus's men into pigs. But Odysseus saved himself by eating a protective herb given to him by the god Hermes. Circe saw that Odysseus was resistant to her magic, and turned his crew back into men again. Circe advised Odysseus to visit the Underworld to find out more about his future. He traveled there, and had a vision in which his homeland was occupied by hostile invaders. The hero decided to hurry home.

But his journey took longer than he had expected. Odysseus first encountered the Sirens, enchanting creatures whose beautiful song lured all passing sailors. He sailed past them by commanding his men to block their ears. After this, Odysseus's ship had to pass between Scylla, a six-headed, man-devouring monster, and Charybdis, a whirlpool. Odysseus was forced to take the painful decision of losing six of his sailors to Scylla, each of whose six heads could only eat one man at a time, rather than have all of them drown in the whirlpool of Charybdis. »

◄ **Odysseus**
Like all Greek heroes, Odysseus was physically strong. But he was also cunning, which helped him overcome the obstacles that beset his voyage.

MONSTERS AND OBSTACLES

Odysseus encountered several obstacles on his journey. The giant Laestrygonians destroyed all the ships in his armada except for his own. When they were trapped in Polyphemus's cave, he and his men tied themselves to the underbellies of the Cyclops's sheep. The next day, Polyphemus let his sheep out to graze, and the Greeks escaped. On Circe's island, Odysseus's men were turned into pigs, thus delaying the voyage.

◄ **The Laestrygonians**
Antiphates, the king of the Laestrygonians, killed and ate one of Odysseus's men. Then all the giants pelted the Greek ships with huge rocks, sinking all but one.

► **The magic of Circe**
The enchantress Circe turned men into animals by giving them a potion and striking them with her wand.

◄ **Odysseus and Polyphemus**
Using a sharpened stake of olive wood, Odysseus put out the single eye of Polyphemus so that he and his men could escape from the Cyclops's cave.

PERILS OF THE SEA

The Greeks were a people who lived mainly on islands and in coastal settlements, and hence were accomplished sailors. They knew well that sea voyages, even in the often calm Mediterranean, had their dangers, and that sailors had to watch out for unfavorable winds, dangerous whirlpools or currents, and jagged rocks. Odysseus had to cope with tempests sent by Poseidon, perilous currents, and some more fantastic dangers. Some of these, like the seductive song of the Sirens, could be deceptive—Odysseus was warned by Circe that the song of the Sirens must be resisted.

> # NEVER YET HAS ANY MAN ROWED PAST THIS ISLE IN HIS BLACK SHIP UNTIL HE HAS HEARD THE SWEET VOICE FROM OUR LIPS.
> Homer, *Odyssey*, Book IX

▲ **Odysseus and the Sirens**
While his sailors blocked their ears, Odysseus had himself tied to the mast so that he could not follow the Sirens.

▼ **Charybdis**
This notorious whirlpool sank all passing ships, but Odysseus steered through the narrow gap between it and Scylla.

THE WORLD OF THE DEAD

Odysseus visited the Underworld to find out about his future. First he consulted the prophet Tiresias, who warned him not to harm the cattle of Helios. Then he met his mother, Anticleia, who told him how his wife and son were suffering at home. Odysseus also met the ghost of Achilles. Finally, he grew fearful and left the Underworld in terror.

► **Achilles**
The ghost of Achilles told Odysseus he would rather live on Earth as a humble laborer than rule among the dead.

THE JOURNEY CONTINUES

Odysseus next stopped at an island where Helios, the sun god, kept his cattle. Although they had been warned not to kill these animals, the sailors slaughtered a few of the cattle. Helios complained to Zeus, who struck their ship with a thunderbolt, killing the crew and shattering the ship. Only Odysseus survived, clinging to the wreckage.

Odysseus was washed up on the island belonging to the goddess Calypso, who wanted him to stay with her. Though he lived there for seven years, Odysseus finally resisted the temptation to stay further, and travelled on. He was then shipwrecked again and washed ashore on the island of Alcinous, the King of the Phaeacians. Here, the goddess Athena contrived to make the king's daughter, Nausicaa, meet Odysseus; and the two were attracted to each other. Odysseus was tempted to stay with her, but finally, longing for his wife and his homeland, Ithaca, he traveled on again.

PENELOPE'S SUITORS

Bruised and greatly aged by his ordeal, Odysseus arrived in Ithaca to find his house full of suitors who, assuming he was dead, were hoping to marry his wife, Penelope, and take over all his

► **Nausicaa**
The princess was with her friends at the seashore when a tired and naked Odysseus appeared before them. He was given clothes by Nausicaa.

► **Odysseus and Calypso**
Promised agelessness and immortality by Calypso, Odysseus was tempted to remain with her forever, but in the end he constructed a raft and resumed his journey home to Ithaca.

lands and wealth. The suitors were living off Odysseus's food and abusing his wife's hospitality, just like the hostile invaders he had seen in his vision in the Underworld. Penelope did not want to marry any of them, so she said she would declare her choice when she had finished weaving a tapestry on which she was working.

Finally, Penelope had to make up her mind. She said she would marry the man who could string Odysseus's powerful bow. No one recognized Odysseus (he revealed himself only to his son, Telemachus) as he took his place with the others. He was the only one who succeeded in stringing the bow. Then Penelope realized the man was her husband. With the help of Telemachus, he killed all the suitors. But, though he loved Penelope, Odysseus, after wandering for so long, found it hard to settle down in Ithaca. Soon he was planning another journey and looking forward to more adventures.

ITHACA

When Odysseus landed in Ithaca, he disguised himself as a beggar to find out what was going on in his house. He discovered that his wife and his son were alive, but they were beset by trouble. Many suitors were pressing Penelope for her hand in marriage. Because they believed Odysseus to be dead, their requests were legitimate, but still their behavior was inexcusable. For the Greeks, hospitality was the greatest of virtues, but the suitors abused Penelope's hospitality and showed no respect for her own sentiments. This abuse justified their eventual killing by Odysseus and his son, Telemachus.

► **Penelope weaving**
Odysseus's loyal wife unraveled a bit of her tapestry every night, to put off the day when she would have to choose between the many suitors clamoring for her hand.

◄ **Death of the suitors**
Odysseus and Telemachus both launched an attack on the suitors, who quaked behind their shields as they fell one by one.

DIVINE INTERVENTION

The gods of Mount Olympus not only influenced the Trojan War, but also had an impact on the adventures of Odysseus. Whenever the hero offended a deity, his journey home was delayed. Poseidon, Helios, and Zeus himself, all hampered the progress of the voyage. After blinding Polyphemus, Odysseus shouted out his real name to the Cyclops as he sailed away. Polyphemus told Poseidon that Odysseus had blinded him, and the sea god unleashed a series of storms to wreck his ships. When Odysseus's men slew the cattle of Helios, Zeus punished them. Though Hermes saved Odysseus from the magic of Circe, the one deity who consistently protected and advised the cunning hero was Athena.

▲ **Helios on his chariot**
The sun god (referred to as Hyperion by Homer) exerted his power when the Greeks ate the meat of his cattle, making the beef bellow as if it were alive.

▲ **Divine protector**
Athena was Odysseus's benefactor. She persuaded Calypso to release him, set up his meeting with Nausicaa, and advised him to disguise himself before confronting his wife's suitors.

SOME WORK OF NOBLE NOTE, MAY YET BE DONE, NOT UNBECOMING MEN THAT STROVE WITH GODS.

Alfred, Lord Tennyson, *Ulysses*, 1842

Poseidon

HOMER

Both the *Odyssey* and the *Iliad* are attributed to Homer, a blind poet who probably lived in the 8th century BCE. Little is known about Homer, and some scholars believe the epics were actually the work of earlier poets, who handed down the narratives by word of mouth, adapting and modifying them before they were written down by Homer himself. The two epics combine story, character, and poetic language so effectively that Homer is considered even today as one of the world's greatest writers.

Homer

MODERN ODYSSEYS

The adventures of Odysseus are immensely popular. Because Homer's epic is a powerful tale with an open-ended conclusion, its material has been used in new ways. One of these "modern Odysseys" is *The Odyssey: A Modern Sequel* (1938), a long poem by Nikos Kazantzakis (1883–1957), describing Odysseus's new adventures. *Ulysses* (1922), a novel by James Joyce (1882–1941), also uses the idea of an odyssey in its story about Leopold Bloom, a native of Dublin, who makes a meandering journey around his home city.

▶ **Joyce's *Ulysses***
Bloom's wanderings take place in the course of a single day. The characters and encounters allude to episodes from the Greek myth.

THE ODYSSEY

THE ARGONAUTS

The myth of Jason and the Argonauts is one of the greatest quest stories in all mythology. It concerns Jason, heir to the throne of Iolcus in northeastern Greece. When Jason was a child, his uncle, Pelias, usurped the kingdom and imprisoned Jason's father, King Aeson. Jason's mother, Alcimede, smuggled him away and entrusted his care to Cheiron the Centaur, who raised him. After Jason grew to manhood, he went to Pelias and demanded the kingdom that was rightfully his own. Pelias said that Jason could only be king if he stole and brought back the precious Golden Fleece from King Aeëtes of Colchis.

THE MYTH

For his journey to Colchis, Jason had a special ship built, named the *Argo*. The ship's timbers included planks taken from a sacred oak tree at the oracle of Zeus at Dodona, making the vessel especially strong. Jason persuaded many of Greece's greatest heroes, including Heracles, Polydeuces, Peleus, and Orpheus, to join him on the *Argo*. This group of heroes became known as the Argonauts.

DANGERS AND OBSTACLES

The heroes faced all kinds of obstacles on their journey, from encounters with attractive women who delayed their quest, to confrontations with the deadly perils of the sea. First, they were seduced by the all-female population of the island of Lemnos, delaying their progress for several months. Then one of their number, Hylas, left the quest when water nymphs pulled him into a well, and his friend, Heracles, distressed at his loss, left the *Argo* to save him. The remaining Argonauts had still more dangerous challenges ahead. They got involved in a boxing match with King Amycus, a formidable fighter who usually killed his opponents. They were saved by the prowess of Polydeuces, who is said to have invented the sport of boxing. In another encounter they met a blind prophet called Phineus who was tortured by the Harpies, bird-like creatures with women's heads, also known as the hounds of Zeus. These frightful beings continually snatched away Phineus's food and pecked at his eyes. Two of the Argonauts chased the Harpies away and in return a grateful Phineus helped them sail through the Clashing Rocks, one of several other perils that they had to negotiate before reaching Colchis.

▲ Harpies
With their hardened beaks and talons and their poisonous droppings, the Harpies were formidable monsters.

CHALLENGES IN COLCHIS

In Colchis, King Aeëtes did not want to lose the Golden Fleece, so he set Jason a challenge—to tame a pair of fire-breathing bulls and use them to pull a plough, dropping the teeth of serpents into the soil as he went. From the teeth, armed warriors would spring up to attack Jason. The hero only succeeded because the daughter of Aeëtes, the sorceress Medea, had fallen in love with him and helped him accomplish the task. Her father, however, still would not let Jason take the fleece. Then she suggested that Orpheus's music would charm the poisonous serpent guarding it and put it to sleep. With the fleece finally in his hands, Jason sailed for home, negotiating hazards such as Scylla and Charybdis, the Sirens, and the giant Talos, who threw huge rocks at the ship until Medea killed him with a deadly glance. At last Jason reached Iolcus and claimed his kingship.

▼ The Argo sets off
Jason wisely decided to take with him some of the strongest heroes in Greece. The crew set off on their perilous quest, cheered by the people of Iolcus.

KEY CHARACTERS

Ancient writings contain several different lists of the Argonauts, but they all agree in including many of the most prominent ancient Greek heroes, such as Heracles, Patroclus, and Peleus, as well as the twins Castor and Polydeuces. Some accounts list the huntress Atalanta as the only woman warrior among the crew. Most of these characters embodied great strength and skill in arms, but such qualities would have been useless without others such as the sorcery of Medea or the music of Orpheus.

◄ Jason
After his successful quest, some accounts state that Jason ruled happily in Iolcus. Others allege that his life was ruined by Medea's scheming.

▲ Medea
As she was a priestess of Hecate, the Underworld goddess, Medea could use her sorcery to help Jason.

◄ Orpheus
Orpheus's entrancing music helped the Argonauts on many occasions throughout their arduous journey.

THE HEROES SHONE LIKE GLEAMING STARS AMONG THE CLOUDS.

Apollonius of Rhodes, *Argonautica 1*

THE GOLDEN FLEECE

Athamas, king of Thebes, had a legitimate son, Phrixus, as well as children by Ino, his mistress. Ino tried to cause the death of Phrixus, so that one of her own children could inherit the throne. Nephele, the mother of Phrixus, arranged for him to fly out of danger to Colchis on the back of a golden ram. Aeëtes, ruler of Colchis, welcomed him, hoping that Phrixus would give him the ram, but he sacrificed the beast to Ares and the priests of Ares displayed the fleece in a garden. It was guarded by a serpent that never slept. Pelias, who sent Jason on his quest, was the cousin of Phrixus.

▲ The flying ram
The ram was such a tireless flyer that it carried Phrixus all the way from Thebes to Colchis, which was said to be at the very edge of the world.

DANGERS AT SEA

Jason and the Argonauts had to pass several of the perilous obstacles that had also been faced by Odysseus on his journey home from Troy—both heroes faced the Sirens, with their alluring music, and Scylla and Charybdis. In addition, Jason had to pass between the Clashing Rocks. The challenges of weather, navigation, and the perils of the sea took the Argonauts on a much longer route than Odysseus's, however. Their journey encompassed the Black Sea, the Danube, the Adriatic, and the Mediterranean.

▲ The Clashing Rocks
This pair of living rocks, said to be at the entrance to the Black Sea, slammed together when a ship tried to pass between them.

▲ The Sirens
The Sirens lured sailors with their seductive song. When the Argonauts sailed by them, Orpheus played his lyre continuously to drown out their voices.

▲ Scylla
The sea nymph Thetis helped the *Argo* to sail past Scylla, the monster who devoured sailors passing through the Strait of Messina.

THE ARGO

Made by the shipbuilder Argus, the *Argo* had a prow with the gift of prophecy given by Athena. The vessel was thus able to take Jason and his companions through a series of deadly perils. The craft had more than one bank of oars so it could be rowed at speed.

The ship with the magical prow

ROMAN GODS AND GODDESSES

The Romans adopted many of the gods of the Etruscans, the people who lived in northern Italy before them, and adapted them to Roman ideas and beliefs. These deities were eventually combined with aspects of gods from lands conquered by the Romans, particularly Greece. Many Roman deities are very similar to those of the ancient Greeks, but they usually have different names and sometimes different myths.

THE TRIUMVIRATE OF ROMAN DEITIES

The ancient Romans gave pre-eminence to Jupiter, Juno, and Minerva, known as the triumvirate. Jupiter began as the Etruscan sky god Tinia, who was then combined with Zeus, the Greek sky god – ruling the heavens like a Roman emperor, Jupiter was "best and greatest." Juno was his wife, and Minerva was the goddess of wisdom, arts, and crafts.

◀ **Jupiter**
Like Zeus, Jupiter was the all-powerful sky god. His weapon was a thunderbolt.

▶ **Juno**
Identified with the Greek goddess Hera, Juno was goddess of women, marriage, and childbirth.

▲ **Minerva**
Minerva shared many attributes with the Greek goddess Athena, but was a more distant deity for the Romans.

ROMAN GODDESSES

The goddesses of the Roman pantheon differed greatly in their roles. The most widely worshipped was Vesta, goddess of the hearth, but all the goddesses had festivals and popular shrines. They were also all originally Italian goddesses to whom the Romans added attributes of Greek goddesses. Vesta was the counterpart of Hestia, Ceres was an old Earth goddess who became equated with Demeter, Diana was a goddess of light and the moon who became identified with Artemis, and Venus was linked with Aphrodite as goddess of love.

▲ **Diana**
Much worshipped by women, Diana was a goddess of savage and wild places as well as children and childbirth.

▲ **Venus**
Worshipped mainly in the spring, Venus was, perhaps surprisingly, most dear to ordinary Roman soldiers who were about to set off on a military campaign.

▲ **Vesta**
The hearth goddess was revered by all Romans. By keeping their fireplace clean and decorated at all times, they hoped that she would bring their home and family good fortune.

▲ **Ceres**
Associated with the Earth, growth, and the Underworld, Ceres was worshipped by some in Greek, stressing her link to Demeter.

ROMAN GODS

The Romans followed a similar pattern with their gods as with their goddesses, identifying the deities of their Italian predecessors with those of the Greeks. Occasionally, however, they imported a Greek god, such as Apollo, who had no Roman parallel. But they tried to make all these deities clearly Roman in character. For example, they portrayed them in Roman clothes or armor, and attributed to most of them a moral rectitude that was very different from the amoral deities of the Greeks.

◄ Cupid
God of love or desire, Cupid was often referred to by Roman poets, but was not worshipped as widely as his Greek equivalent, Eros.

◄ Apollo
The Romans had no early equivalent to Apollo, and lifted this god of music, prophecy, cattle, and light straight from the Greek pantheon.

▲ Asclepius
The "best of physicians," Asclepius was the god of medicine and was equally popular in both ancient Greece and Rome.

▲ Bacchus
Counterpart of the Greek god Dionysus, the vine and honey god Bacchus was identified with Liber, the ancient Roman wine and fertility god.

◄ Mars
Long honored in Italy as a god of war and farming, Mars was the most important Roman god after the triumvirate. He became identified with the Greek god of war Ares.

▲ Mercury
An ancient god of trade, exchange, and transport, Mercury took on many traits of the Greek heavenly messenger Hermes.

▲ Neptune
The Romans were not great seafarers; Neptune was originally a god of water and rivers that the Romans later linked to the Greek sea god Poseidon.

➤ Vulcan
God of fire and blacksmiths, Vulcan was a version of the Greek Hephaestus. Originally a god of volcanoes, he was also worshipped to prevent fires.

ROMAN GODS AND GODDESSES

53

AENEAS AND THE ORIGINS OF ROME

A Trojan prince, Aeneas was the son of a mortal father, Anchises, and Venus, the goddess of love. He was a great hero and leader, whose escape from Troy and arrival in Rome was the result of prophecy, adventure, and divine intervention.

Although Aeneas did not actually found their city, the Romans saw him as the founder of their race. His remarkable life was celebrated in the epic poem, the *Aeneid,* by the great Roman poet Virgil (c.70–19 BCE).

THE MYTH

Aeneas had been told of two prophecies that would shape his life. The first said he would be the founder of a great dynasty, and the second, that he would destroy the city of Carthage in northern Africa. When the Trojan War ended, he began a journey to fulfil his destiny. Aeneas took with him his father, Anchises, who had been wounded in battle, but he died on the journey. Crossing the Aegean Sea, Aeneas and his friends visited the land of the Cyclopes—the aggressive one-eyed giants—from whom they escaped and set sail again. The goddess Juno, rival of Venus, did not want Aeneas to reach his goal, so she ordered Aeolus, god of the winds, to raise up a storm and wreck his ship. The waves washed up Aeneas and his men on a shore near Carthage.

◄ Wounded hero
Aeneas fought bravely during the Trojan War and was wounded by the Greek hero Diomedes. After Hector died, Aeneas played a leading role in the Trojan forces.

FROM CARTHAGE TO ITALY

Upon his arrival in Carthage, Aeneas was taken to the court of Queen Elissa and, due to the intervention of the goddess Venus, the two fell in love. But when Mercury, the messenger of the gods, reminded him of his destiny, Aeneas left Carthage and Elissa killed herself in despair.

Landing on the west coast of Italy, Aeneas found himself near Cumae, home of the Cumaean Sibyl, a prophetess who lived near the entrance to the Underworld. Aeneas visited the Underworld to see his father again, but while he was there, the Sibyl showed him a vision of the future of Rome. When he saw the vision, he was convinced that he should continue on his journey to establish the Roman race, so he went to Latium, the region on the banks of the River Tiber.

IN LATIUM

After arriving in Latium, Aeneas met the local king, Latinus, and the two agreed on a treaty that allowed Aeneas to marry the king's daughter, Lavinia. However, the princess was already betrothed to Turnus, the King of the Rutilians. An enraged Turnus declared war and the two sides fought for months. In the end, Aeneas killed Turnus and was able to unite the two states. From then on, the people of Latium, the Rutilians, and Aeneas's followers from Troy lived together peacefully and formed the race from which the Romans—including Romulus and Remus, the founders of the city of Rome itself—were descended.

◄ Aeneas and Anchises
Aeneas had to carry his wounded father on their journey, but Anchises died when they reached Sicily, where his son held lavish funeral games.

DIDO OF CARTHAGE

Later known as Dido, Elissa was married to Sichaeus, the King of Tyre. After his death, her brother took over the throne and she left the city. Eventually, she arrived on the North African coast, where she asked the local people for an area of land that could be bounded by a bull's hide. When they agreed, she cut a hide into thin strips, joined them together, and claimed a large area of land. She established the city of Carthage and ruled over it happily until Aeneas left her to go to Latium.

◀ **Death of Elissa**
When Aeneas left her, Elissa climbed on to a funeral pyre and stabbed herself to death. Her people gave her the name Dido, meaning "brave one."

▲ **Aeneas's ship**
A storm whipped up by Aeolus, god of the winds, blew Aeneas's ship to Carthage—the hero was under the influence of fate and the gods throughout his journey.

THE DESCENDANTS OF AENEAS

Aeneas played an important role in Roman mythology, not only because the Romans saw him as the founder of their race but also because, as the son of the goddess Venus, he enabled them to trace their lineage back to the gods. This link was immensely significant for the Romans, because it gave their ruler—in both Italy and their wider empire—a kind of legitimacy that put them on a level above the other rulers they had conquered or supplanted. In addition, certain influential Roman families, notably that of Emperor Julius Caesar (c.100–44 BCE), claimed a direct family link with Aeneas and with the gods.

▶ **Julius Caesar**
The Roman military leader and dictator, Caesar, a member of the family of Julius, claimed to be a descendant of Aeneas's son, Ascanius.

THE CUMAEAN SIBYL

The Sibyls were women who were skilled in prophecy. They often lived at places on the borders of the Earth and the Underworld, or where the worlds of the gods and humans came together. They used their proximity to the gods to predict the future. One of the most famous Sibyls lived at Cumae. She had been a stunningly beautiful young woman, with whom Apollo had fallen in love. He granted her a gift in return for her favors and she asked for immortality. But when she rebuffed Apollo, he condemned her to an eternal old age. When Aeneas came to consult her, she was a pathetic creature said to be about 700 years old.

▲ **The Cumaean Sibyl**
At the beginning of her prophetic career, the Sibyl of Cumae was a beautiful young woman who entranced both gods and mortals.

◀ **Aeneas and the Sibyl**
When Aeneas travelled to the Underworld from an entrance near Cumae, the Sibyl acted as his guide.

ROMULUS AND REMUS

The twins Romulus and Remus were the sons of a vestal virgin, the daughter of a usurped king of Alba Longa, who had broken her vows. Condemned to be drowned in the River Tiber, the brothers were found by a wolf that suckled them until a shepherd discovered and adopted them. When the twins grew up, they discovered their parentage and fought to restore Alba Longa to its rightful ruler. Later, they set out to found Rome, a new city on the banks of the Tiber.

She-wolf suckling Romulus and Remus

▲ **Thor fighting the serpent Nidhogg**
In Norse mythology, serpents are the enemies of deities and heroes.
Here, one of the most notorious, Nidhogg, rises from the ocean but
is attacked by the great god Thor, who wields his famous hammer.

NORTHERN EUROPE

The early cultures of far Northern Europe produced a fascinating body of myths about the creation of the cosmos and the lives and adventures of their deities. The influence of these great stories eventually spread far and wide.

Between the late 8th and early 11th centuries, the Viking raiders of Denmark, Norway, and Sweden became famous for their ruthless attacks on the coastal communities of Western Europe and for their daring voyages of exploration in longships. Although these Norsemen developed writing that used angular symbols called runes, they did not at first produce a great written literature. However, they did have a rich oral tradition, which produced some of the most enthralling stories in all world mythology.

NORSE DEITIES AND HEROES

The great Norse myths deal with great themes: the creation of the cosmos, the wars and loves of the deities, and the coming of the end of the world. They imagine different races of mythical beings—from giants to dwarfs—who live in different worlds that are parallel to our own home world, which is known as Midgard. The culture of the deities is warlike and heroic, and the real and mythical worlds meet at Valhalla, the great hall of the leading deity Odin, where the souls of deceased human heroes find their heavenly reward.

The stories of the Norse deities were mainly passed on by word of mouth. Some myths were written down by monks in monasteries as early as the 8th century, but most were first recorded in the 13th century. By this time, Norse travelers had even colonized Iceland, and it was

Icelandic writers who wrote down the myths and traditions of the Norse people. Their greatest writings included the *Prose Edda*, by Snorri Sturluson, who recorded all he could find of the Norse myths, and the *Poetic Edda*, written by an unknown hand, which adds further tales to the canon. Other Icelandic writers wrote prose sagas—texts that tell the stories of prominent Norse families and mix mythology and history.

GREAT INFLUENCE

Norse myths and culture proved influential for centuries. The Anglo-Saxons, who came from mainland Europe and settled in England in the 5th century, told stories that were derived from Scandinavia and sometimes even set there. The best-known example is the great Anglo-Saxon poem *Beowulf*, a tale of fantastic heroism and monster slaying set among the Danes and the Geats; the latter were probably the people of Sweden. In the Middle Ages, Norse myths also spread south to Germany, where stories of heroes influenced a great many poets and dramatists.

OTHER TRADITIONS

Meanwhile, other parts of Northern Europe had quite separate traditions of myth and legend. One of the richest came from Finland. Here, a large body of complex myths about the creation of the universe and the adventures of the early gods was handed down from generation to generation by word of mouth. Only in the 19th century did the Finnish scholar Elias Lönnrot write the stories down and combine them into a single, vast poetic epic called the *Kalevala*. This masterwork of storytelling became a symbol of Finland's national identity and has since been translated into many different languages, finally bringing the myths and legends of this small country to a worldwide audience.

▲ **Early Viking pendant**
This small silver pendant represents the head of either a Viking hero or one of the Norse gods. The figure wears an elaborate crested helmet.

▶ **Viking longship**
Short of good land to farm at home in Scandinavia, the Vikings traveled widely to find new territory in swift, streamlined longships. These well-built craft were known as "dragon-boats" because of their curving, dragon-like carved prows.

NORSE ORIGINS

Like all creation myths, Norse stories about the origin of the world attempt to explain natural phenomena. The earliest surviving accounts of Norse myths come from Icelandic writers. They set their creation story in a land where ice and fire come together as they do among the glaciers and steaming volcanoes of Iceland. To the north is the land of ice and snow, and to the south is a world of seething fire and flames. Life, in the form of the first giants, emerges from the interaction of these two opposing forces.

▲ **Audhumla**
The primal cow Audhumla nourished the giants with four streams of milk that flowed from her udders, increasing their strength and their brutality.

THE MYTH

In the beginning there was nothing but a vast void called Ginnungagap. Gradually, two realms appeared on either side of this void. Muspelheim, a region of heat and fire, formed in the south; Niflheim, a place of cold and ice, came into being in the north. In the center, between these two places, the hot air of Muspelheim met the cold air of Niflheim and the ice started to melt. Slowly the dripping ice formed the shape of a huge and monstrous being, a frost giant called Ymir.

THE GIANTS AND AUDHUMLA

Ymir slept and as the warm air from Muspelheim played across his body, he started to sweat. From his sweat other frost giants emerged—one male and one female from under his left arm, and another six-headed male from his legs. Meanwhile, the ice continued to melt into the shape of a huge cow called Audhumla, and her milk fed the first frost giants. Audhumla licked the ice and drank the water as it melted. As she licked away, a giant's head appeared, followed by his body, and after three days another giant was freed from the ice. So now there was a small group of frost giants who settled down in Niflheim. Buri, the first giant whom Audhumla had freed from the ice, had

▲ **Ash trees**
The first man and woman—Ask and Embla—were said to have been created from an ash and an elm trees.

a son named Bor, who married Bestla, daughter of a giant named Bölthorn. The couple had a trio of children named Odin, Vili, and Ve, who became the first three of the Norse gods, with Odin as their leader.

THE CREATION OF THE WORLD

The three gods were always battling Ymir, who frequently attacked them. Finally they got together and killed him. A flood of blood from Ymir's veins drowned all the frost giants except for Bergelmir (Ymir's grandson) and his wife, who escaped in a boat made from a tree trunk and settled in a place called Jotunheim. The three gods then made the Earth from Ymir's flesh, turning his unbroken bones into mountains. His blood became the rivers, lakes, and sea, and his skull the great dome of the sky. They threw sparks from Muspelheim high into the air to form the sun, the moon, and the stars. The gods then created the first man, called Ask, from an ash tree, and the first woman, called Embla, from an elm tree.

THE CREATORS

Odin, Vili, and Ve, the creator deities of Norse mythology, were the first of the Aesir, or sky gods. They lived in a fortress called Asgard at the highest point in the cosmos. Together they fought a long war with another group of gods, the Earth or fertility deities known as the Vanir, who were led by the sea god Njörd and his two children, Freyr and Freyja. The war was a stalemate, and the two sides agreed to a truce with the exchange of hostages. The Aesir sent two of their gods, the dull Hoenir and the wise Mimir, as hostages from their side. Unhappy with this exchange, the Vanir beheaded Mimir, and sent his head to the Aesir. Odin, who was always in search of wisdom, preserved the head and recited charms over it, and it advised him henceforth.

◄ The Aesir
Of the three leaders of the Aesir, Odin (meaning "frenzy"), a shape-changer who possessed superhuman strength in battle, is the most prominent in myths. By contrast, Vili (meaning "will") and Ve (meaning "sacred enclosure") are more shadowy figures who accompany Odin on his adventures.

▲ Sleipnir
Odin rode a grey, eight-legged horse called Sleipnir. The creature was known as the best and fastest of steeds, giving Odin a great advantage in battle.

ODIN WAS THE CLEVEREST OF ALL ALL OTHERS LEARNED FROM HIM.

Snorri Sturluson, *Ynglinga Saga*, c.1225

▼ Norse spear
The spear was one of the weapons commonly used by Norse warriors. Odin had a spear called Gungnir, which never missed its target.

Ask   Embla

ASK AND EMBLA

Most creation myths narrate the origin of a primal couple from whom the human race is descended. According to Norse mythology, Odin, Vili, and Ve were walking along a beach when they came upon two trees. They created Ask from the ash tree and Embla from the elm tree. Then each of the gods gave them a gift. Odin breathed life into them, Vili gave them thoughts and feelings, and Ve provided them with sight and hearing. The pair became the ancestors of all humans. They lived in Midgard (Middle Earth), the home created for them by the gods. It was protected by fortifications constructed from the eyebrows of Ymir.

RUNES

Early Norse writers used letters called runes, made up of vertical and diagonal strokes, to carve inscriptions in stone. Odin is said to have created the runic alphabet. Impaled on his own spear, he hung from Yggdrasil, the world tree, for nine days until the runes appeared before him. Runes were believed to have magical powers. Some of these rune stones combined runic inscriptions with mythological images. The one below shows Odin with the Goth king, Ermaneric, among whose family the god made trouble, leading to the death of Ermaneric's son.

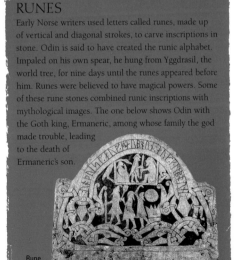

Rune stone

THE NORSE GODS

The principal Norse gods were descended from the race of giants who were the first inhabitants of the universe. The oldest and most powerful of the Norse deities was Odin, and many of the other gods—such as the thunder god Thor, and Balder, god of beauty and light— were his descendants. Several other gods and goddesses, including the shape-changing god Loki, descended from the giants, via a separate line. Another branch, not connected to the main tree, included a number of fertility deities, such as the weather god Freyr and his sister, Freyja, goddess of love.

AUDHUMLA

BURI

BOR — BESTLA

VILI

VE

FRIGG

ODIN

Frigg

Odin

Freyr

NJORD — SKADI

BALDER — NANNA

HOD

FORSETI

Balder

FREYR

FREYJA

Hod

Fenrir

YMIR

GIANTS

SIGYN — LOKI — ANGRBODA

NARVI   VALI

HEL   FENRIR   JORMUNGAND

EARTH — GRID

VÍDAR

SIF — THOR

MAGNI — MODI

HERMOD   BRAGI — IDUN   TYR

Loki

Sif

Tyr

Thor

Bragi   Idun

LOKI

Loki was the trickster of the Norse pantheon and the husband of the goddess Sigyn. He represented disorder, mischief-making, and irrationality, and always stood in the way of those who wanted to bring order and calm to the universe. Some said he interfered in the lives of humans too, and he was often blamed for giving ordinary people the desires and passions that caused problems in their lives. A shape-changer with an insatiable sexual appetite, his tricks ranged from simple pranks to cold-blooded murders.

THE TRICKS OF LOKI

A blood brother of Odin, Loki had three wives who bore him many children, but this was not enough for him. So he used his power of shape-changing to have affairs with goddesses, giants, humans, and animals. Loki also had a rapacious appetite for food, and even killed a dwarf called Otr for the salmon that he had caught. However, he occasionally used his trickery to help the gods. For instance, he hatched a plot to retrieve Thor's hammer, which had been stolen by the giant Thrym. The giant was willing to return the hammer only if the gods let him marry the goddess Freyja. So Loki suggested that Thor disguise himself as Freyja and go to the wedding dressed as a bride. Before the ceremony, Thrym brought out the hammer and Thor snatched it from him.

◀ **The shape-changer**
Although he is usually portrayed in human form, Loki's many disguises included a flea, a fly, a salmon, and a seal. To disguise himself as a bird, he stole Freyja's cloak of feathers.

▲ **Loki and Sif**
When Loki cut off the golden hair of the corn goddess Sif, the crops would not ripen. Sif's husband, Thor, threatened to kill Loki as a result.

▲ **Skilled Norse dwarfs**
Norse dwarfs were skilled craftsmen. When Thor threatened Loki for cutting Sif's hair, the trickster persuaded a dwarf to make new hair for the goddess.

THE DEATH OF BALDER

Balder was the son of Odin and Frigg, and the most handsome of all the gods. One night he had a dream that he would die. When Frigg found out about it, she made every living thing—animals, trees, and plants—promise not to harm her son. But while doing this, the goddess forgot to ask one plant, the mistletoe. Assuming that Balder was invincible, the gods often used him as a target for knife-throwing and archery. One day, they were hurling around all kinds of objects, such as rocks and branches. Loki had craftily learned from Frigg the secret that Balder was not immune to the mistletoe. He sharpened a twig of mistletoe to make a dart, placed it in the hand of the blind god Höd and helped Höd aim it at Balder. The dart pierced Balder's heart and killed him.

HANDSOME IN APPEARANCE, WICKED IN CHARACTER, AND VERY CHANGEABLE IN HIS WAYS.

Snorri Sturluson, *Prose Edda*, c.1220

▲ **Mistletoe**
The evergreen plant mistletoe, which bears fruit in the winter, is often regarded as a symbol of new birth. Ironically, it caused the death of Balder, beloved of the gods.

◄ **The punishment of Loki**
Loki was punished for causing Balder's death by being bound with the entrails of his son. The giantess Skadi placed a snake above him, which dripped venom onto him.

TRICKSTERS FROM OTHER CULTURES

Most mythologies have a trickster figure, a god who likes to play pranks on other deities or cause widespread chaos. These figures often have a large appetite for sex, food, and mischief. Such tricksters are usually a source of great amusement, but their pranks, like many of Loki's, can also have serious consequences. Some tricksters are also heroes and carry out brave deeds, like the Hindu god Hanuman. They may also be culture heroes, figures who bring the skills of civilization—such as fire- making, cooking, and medicine—to the human race.

► **Enki**
The creator god of Mesopotamia was also a trickster with an insatiable sexual appetite that even extended to his own daughter and granddaughter.

◄ **Hanuman**
The son of the Hindu wind god Vayu, Hanuman once tried to swallow the sun. A trickster in his youth, he later became a staunch devotee of Lord Rama.

► **Ananse**
This West African spider god was credited with teaching humans such skills as fire-making, but he was also an incorrigible trickster.

◄ **Coyote**
Appearing in many North American myths, Coyote loved making mischief and once blew out the light of the moon.

LOKI

KALEVALA

The *Kalevala*, an epic poem, is based on the traditional oral poetry of eastern Finland and is the national epic of the country. It tells of the creation of the world, and about rivalries between the country of the Finnish people (Kalevala) and the Northland (Pohjola). It also describes how three Finnish heroes—Väinämöinen, Ilmarinen, and Lemminkäinen—woo the princess of the Northland.

THE MYTH

The story begins with Ilma, the air, who existed before time began. She had a daughter called Luonnotar, who wandered ceaselessly through the clouds made by her mother. After many years she fell, exhausted, into the ocean.

VÄINÄMÖINEN AND THE GIANT

Luonnotar floated in the water for 700 years. Without her knowledge, the lapping water made her pregnant; but her pregnancy was so prolonged that her child, Väinämöinen, had already become an old man while still in her womb. After his birth, Väinämöinen swam across the waters until he reached the land that was to become Finland. He had started to make a home for himself there when he was challenged by a giant named Joukahainen. At first the two quarreled violently, but Väinämöinen, who was a skilled musician, defeated the giant in a musical contest and won the hand of Aino, Joukahainen's sister, in marriage. However, Aino did not want to marry an old man, and thus chose to drown herself rather than submit to this alliance. So Väinämöinen decided to go to Pohjola, the Northland, to find himself a wife.

▶ **Väinämöinen**
The central character of the *Kalevala* is an unusual hero, an old man who possesses sheer determination and an outstanding musical gift.

IMPOSSIBLE TASKS

The journey to Northland was long and arduous, but finally Väinämöinen reached Pohjola and met its ruler, Louhi. She promised Väinämöinen that he would be allowed to marry her daughter if he could make a sampo, a magical mill that could produce salt, flour, and gold. Väinämöinen agreed to try, in spite of the fact that such a machine had never been made. He returned to Finland to make the sampo, but on the way he met Louhi's daughter, the Maid of the North, and asked her to marry him without the sampo. She agreed—provided that he accomplished a few more apparently impossible tasks, including peeling a stone, knotting an egg, splitting a hair with a blunt knife, and making a boat out of a weaving shuttle. Väinämöinen was distracted from these tasks by spirits sent by Louhi, and so he asked his brother, Ilmarinen, who was a master craftsman, to make the sampo for him. After a lot of hard work, Ilmarinen managed to forge the sampo. He was then asked to perform some more tasks, including ploughing a field full of vipers. When he succeeded, he was allowed to marry Louhi's daughter. Väinämöinen had forgotten that it was the maker of the sampo who would win the hand of the Maid of the North, so he was disappointed in love once more. ≫

▶ **Louhi**
With magical powers, including the ability to fly, Louhi, the ruler of the Northland, made a formidable figure. She would have been even more powerful if she had kept hold of the sampo.

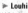

KEY CHARACTERS

The *Kalevala* is a collection of many Finnish legends with several characters. Among these, Väinämöinen is present throughout, and at the end he leaves behind the kantele, his musical instrument, as a symbol of continuing Finnish culture. His brother, Ilmarinen, is a blacksmith-sorcerer. Lemminkäinen is the poem's trickster figure. His many sexual encounters in his quest for a wife are typical of tricksters in myth. But he is also brave enough to visit the Underworld to kill the Swan of Tuonela in a bid to win Louhi's daughter.

▶ Ilmarinen
One of Ilmarinen's tasks is to plough a field of serpents. The Maid of the North helps him in this task by telling him to forge a special plough and use his magic to subdue the serpents.

SLOWLY WAKES THE SON AND HERO, RISES FROM THE DEPTHS OF SLUMBER, SPEAKS AGAIN IN MAGIC ACCENTS.

Elias Lönnrot, *Kalevala*, c.1849

▶ Lemminkäinen
When Lemminkäinen is killed on his perilous visit to the Underworld, his mother is able to reassemble his body, then give him back the breath of life.

THE FINNISH CREATION STORY

While Luonnotar was floating in the ocean, a duck swam by and laid her eggs on Luonnotar's knee, which was sticking out of the water. Then the bird settled down to hatch them. When Luonnotar moved, the duck was frightened and flew off. The eggs rolled away and broke, and from them the world was created. One half of the shells fused together to make up the sky and from the other half the land was created. The yolk was transformed into the sun and the albumen became the moon.

Primal duck

◀ Luonnotar
The myth's creator figure is passive, and the creation from the duck's eggs happens by accident. Some versions claim that it was an eagle that laid its eggs on her knee.

THE SAMPO

Described as a mill that would produce salt, flour, and gold, the sampo was a strange object made from many bizarre components. It was finally forged by Ilmarinen after his initial attempts produced a crossbow, a boat, a heifer, and a plough, which he threw back into the fire. The sampo has two symbolic qualities: it is the bride price of Louhi's daughter, and it also represents the wealth of the Finnish people.

Plough

Boat

Crossbow

Heifer

RECLAIMING THE SAMPO

Ilmarinen and Louhi's daughter did not stay together for long. The Maid of the North was killed soon after the marriage because she had ill-treated a magician called Kullervo (*see opposite*). Ilmarinen wanted to marry Louhi's other daughter, but Louhi refused. So Ilmarinen returned to Finland and the people of Northland kept the sampo.

Väinämöinen and Ilmarinen thought it was unfair that Louhi and her people had kept the sampo and the riches it provided. They decided that if they could not find a wife in Northland, at least they could ensure prosperity for their homeland by stealing the sampo back. So the two brothers set sail for the North, taking with them Lemminkäinen, the adventurer and trickster. Lemminkäinen had once gone to Pohjola to woo one of Louhi's daughters, and there he had been given some tasks to accomplish. One of these was to kill the Swan of Tuonela in the Underworld; Lemminkäinen

The escape
Väinämöinen and his companions had to fight off an infuriated Louhi who pursued them in the form of a gigantic bird.

The last journey
The poem suggests that Väinämöinen's last journey in a boat, travelling up the sunbeams, is to a kind of halfway land between the Earth and the sky, from which he will one day return.

was killed there, but restored to life by his mother. Now he sought revenge against Louhi. During their voyage the three heroes caught a fish and Väinämöinen made a kantele, a magical harp-like musical instrument, from its backbone. It had the power to charm its listeners and put them to sleep.

When they arrived in the Northland, Väinämöinen played a tune on the kantele and lulled Louhi and her followers into a deep sleep. Then they soon got hold of the sampo and set sail for home. Unfortunately, just then Lemminkäinen began to sing a loud and triumphant song that woke up Louhi and her people. Enraged, Louhi sent storms to wreck their boat and transformed herself into a monstrous bird of prey to pursue them. In the tumult, the sampo was broken into many pieces, some of which sank to the bottom of the sea.

Väinämöinen gathered as many of the pieces of the sampo as he could. Although he and his brother realized that they would never be able to recreate it, they felt that even its magical parts might bring prosperity to their country. Väinämöinen bequeathed these fragments to the Finnish people. By now a very old man, he realized his powers were waning. He sailed away from this life, but it is said that he will return whenever his people need him.

FINNISH NATURE SPIRITS

With its deep lakes and dense forests, Finland presents a dramatic and sometimes harsh landscape. Its early poets and storytellers responded to this environment by imagining a host of nature spirits who represented the character of their land. One of the best known spirits is Tapio, the god of forests, who typifies this response to the landscape—some accounts say that his beard was made of trees while his eyes were bottomless lakes. He was so closely identified with Finland that sometimes the country was called Tapiola. Pellervoinen was another such nature spirit, a harvest god who presided over fields and meadows.

◄ Tapio
In the *Kalevala*, Lemminkäinen appeals to Tapio to help him catch the moose of Hisi in the forest, one of the tasks he has to accomplish to marry Louhi's daughter.

► Pellervoinen
A spirit of fertility, Pellervoinen appears at the beginning of the *Kalevala*. He sows the seeds in swamps and barren lands from which the trees of Finland grow.

THE TALE OF MARJATTA

At the end of the *Kalevala*, the story of Marjatta is told. Marjatta, a virgin, became pregnant after eating a berry and gave birth to a son. Since the child had been born out of wedlock, Väinämöinen wanted the baby killed. But the sky god Ukko, after hearing certain details of Väinämöinen's own past, declared instead that Marjatta's child should become the king, replacing Väinämöinen as the ruler of Finland.

▲ **Berries**
The Finnish word for berry, *marja*, is similar to Marjatta and Maria. In the *Kalevala*, the berry calls to Marjatta, pleading with her to pluck it.

▶ **Marjatta with her baby**
The birth of Marjatta's child signals the arrival of a new age. The story of Marjatta takes the *Kalevala* into a new direction. It is an allegory that points to the coming of Christianity to Finland.

THE CURSE OF KULLERVO

Kullervo and his sister had been sold into slavery by their stepfather. Kullervo worked for the Maid of the North, who treated him very badly. One day, she baked a stone in his bread. He broke his magic knife trying to slice the bread. Enraged, he cursed his cruel mistress and transformed her cattle into wild animals, which tore her to pieces. Kullervo was heading home when he met and fell in love with a girl. The two made love, but later they discovered that they were brother and sister, and the girl committed suicide. Kullervo then tracked down his mother and stepfather and killed them before taking his own life.

Magic knife

▶ **Kullervo**
The story of Kullervo is a powerful tragedy in which a hero of great promise is subjected to a cruel fate for no apparent fault of his own.

JEAN SIBELIUS

Finland's best-known composer, Jean Sibelius (1865–1957), was inspired by the traditional poetry of his country, especially the *Kalevala*. His compositions include the tone poem *Pohjola's Daughter*, and a choral symphony based on the story of Kullervo. Through these works he became closely associated with Finland's national identity.

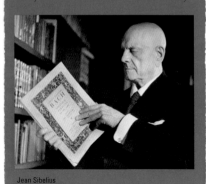

Jean Sibelius

> ## TEAR AND KILL THE WICKED HOSTESS, TEAR HER GUILTY FLESH IN PIECES, WHEN SHE COMES TO VIEW HER CATTLE.
>
> Elias Lönnrot, *Kalevala*, c.1849

TUONELA

The Finnish Underworld, or Tuonela, was the realm of Tuoni and Tuonetar. It was a place of darkness and silence, surrounded by dense thickets, deep forests, and a dark, icy river. These defences made it difficult to escape from Tuonela, and most of those who entered here were eaten by a monster called Surma. Any soul that survived was given the beer of oblivion, which made them forget everything about their life on Earth. The only mortal to visit Tuonela was Lemminkäinen. There, he was killed by a water snake, and torn to pieces by one of Tuoni's children.

◀ **The Swan of Tuonela**
Lemminkäinen's task was to shoot the swan that swam in the dark river surrounding Tuoni's kingdom.

BEOWULF

The life of the hero Beowulf is depicted in the great Anglo-Saxon poem of the same name, a work that champions the values of honor, valor, and friendship. The poem begins with the story of young Beowulf, a warrior of the Geats, a people from southern Sweden. He is a man with the strength and courage to defeat the most terrible opponents. *Beowulf* goes on to describe how the hero slays the monsters that terrorize the Danes. Later, he becomes the Geatish king and enjoys a long reign before facing his final challenge and a heroic death.

THE MYTH

As a young man, Beowulf travelled to Denmark. For many years, King Hrothgar of Denmark and his people had been terrorized by a monster called Grendel. It would break into Hrothgar's palace hall at night, kill some of the sleeping warriors, and carry them off for food. Beowulf offered to fight the monster, and laid a trap for Grendel, mortally wounding the creature, and eventually killing it. King Hrothgar was overjoyed and bestowed many gifts on Beowulf.

GRENDEL'S MOTHER

Grendel's death infuriated his monstrous mother, and she attacked the people in Heorot, seeking revenge. She lived in a lake, so Beowulf dived into its murky depths to challenge and fight her. It was a long, hard struggle for Beowulf because he could not manage to penetrate the monster's thick, scaly hide with his sword. In the end, he was able to take a weapon from the creature's armory and stab her with it, killing the monster and ensuring peace for the Danes. After this triumph, Beowulf returned to the land of the Geats, where he was made king and ruled his people for 50 years.

BEOWULF AND THE DRAGON

When Beowulf was an old man, he was faced with the prospect of battling yet another monster, one that was attacking the Geats. A dragon had guarded a hoard of treasure in an ancient burial mound for hundreds of years. When a thief entered the mound and stole a precious cup from the hoard, the enraged dragon went on the rampage. So Beowulf and a group of his bravest warriors set out to confront the beast. Beowulf carried a strong metal shield to protect himself from the dragon's hot breath, but his sword was unable to pierce the beast's scaly skin. His warriors began to desert him one at a time, fleeing in terror, and it seemed that Beowulf would be defeated when the dragon grabbed him by the neck.

A faithful warrior named Wiglaf, who had remained by Beowulf's side, then stabbed at the monster's belly with his sword, while Beowulf attacked the dragon with his knife. The combined effort weakened the dragon and it fell down dead. The monster had been slain, but not before the creature's hot, venomous breath had poisoned Beowulf, and he lay dying. With his death imminent, Beowulf declared Wiglaf as his successor and bequeathed his treasures, weapons, and armor to the young hero who had helped him in ending the menace.

▼ **Beowulf, the monster-slayer**
During his clash with the monster Grendel, Beowulf demonstrated his almost superhuman strength by tearing off one of the creature's arms.

MONSTERS

The monsters in *Beowulf* and in other Northern European myths are creatures whose strength exceeds that of ordinary human warriors. They lurk in dark places, such as the bottom of the lake where Grendel's mother had her lair, and their very appearance is hideous enough to frighten most people. Dragons have a thick, scaly skin, which is invulnerable to most weapons, and they breathe fire, which is poisonous and hot. Their form is often described as serpent-like, but some also have wings. In general, these creatures were conceived to emphasize the heroism of the valiant warriors who defeated them. But in *Beowulf*, there is also a Christian tone to the poem; the monsters are seen as heathen or non-Christian creatures that fight the heroes, who are godly and righteous.

◀ **Gruesome Grendel**
The monster Grendel is often portrayed as a hideous beast that would carry off its Danish victims to an underwater lair and subsequently feed on them.

WIDE WAS THE DRAGON'S WARRING SEEN, ITS FIENDISH FURY FAR AND NEAR, AS THE GRIM DESTROYER THOSE GEATISH PEOPLE HATED AND HOUNDED.

Beowulf, c.11th century

▲ **Slaying the dragon**
It took two heroes, Beowulf and Wiglaf, to kill the dragon that attacked the Geats. By staying by his leader's side, Wiglaf showed that he was a true hero, brave and loyal enough to inherit the Geatish throne.

BURIAL TREASURE

Anglo-Saxon poetry mentions treasures such as rings and jewels, which a king would bestow on his bravest warriors. Also, when great Anglo-Saxon kings died, they were buried with some of their treasures. The largest such collection of precious items was unearthed at a ship burial at Sutton Hoo in eastern England in 1939. This was the grave of an unknown East Anglian king (possibly Redwald, who died c.627), and the collection had both Christian and non-Christian items, showing a mixture of beliefs.

Anglo-Saxon coins

Anglo-Saxon helmet

▲ **Sutton Hoo treasure**
Besides the gilt bronze helmet, coins, and gold buckle (above), the Sutton Hoo burial contained a jeweled sword, a royal scepter, silver dishes, and drinking vessels.

THE ANGLO-SAXONS

After the Romans left Britain in the 5th century CE, the southern part of the country was ruled by invaders from northern Germany and Denmark, who came to be called the Anglo-Saxons. Their language, known as Anglo-Saxon or Old English, was a Germanic tongue that later evolved into modern English. Anglo-Saxon monks and scholars used Old English to compose works of prose, riddles, a history book called the *Anglo-Saxon Chronicle*, and poems on heroic and religious subject matter.

Beowulf manuscript (10th century)

MAGNUS ARTURUS REX
POTENTISSIMUS ANGLIAE

DOMINUS LUNCELOT DU L
EQUES INVICTUS

▲ **King Arthur as a medieval English monarch**
Although said to be a king of earlier times, Arthur has often been seen as the ideal medieval
English monarch and was frequently portrayed as such in medieval costume, as in this 1862
stained glass representation by the noted Victorian artist William Morris (1834–96).

WESTERN EUROPE

The ancient Celts were an early European people who had an influence on mythology that lasted for hundreds of years. From their shadowy early deities to their later tales of heroes, their myths still fascinate people to this day.

The ancient Celts were a group of tribes, probably originating from Central Europe, who expanded across the whole continent between the 5th century BCE and the growth of Roman power in the 3rd century BCE. Although there was no Celtic empire, there were Celtic settlements in areas as far apart as Spain and Turkey, and at many places in between. But as the Roman Empire expanded, the Celts were pushed out to the edges of Europe, particularly to Ireland, Wales, Scotland, and parts of western France. These areas are the heartlands of the early Celtic mythology that has come down to us through the centuries.

CELTIC MYTHS

The early Celts did not leave written records. Their Roman conquerors described them as being warlike and barbarous, though this was probably a highly biased view. The Romans did, however, record a certain amount of information about early Celtic deities. Archaeological remains from this time—including sites such as burial mounds, around which local legends have grown—have added to our knowledge of these elusive ancient people and their beliefs. Much later, between the 11th and 14th centuries, a few monks in Wales and Ireland wrote down what they knew of the stories of the Celts. These tales—of the Irish gods, of Irish heroes such as Cúchulain, and of Welsh myths recorded in

▲ **Bryn Celli Ddu burial site**
Ancient burial mounds like this one on the Isle of Anglesey (c.2000 BCE) were thought to be magical, and their entrances seen by some as gateways to the Otherworld.

the books known as the *Mabinogi*—are windows into an enthralling mythical world. They tell of magic and sorcery, of remarkable transformations, of fantastic giants, and of journeys into an Otherworld, where time stands still and people are perpetually youthful. These stories have been much retold over the centuries, and have inspired poetry in many Western European languages.

ARTHURIAN LEGENDS

Another group of myths appeared for the first time in the Middle Ages. These concern King Arthur, a legendary king of Britain who may have been based on a real 5th or 6th-century king or chieftain, although the evidence is scanty. Beginning with Geoffrey of Monmouth (d.1155), a number of writers set down the deeds of King Arthur and his followers. These early versions of the legend vary, but all portray Arthur as a brave and virtuous king who is betrayed by his relative, Mordred. Further elements—the round table and its knights, the search for the Holy Grail, and subplots about the king's various followers—were added to later versions of the Arthurian legends.

During the Middle Ages, poets and prose writers both in Britain and abroad became fascinated with the stories of King Arthur and his associates, or the "Matter of Britain" as these legends became collectively known. Writers from the French poet Chrétien de Troyes to the English prose writer Thomas Malory were famous for recording—and also adding to—the stories of Arthur, as well as other tales of chivalry. In the process, the various knights of the Round Table acquired stories that sometimes became more important than those of King Arthur himself. Sir Gawain, who beheads a mysterious Green Knight, and Sir Lancelot, who becomes the lover of Arthur's queen, Guinevere, are well-known examples. Centuries later, people all over the world are still reading versions of these stories with great fascination.

◀ **Celtic cauldron**
Cauldrons play a key role in several ancient Celtic myths. This is the Gundestrup Cauldron, a 1st-century BCE metal vessel from Denmark, on the edge of the Celtic world. It is covered in images of Cernunnos, Lord of the Beasts.

MYTHS OF THE ANCIENT CELTS

The territory of the ancient Celtic people stretched from Britain, across France and Germany, to Central Europe. Although they were not literate to begin with, these people had a highly developed culture, and excavations of their graves and religious sites show that they worshipped many different gods and goddesses. The Romans, who eventually conquered most of their lands, left descriptions of some of the Celtic deities and religious rituals, and identified many of those deities with their own.

THE GOOD STRIKER

Sucellos, whose name means "the Good Striker," was found in various parts of the Celtic world, especially in Gaul (modern-day France) and Britain. Often said to be a deity of agriculture and forests, his precise significance is still unknown. He is usually depicted as a long-haired, bearded figure, carrying a hammer in his left hand. His main attribute is this hammer, but the symbolism associated with it is unclear; it may have been a weapon, a tool used in one of the crafts, or simply a symbol of the deity's power. Sucellos is generally portrayed as standing with his consort, the goddess Nantosuelta, who carries a dish (perhaps a piece of ritual equipment) and a long pole topped with a house (which may indicate that she was a domestic goddess).

◀ **Symbol of Sucellos**
Sucellos presided over the grape harvest, sometimes carrying a pot or a barrel to store wine made from the grapes.

▲ **Nantosuelta**
The goddess Nantosuelta may have been associated with prosperity, wellbeing, and domestic life.

◀ **Sucellos's hammer**
The hammer or mallet usually carried by Sucellos is the reason for his title, "the Good Striker."

▲ **Cernunnos**
The Horned God or Cernunnos was often depicted as the "Lord of the Beasts," surrounded by animals that included a bull, stag, wild boar, and serpent.

THE HORNED GOD

Cernunnos is known as the horned god because he took the form of a man with the horns (and sometimes the hooves and ears) of a stag. He is usually shown with long hair and a beard, often wearing a neck-ring, or torc, which is the Celtic sign of noble birth. Cernunnos seems to have been widely worshipped in Celtic Europe, and was probably a "wild" god like the Classical Pan. His horns suggest that he was a deity of fertility, and to emphasize this point, he was associated with symbols such as the cornucopia (horn of plenty), with fruit, and with containers of grain. This function probably encompassed both sexual fertility and the fecundity of the fields.

Neck-ring or torc

THE THUNDERER

Taranis was a sky god and a major deity in Celtic Britain; he was apparently much worshipped when the Romans invaded the island in the 1st century CE. Latin writers described him as a god of war and likened him to Jupiter; the common attribute between Taranis and Jupiter being the control of thunder. The Celts also had a sky god who was represented by a wheel or disc and who governed the sun. Sometimes, this wheel god is equated with Taranis. The Romans observed that worshippers of Taranis comprised a cruel cult. The Celts made sacrifices to Taranis, with the offerings sometimes including humans who were burned alive in wooden boats or left to drown in bogs. This form of worship may confirm that Taranis, although a sky god, was related to the Romano-Celtic god Dis Pater, an Underworld deity.

▲ Wheel of Taranis
The spoked wheel, representing both the sun's rays as well as its movement, was used in the Celtic world to represent the sun and its deities, possibly including Taranis.

◀ God of the sky
This sky god, with his wheel and lightning bolt, may represent a deity who is a combination of Taranis and Jupiter, the sky god of the invading Romans.

◀ Lightning of the gods
The Celts considered thunder and lightning to be evidence of the supernatural activity of the gods, and treated places struck by lightning as sacred spots.

GOD OF FIRE AND LIGHT

Belenus, also known as Bel or Belus, was a Celtic god of light and the sun. All his names include an element meaning either "bright" or "shining." A widely worshipped deity across much of Europe, Belenus had shrines that were located as far apart as Britain, Austria, and Italy. Being associated with healing as well as the sun, Belenus is also believed to be the Celtic equivalent of Apollo. As with Apollo, some of Belenus's shrines were built near springs, where worshippers went to drink water in the hope of a cure. The springtime feast of Beltane in Celtic Britain, during which fires were lit to mark the lengthening of the days and the better weather, may have been linked with the worship of Belenus.

◀ God of the sun
The lines surrounding Belenus's head may depict the warm, glowing rays of light emanating from the sun god.

TRIPLE DEITIES

The Celts were fascinated by things that came in threes. They made images of bulls with three horns and gods with three faces or heads. The Welsh and Irish wrote triads, poems with three lines that described three concepts. And Celtic legends often speak of people with three sons or daughters. Gods and goddesses also came in groups of three. A number of Celtic carvings and reliefs show a trio of female deities standing together. This trio of goddesses or "triple mother" seems to have been considered particularly powerful by the Celts. They represent both human fertility and the bounty of the earth, and have dominion over human life and well-being. They also seem to symbolize the span of human life—many trios of goddesses take the form of women of different ages.

◀ Triple deities
Celtic reliefs often showed the trio of goddesses carrying baskets that probably contained fruits or vegetables, representing the bounty of the Earth.

THE ULSTER CYCLE

One of the most famous and compelling Irish myths involves the deeds of the men of Ulster, in Northern Ireland. The great hero of the Ulster Cycle of myths is Cúchulain, a fearless warrior. He was known for his terrifying battle frenzy, when his eyes glared and his voice roared, and his spear was considered to be almost invincible. His story includes a remarkable childhood, a long period at war with Ulster's rival Irish kingdom Connaught involving dramatic single combats, and a heroic death.

THE MYTH

King Conchobar of Ulster had a retinue of 150 boys who were training to be warriors. His nephew, Cúchulain, wanted to be a part of the band, but the boy's mother insisted that he was too young. Angry at being left out, Cúchulain set off to join the other boys, but they ridiculed him for being too small, and attacked him. Cúchulain went berserk—his head grew so hot that a red glow surrounded it, and he began to snarl fiercely. His attackers ran away, quaking with fear. Conchobar was impressed with his young nephew's power, and he recruited the boy into his service at once.

As a young man, Cúchulain wooed Emer, considered to be the most beautiful woman in Ireland. But Emer's father, Forgall, did not approve of the match; he wanted someone better for his daughter. Forgall persuaded Conchobar to send Cúchulain to Scotland to study the art of war from a famous warrior-woman called

▶ **Bull of Cooley**
Bulls were a symbol of power or wealth, so Maeve stole the bull of Ulster to get even with her husband.

Sgatha. When Cúchulain returned, Forgall barred him from entering his fortress, but the warrior scaled the walls and carried Emer away.

CÚCHULAIN AT WAR

Queen Maeve of Connaught owned a great white-horned bull, which was one of her most prized possessions. One day, it defected to the herd of her husband, King Ailill, so she stole the Brown Bull of Cooley, one of the finest creatures in Ulster. The men of Ulster wanted to retaliate but they were suffering from an ancient curse that made them ill at times of difficulty. Only Cúchulain remained immune to the curse due to his divine birth; his father was the sun god Lugh. He took on some of Connaught's best warriors in single combat, and they fell one by one. Then he climbed into his chariot and ran amok among the rest of the rival army, killing many others.

Queen Maeve continued to send reinforcements, including Cúchulain's friend, Ferdiad, who was fighting on her side. The hero prepared for battle again, but this time the signs were ominous. His wine turned to blood and he saw a girl weeping and washing bloodstained clothes. Cúchulain knew then that his death was imminent, but he killed many of the enemy, including Ferdiad, until a spear pierced his body. He dragged himself to a standing stone and bound himself to it, so that he would die on his feet. A crow—said to be Morrigan, the death goddess—landed on his shoulder, and he died.

◀ **Ferdiad's death**
Beguiled into fighting for Maeve, Ferdiad pushed Cúchulain into a fjord, but was finally slain by him.

ORIGINS OF CÚCHULAIN'S NAME

Originally named Sedanta, Cúchulain was the son of a mortal woman, Deichtine, and the Irish sun god Lugh. While still a boy, Conchobar invited him to a feast held by a blacksmith named Culann. He arrived late, and when Culann's guard dog attacked him, he killed it with his bare hands. To placate the blacksmith, the boy offered to act as a guard until Culann could breed another dog. Thus, he was given the name Cúchulain, "the hound of Culann."

◄ **The killing of the hound**
Cúchulain came to be associated with dogs, creatures that were seen as both strong and loyal, after killing Culann's hound.

► **Lugh, the sun god**
Chief of the Irish gods, Cúchulain's father was a great warrior, and skilled in the arts. He gave his great strength and power to his son.

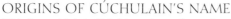

SEDANTA GRABBED THE HOUND BY ITS LEGS AND SMASHED ITS HEAD ON THE STONE COURTYARD.

ULSTER AND CONNAUGHT

Irish myths tell how the land was invaded by legendary races; one of these, known as the Fir Bolg, divided Ireland into five provinces: Ulster, Leinster, Connaught, Munster, and Meath. Much later, Ulster and Connaught became great rivals, and their rivalry was described in a great Irish epic poem, *Táin Bò Cuailgne* (The Cattle Raid of Cooley), written around the 8th century. A source for many stories about Irish heroes, the poem explains how Maeve lost her bull to her husband, leading her to steal the bull of Ulster.

▲ **King Conchobar**
A man of great power and wisdom, the ruler of Ulster was said to be the son of a druid.

▲ **Queen Maeve's warning**
Although she was warned about her defeat, Queen Maeve nevertheless stole the Bull of Cooley and forced the men of Connaught to fight against Ulster.

DEIRDRE OF THE SORROWS

A tragic myth associated with Conchobar is that of Deirdre, the daughter of the king's bard. It was predicted that she would be very beautiful, so Conchobar had her brought up in seclusion, intending to marry her later. One day, she saw the king skinning a calf and a raven drinking its blood. She declared that she would marry someone with hair like the raven's feathers, cheeks like the calf's blood, and a body as white as snow. Naoise, one of Conchobar's knights, was such a man. The two fell in love and eloped. The king enticed them back and had Naoise killed. He tried to persuade Deirdre to marry him, but she opted to kill herself instead.

▲ **Deirdre and Naoise**
To escape King Conchobar, Deirdre and Naoise fled across the sea to Scotland, but even there they were not safe from Conchobar's clutches.

◄ **Fergus mac Róich**
The great Ulster warrior Fergus mac Róich, who has a role in many Celtic tales, was sent to escort Deirdre and Naoise home. He was later killed in a lake by the jealous ruler of a Connaught district.

MAGICAL WORLDS

Ancient Celtic literature abounds with stories of people visiting magical worlds that are separate from but close to our own. The denizens of such Otherworlds do not age, and live a pleasant life, free of pain and despair. Time

telescopes in their world so that hundreds of human years pass by quickly, unnoticed by the visiting mortals. But, although life in the Otherworld is tranquil and idyllic, visitors generally feel a fatal longing to return home.

THE LAND OF THE YOUNG

Oisín was the famous son of Finn mac Cool and one of the Fian, a group of warriors who fought for Ireland. Once, when hunting, he met a beautiful woman called Niamh Chinn Óir (Niamh of the Golden Hair), riding a white horse. Niamh professed her love to Oisín and asked him to accompany her to Tir na nÓg, the "Land of the Young," of which she was queen. On the way to this magical world, Oisín killed a giant, and having shown his bravery, was given Niamh as his bride. The couple lived happily for centuries, but Oisín eventually grew homesick and decided to visit Ireland. He discovered that much had changed since his departure. Niamh had warned Oisín not to dismount from his horse in Ireland, but he forgot when he saw some men needing help to lift a boulder. As soon as his feet touched the ground, he became old and died.

▲ **Oisín**
Besides being a warrior and a shape-changer, Oisín was the poet of the Fian, and many of the adventures of Finn mac Cool and his people are told from Oisín's point of view.

▶ **Queen of Tir na nÓg**
Niamh Chinn Óir was a young woman of exceptional beauty, who would ride across Ireland on horseback. She ruled a land where nobody aged or fell sick but where the years passed by like minutes.

◀ **Oisín and the boulder**
Oisín saw two men struggling to raise a boulder as he passed on his horse. But when he stepped down from his mount to help them, he aged 300 years in a few moments.

THE LAND OF WOMEN

Máel Dúin was an illegitimate child. One day he learned that his father had been slain by raiders and set off to seek the killers. He and his 17 companions visited many islands, each with amazing inhabitants, including enormous birds, fighting horses, and other wonders. Finally, the travelers reached the "Land of Women," where the queen married Máel Dúin and offered her daughters as wives to his crew. After staying there for three months, the men wanted to return home. But every time they set sail, the queen threw a length of twine that stuck to Máel Dúin's hand, and she pulled them back in. Finally, another sailor caught the twine and the others cut off his arm to help them escape.

◀ **Isle of the maidens**
The land that Máel Dúin and his companions found was populated only by women, all of whom were eager for the visiting men to stay with them.

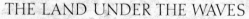

◀ **Celtic ship**
Máel Dúin and his crew travelled in a ship that, like Viking ships, was equipped with a sail and oars for use when there was no wind.

▲ **Fountain of knowledge**
According to legend, there was a fountain in the "Land of Promise" whose waters were said to grant secret knowledge to the drinker.

▲ **Voyage of St Brendan**
The Irish saint, Brendan, lived in the 6th century and traveled widely. On one voyage he supposedly landed on a whale, believing it to be an island.

THE LAND OF PROMISE

Set far across the sea, Tir Tairngire, or the "Land of Promise," was the place most sought after by explorers. It was a paradise where life was easy and where visitors could acquire magical skills. Some believed that Manannán mac Lir, a sea god and a great warrior, was the ruler of Tir Tairngire, although others thought he merely traveled there, taking with him his young son, Mongán, who stayed here for years and gained much secret knowledge. One of the explorers to reach this land was a Christian saint, Brendan, who journeyed in a boat along with 14 companions. It was one of many marvelous islands that Brendan was said to have visited in a series of travels that may have included expeditions to Iceland.

THE LAND UNDER THE WAVES

There are a number of Celtic tales about the "Land under the Waves," a city or country submerged in the sea. The most famous tale is the story of Ys, off Brittany. This was a prosperous city that was protected from the waves by a strong dyke built by a saintly king called Gradlon Meur. But Gradlon had a wicked daughter called Dahut. Different versions of the story depict her as having opened the sluice gates after either getting drunk or being persuaded by another evil character to do so. Consequently, in all versions of the myth, the sea rushed in from every side and Ys disappeared forever beneath the waves. Some believed that life went on in the strange submarine world of the vanished city.

▲ **The submerged city**
According to the legend of Ys, people who traveled along the Breton coast could hear the bells of the city's churches ringing below the waves.

THE MABINOGI

The four branches, or parts, of the *Mabinogi* (often called the *Mabinogion*) comprise a rich treasury of Welsh myths and legends about early Celtic deities and heroes. These tales were first written down in the 12th century. The four branches deal with: the adventures of Pwyll, prince of Dyfed, especially his visit to the "Otherworld"; the children of the sea god Llyr, Brân and Mananwydan; and other stories, including that of Blodeuwedd. Some of the characters, such as Brân, developed further in the retelling of stories beyond the *Mabinogi*. Christian writers called him "Brân the Blessed" and said that he brought Christianity to Wales.

THE WIFE MADE FROM FLOWERS

Lleu Llaw Gyffes (Bright One of the Skilful Hand), the son of Arianrhod, lived under a curse: his mother, Arianrhod, had declared that he would never be able to have a human wife. However, Gwydion, Arianrhod's brother, was a magician, and he decided to help his nephew. He sought the assistance of another magician, Math of Gwynedd. Together they used their powers to create a beautiful woman called Blodeuwedd from the flowers of the meadowsweet, broom, and oak. They wanted Blodeuwedd to be Lleu Llaw Gyffes's wife, but she fell in love with another man, Gronw Pebyr, who killed Lleu. As he died, Lleu turned into an eagle and flew to an oak tree. Gwydion eventually came to his rescue and transformed him back into his human form. Lleu sought out and killed Gronw, and became the Lord of Gwynedd (North Wales).

▼ **Blodeuwedd**
The name Blodeuwedd means "flower face" and symbolizes her captivating physical beauty as well as the wild flowers from which she was conjured up.

▶ **Oak tree**
The Celts considered the oak to be magical. Priests used its wood for their wands and the mistletoe growing on it for their rituals.

◀ **Owl**
Once Blodeuwedd's treachery was discovered, Gwydion punished her by turning her into an owl.

BRÂN THE BLESSED

Brân, also known as Bendigeidfran, was depicted in many different ways by the ancient writers of England and Wales. To begin with, he was portrayed as a sea god, who was seen striding above the waves. Later, he was described as a mighty British king and leader, who lived at a time when the people of Britain were waging a war against Ireland. His valor and strength helped the British defeat the King of Ireland, even though Brân's forces were outnumbered and he was fatally wounded. After the battle, Brân informed his men about his impending death and instructed them to cut off his head and take it back to Britain, where it would protect them from future invasions. To the astonishment of his companions, Brân's head constantly talked to them all the way back to London, where they buried it, and it continued to act as their guardian.

▲ **Poisoned spear**
Normal weapons could not hurt Brân, but in the battle against the Irish he was mortally wounded by a poison-tipped spear.

▲ **Brân the giant**
As a king, Brân was known to be a giant of superhuman strength. He possessed a magical cauldron that could revive the dead; eventually it passed into the hands of the Irish.

▶ **Castell Dinas Bran**
These ruins in Llangollen, North Wales, now amounting to just a few stones and earthworks, were believed to be the home of the giant king, Brân.

RHIANNON AND PWYLL

Pwyll, a prince of Dyfed, fell in love with the beautiful Rhiannon, but her family wanted her to marry another man, Gwawl. Pwyll and Rhiannon married without the consent of her parents, who refused to recognize this marriage. Soon the couple had a son, but members of Rhiannon's family stole the baby and accused Rhiannon of murdering her son. As punishment, Pwyll made his wife stand on all fours like a horse and offer rides to whoever passed by. Meanwhile, Pwyll visited a princely neighbor who had been losing foals mysteriously from his stables. Pwyll stood guard outside the stables, caught the monster who had been stealing the foals, and cut off its arm in the ensuing struggle. Upon returning to the stables, Pwyll discovered his son lying in the straw. He took him home to Rhiannon, who named him Pryderi or "care."

▼ **Rhiannon**
Pwyll was initially attracted to Rhiannon when he saw her on a white horse. Rhiannon was associated with horses because she was a human incarnation of the Celtic horse goddess Epona.

▲ **Pryderi**
Found across stories of the *Mabinogi*, Pryderi was a virtuous character who may have affected the portrayals of Perceval in the Arthurian legends.

KING ARTHUR AND HIS KNIGHTS

The legend of King Arthur and the Knights of the Round Table has captured the imagination of writers down the ages. There have been different versions of the story told by British, German, and French authors, but all of them portray Arthur as a wise, just, and brave ruler. The tales extolled the ideals of honor, chivalry, and bravery exemplified by this perfect king and his valiant knights.

THE MYTH

Arthur was the illegitimate son of King Uther Pendragon of Britain and Queen Ygern of Cornwall. Hence he was brought up in secret, away from his parents. However, Uther gave Arthur a chance to become his heir. The king embedded a sword in a block of stone and declared that whomever pulled it out would rightfully become the future King of Britain. Many knights tried to recover the sword but failed, until one day Arthur arrived and removed it easily. Later, when the sword was damaged in a duel, Arthur was given a new sword—the mythical "Excalibur"—by the "Lady of the Lake," a figure shrouded in mystery in the Arthurian legends.

THE KING AND HIS KNIGHTS

Arthur was an honorable king who ruled wisely. He was deeply in love with the beautiful Guinevere, whom he took for his queen. He had many brave knights as his followers, and they discussed matters of state sitting together around the famous Round Table in the castle at Camelot. Many of these knights set out on a quest to find the Holy Grail, the cup used by Jesus Christ before his death, which is considered one of the most important Christian relics in history. However, only

▶ **King Arthur**
The mythical ruler is depicted as strong, athletic, and well-versed in the art of warfare. He was the ideal king who presided over a golden age of chivalry.

Galahad, Perceval, and Bors succeeded in completing the quest. According to some versions of the story, they eventually found the Holy Grail and took it to the city of Jerusalem.

ARTHUR'S DEATH

Meanwhile, problems were brewing at Camelot. One of Arthur's trusted knights, Lancelot, fell in love with Queen Guinevere, and they had a secret affair. When Arthur found out, he banished Lancelot, who was also his dearest friend. Subsequently, Arthur's son, Mordred, decided to challenge his father for control of the kingdom. Many warriors on both sides perished in the fierce battle; those left alive included King Arthur and Mordred, who continued to fight each other relentlessly. Arthur finally killed his treacherous son, but was himself gravely wounded. Knowing that he was nearing death, Arthur sailed to a place called Avalon (the "island of apples"), where he fell into a long, death-like sleep. It was believed that Arthur would return to rule once again when Britain was in dire trouble and in need of a great leader. Thus, he came to be known as the "Once and Future King."

◀ **The sword in the stone**
Pulling the sword out of the stone was an apparently impossible task. Only a hero could succeed, and when Arthur did so, people were convinced that he was the rightful king.

KEY CHARACTERS

Many characters are involved in the Arthurian legends—some are forces of good, while others bring about the destruction of Arthur's court at Camelot. Besides most of the knights (*see right*), a key figure on the side of good is Merlin—a wizard, prophet, and Arthur's mentor. Flawed characters include Lancelot, a chivalrous knight with one serious moral defect—his love for Queen Guinevere. Lancelot also fails Arthur because he arrives too late to help the king in his battle with Mordred. In some versions of the story, Lancelot becomes a priest upon finding out that Guinevere has repented and become a nun.

▲ **Queen Guinevere**
The different versions of the story vary in the degree of blame assigned to Guinevere for betraying Arthur by having an affair with Lancelot.

▲ **Mordred and Arthur**
The battle between the two rivals, son and father, over the throne of Camelot, culminated in a single combat in which Mordred was killed and Arthur received a fatal wound.

PERCEVAL

A young man of noble birth, Perceval became a knight after proving his worth at King Arthur's court. The Grail legends portrayed him as rather naive, a "pure fool." It was this purity, however, that made him worthy of the Grail and helped him resist the seduction of Kundry, a mysterious figure sent to distract him from the Grail quest. His story inspired Richard Wagner's opera, *Parsifal*, where he heals the mortal wounds of Amfortas, the guardian of the Holy Grail.

The Holy Grail

◄ **Kundry and Perceval**
A female shaman-figure, Kundry was sent to corrupt the Grail knights, but failed to seduce Perceval.

THE KNIGHTS

The Knights of the Round Table were chivalrous men. They were fair in their dealings with others, courteous to women, and helpful to people in need. They were daring and killed monsters and defeated outlaws. There were many tales of their deeds, such as Galahad's quest for the Holy Grail; the adventures of Arthur's nephew, Gawain; the exploits of Pellinore; and the deeds of the naive Perceval. Some stories were about their loves, others about their involvement in political disputes.

▶ **Lancelot**
The dashing Lancelot was brought up by the "Lady of the Lake," who gave him a shield with three stripes that would magnify his strength in battle.

▲ **Galahad**
The son of Lancelot, Galahad was celibate and pure at heart. He was truly worthy of finding the Grail, although the quest was long and weary, and he died soon afterwards.

THE ROUND TABLE

Descriptions of the circular table in Arthur's castle at Camelot vary—some said it could seat 100 or more knights—but the key principle always remained constant: every knight had equal prominence. One particular seat, known as the "Siege Perilous," or the "Seat of Danger," was traditionally left empty because it was believed that the knight to sit on it would find the Holy Grail, and die, thereby ending the days of the Round Table.

Knights at the Table

▲ **The seductive spirits of lakes and streams**
Water sprites, who were said to inhabit streams and lakes in Central Europe, were
famous for playing seductively sweet music in an attempt to lure unwary passers-by,
such as these pretty young peasant girls, into their underwater lair.

CENTRAL AND EASTERN EUROPE

Central and Eastern Europe is home to a fascinating blend of myths and folk tales that reflect both the area's rich natural environment and its diverse heritage of belief systems, from animistic to Christian.

Ranging from the Czech Republic in the west to Russia in the east, Central and Eastern Europe is a region of varied peoples and traditions. Many of the people living in the western part of the area see their roots as Celtic, but the dominant mythology of the region belongs to the Slavs, who between the 5th and 7th centuries spread across Europe from their ancestral homelands in Bulgaria, eastern Slovakia, and neighboring territories.

▲ Decorated Easter eggs
Decorating eggs at Easter is a traditional custom in the Czech Republic. Today, such eggs symbolize the Resurrection, but they are also pre-Christian symbols of rebirth.

EARLY SLAVIC MYTHOLOGY

The beliefs and myths of the early Slavs centred on notions of good and evil and the role of their ancestors. Human life was understood to be a struggle between light and dark, and the dead were seen as spirits who looked after their family's household. These ancestors lived in the Otherworld, but could be contacted by priests who played a role similar to that performed by shamans in other cultures.

The early Slavs also recognized a group of deities, most of whom presided over the elements and parts of the natural world. Svarog, the most powerful deity, was a sky god and god of light. He had two sons, Dazhbog and Svarozhich, who governed the sun and fire respectively. Perun, the thunder god, and Stribog, god of the winds, were also prominent in the Slav pantheon. A pair of fertility goddesses, the Rozhanitsy, presided over the growing of crops and the harvest.

In addition to the deities, the mythology of Central and Eastern Europe is full of other supernatural beings who act as spirits of places of power. In a countryside of dark, ancient forests, deep lakes, and many rivers, it is not surprising that many of these are spirits of woods and water. Water sprites and similar creatures haunt lakes in numerous myths from the region. They are dangerous to travelers, luring them into the water. Forest spirits work in a similar way, leading people astray so that they become lost among the trees.

MALIGN BEINGS

This part of Europe is also home to a host of powerful and often malign supernatural beings—notably witches, werewolves, and vampires—that have become famous far from their homelands. They are also seen as enemies of the faith that swept through the Slavic world in the 9th and 10th centuries, namely Christianity. Christian missionaries dismissed the ancient deities and spirits, but many Slavs simply combined the old with the new: vampires may be thwarted by a Crucifix, and Easter is celebrated by decorating eggs, pagan symbols of rebirth and renewal.

▲ Sadko on the shores of Lake Ilmen
One Russian folk tale tells of a poor man called Sadko who played his *gusli*, or lyre, by the side of a lake. This so pleased the Sea King that the spirit helped Sadko win a wager that there were fish with golden fins to be caught in the lake, so making Sadko rich.

LEGENDS OF THE WITCH

The folklore of the Slavs often reflects their ancestors' anxieties about evil, the unknown, and the dangers of the forest. There are many tales of witches, who were believed to be sinister women living in these forests, and who preyed on innocent people, or upset family relationships or the social order.

Foremost among such evil characters is Bába Yagá, a witch who appears in Russian legends, and in similar tales found across Central Europe, where her name varies slightly. However, her rapacious appetite for the flesh of young children stays consistent, though many of her victims manage to outwit her.

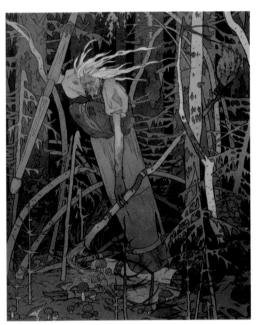

Bába Yagá
The wicked old witch would use her mortar and pestle to travel in the forest, where she would hide among the trees, waiting to ambush unwary victims that walked past her.

◄ **Roses for wishes**
Some legends of Bába Yagá say that the witch could grant people their wishes if they were offered roses, although most stories warn that it was still risky to trust the witch.

BÁBA YAGÁ

The witch called Bába Yagá was depicted in stories as a wrinkled old woman sitting quietly on a wooden bench or keeping warm by her stove. When traveling, she would step into a large mortar and push herself through the sky with a pestle, starting violent storms as she flew. She specially looked out for young children, whom she liked to capture and eat. Some people believed that the witch could turn people to stone with her gaze, turning them back into flesh at her home to feed on them. Bába Yagá used the bones left over after her feedings to build a gruesome and enchanted house for herself, which terrified people for miles around. Even its fence was decorated with the skulls of the children she had killed, and she would light these skulls up like lanterns.

◄ **Horror house**
Bába Yagá's house had a pair of hen legs at its base with which it could run around and chase people at the witch's command.

VASSILISA

Vassilisa was a young girl who lived with her elderly parents in a village. Her mother fell ill and, before dying, gave Vassilisa a magic doll, which would advise her if she offered it good food to eat. Vassilisa's father remarried, but her stepmother and stepsisters did not like Vassilisa and made her do all the hard work at home. One day, when a taper was needed to light the lamps in the house, Vassilisa's stepmother sent her to get some from Bába Yagá, who, instead of giving her some, set the girl some impossible tasks, such as picking out only peas from a mixture of peas and poppy seeds. Vassilisa was able to successfully complete all the tasks with the help of her doll, but Bába Yagá kept devising more for her to do. Seeing no other way of escape, Vassilisa stole away from the house at night while the witch slept, taking with her one of the glowing skulls from Bába Yagá's fence.

▲ Vassilisa and the skull
When Vassilisa returned home with the skull that she had stolen from Bába Yagá's fence, its glowing eyes shone on her stepmother and stepsisters, turning them to ashes.

▲ The powerless crow
Some versions of the story say that after Vassilisa's escape, the witch was turned into a crow and she lost all her powers.

▶ The witch's cat
Bába Yagá's black cat was ill-treated by her, so it helped Vassilisa escape her clutches.

MARIASSA

There was once a young girl called Mariassa, whose stepmother sent her to Bába Yagá to borrow a needle and thread. Luckily, the girl initially called on her aunt, who told Mariassa how to avoid the jaws of Bába Yagá's dog and how to talk to her cat. Mariassa asked the cat for a way out when the witch tried to imprison the girl, and it told her to run away with a towel and a comb. Mariassa escaped, and when she heard the witch approaching, she threw down the towel, which turned into a river, and the comb, which became a forest, thus trapping Bába Yagá.

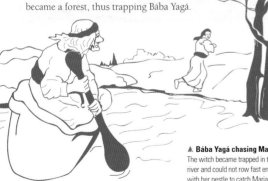

▲ Bába Yagá chasing Mariassa
The witch became trapped in the swift river and could not row fast enough with her pestle to catch Mariassa.

WITCH BURNING

With the arrival of Christianity in Central and Eastern Europe, witches came to be regarded as evil women who performed the Devil's work. Many women suspected of being witches were burned at the stake, most of whom had nothing to do with witchcraft at all. Making models of witches that are burned on May Day is still a popular custom in Central Europe. Such customs, associated with the many rituals that celebrate the arrival of spring, are also held in remembrance of those who died.

A 16th-century engraving of a witch burning

GODS AND GODDESSES OF LOVE

Most of the world's mythologies have deities responsible for love, some of whom began life as fertility gods or goddesses. Many love deities are sexually promiscuous, pursuing their own love affairs as well as encouraging those of others—sometimes making mischief by causing ill-matched couples to fall in love. Other love deities are more concerned with guiding women through pregnancy and childbirth.

▼ Eros
Son of the war god Ares and the love goddess Aphrodite, Eros was the Greek god of erotic desire. He shot golden arrows that made people fall in love.

◄ Cupid
The Roman equivalent of Eros, Cupid inspired many love affairs. One of his intended victims, the mortal woman Psyche, was so beautiful that he fell in love with her himself.

➤ Kama
Son of Vishnu and the goddess Lakshmi, the Hindu love god Kama is a handsome young archer who rides on the back of a parrot. He is married to Rati ("passion").

▲ Shiva
The Hindu god Shiva is sometimes seen as an ascetic, but is also associated with erotic love and worshipped in the form of a *linga*, or phallus.

▲ Semara
The god of love in Bali, Semara lives in the Floating Sky, one of the six heavens located above the Earth. He turned love into a physical pleasure for people so that they would want to have children.

➤ Oenghus
The Irish god Oenghus was known as a god who would help those in love. He fell in love himself with a beautiful swan maiden and took the form of a swan to visit her.

Aphrodite
Known for her beauty and her affairs with mortals and gods, the Greek goddess of love Aphrodite was often accompanied by her son, Eros.

Venus
The Roman goddess of love, Venus began as a spring fertility figure and a patron of gardeners, then became identified with Aphrodite.

Inanna
The name Inanna belonged to an early Mesopotamian love goddess and was also used in many of the Sumerian cities for the goddess known as Ishtar, or Astarte.

Hathor
The Egyptian goddess Hathor, who often took the form of a cow, was a protector of women, patron of lovers, and goddess of both conception and childbirth.

Bastet
Bastet began as a warlike, lion-bodied figure, but in the more sensual form of a domestic cat she was an Egyptian goddess of sexual love. Sometimes she even appeared with her kittens, to symbolize her role as a fertility goddess.

Ishtar
The Babylonian goddess of war and fertility, as well as love, Ishtar was worshipped in Canaan and Egypt as Astarte. Brave as well as beautiful, she was sometimes identified with the planet Venus.

Freyja
With a name meaning simply "lady," the Norse goddess Freyja was especially associated with love. She had many lovers, including mortal kings as well as gods.

Xochiquetzal
Xochiquetzal and her consort Xochipilli were the Aztec goddess and god of flowers. Xochiquetzal had an additional role as goddess of love and childbirth.

87

SLAVIC GODS OF POWER

The ancient Slavs, who lived in and around Russia, had numerous deities who ruled with great power over the Earth. Their control extended all the way from the sky, where the thunder god Perun held sway, to deep down into the Earth, the domain of Mati Syra Zemlya. The Slavs worshipped these gods by giving them offerings and assigning special days to them, occasions that combined holiday with devotion. Although their myths were orally transmitted, many of these powerful stories survived the coming of Christianity.

PERUN

Perun was the god of thunder and lightning. Although he was primarily a war god and his power was terrifying, he also represented the forces of good. When the sun was threatened by storm clouds that concealed it in their shadows, Perun smashed them with his thunderbolt, allowing the sun to reappear and ensuring that life on Earth could continue. The Slavs believed that humanity was constantly threatened by Veles, the god of the Underworld, who was always stealing cattle, kidnapping people, or otherwise causing mischief. At such times, Perun would strike him with his thunderbolt, sending the evil god hurrying back to his refuge. When Christian missionaries came to the Slavic regions, some of the attributes of Perun were transferred to the prophet called Ilya, or Elijah.

▲ **The sky god**
In addition to his weapons and his eagle, Perun was associated with many other attributes. Among the most important of these were the stone and metal that Slavic people used to make weapons.

▲ **The world tree**
In Slavic mythology, the world was represented as a vast oak, with the Underworld in its roots. Perun was symbolized by an eagle that sat in the uppermost branches of the tree.

▲ **Veles the dragon**
The Slavs imagined Veles, the god of the Underworld, as a dragon or serpent, who spent much of his time coiled among the roots of the sacred oak tree.

BYELOBOG AND CHERNOBOG

A benevolent god, Byelobog, and a wicked god, Chernobog, are two of the most ancient deities of Slavic mythology, and some creation stories describe how the pair created the universe together. But the two fell out and were said to be perpetually at war, appearing at regular intervals to fight one another. Because this conflict between good and evil was eternal, they were seen as similar to, and possibly derived from, the Persian deities Ahura Mazda and Ahriman. Byelobog was held in special regard because he was one of the most prominent companions of the sun god Dazhbog. People said that he was also a god of sunshine and warmth, and that if worshipped, he would protect their wheat and ensure a good harvest. Sometimes he was depicted as a kindly, white-bearded old man, and sometimes as a powerful light.

▲ The god of light
The ancient Slavs closely associated the life-giving light and warmth of the sun with the benevolent god, Byelobog – especially after enduring a long, cold, dark night.

▶ The god of darkness
As the god of darkness, Chernobog was most powerful during the "waning" phase of the year, when the nights are longer and the days become shorter.

MATI SYRA ZEMLYA

The Slavic Earth goddess was called Mati Syra Zemlya (Damp Mother Earth). Normally, she was not given a specific form, but her spirit was said to be embodied in the fertile earth beneath the feet of her devotees. Even though she usually lacked a shape, she was seen as vibrantly alive and, therefore, helped everything in the soil to come to life. On certain occasions when she did take human form, she was said to appear as a woman with dark, earth-colored skin, wearing traditional clothes, who would visit people's houses and bless them. On the holy days on which she appeared (notably 1 May and 24 June), no one was allowed to plough the soil. People worshipped her by digging a hole in the ground and putting in offerings of bread and wine.

◀ Ears of wheat
In addition to representing the fertility of the soil, Mati Syra Zemlya was also said to be present in the crops that grew on the ground, especially in the ripe ears of wheat.

▶ The rescue of Kranyatz
When the flood waters continued to rise, Kurent offered Kranyatz his walking stick, actually a vine, and pulled him out of danger.

KURENT

Kurent was the Slavic god of wine. A popular myth tells how the first humans enjoyed an easy life in a valley irrigated by seven rivers that flowed from an egg. They became greedy for more water and broke the egg, causing a great flood. All the people drowned, except for Kranyatz, a watchman, who was saved by Kurent. Later, Kranyatz argued with the god over who should rule the Earth, and after various trials, emerged as the winner. But he got carried away and climbed the mountain where the gods lived. He ate some meat that belonged to them, and got drunk from the wine given to him by Kurent. The gods kicked him down the mountain and he lost his power.

▲ Kurent mask
In Slovenia, sheepskin masks depicting Kurent are worn at the Kurentovanje carnival that is held to celebrate the arrival of spring.

WEST AND CENTRAL ASIA

▶ **Assyrian carved relief**
The palaces and temples of the
Assyrian Empire were adorned
with carved stone reliefs. Many
of these reliefs showed mythical
creatures—such as the winged
bull depicted here—which the
Assyrians regarded as guardian
figures who watched over the
building, protecting it from evil.

WEST ASIA

West Asia was the site of some of the world's earliest cities, where riches from agriculture and trade, and the development of writing and organized religion, produced flourishing cultures that recorded their many myths.

The first great cities of West Asia, or the Middle East, sprang up from as early as about 2600 BCE in Mesopotamia, the land between the Tigris and Euphrates rivers in what is now Iraq. Cities such as Ur, Uruk, Babylon, and Ashur all developed powerful political systems, together with a highly organized religion that was based around imposing mud-brick temples known as ziggurats. The development of trade and taxation systems meant that it was necessary to keep records of what people owned, so the Mesopotamians developed a highly sophisticated writing system, too. They wrote by making cuneiform, or wedge-shaped, marks with a reed stylus in small, handheld tablets of wet clay, which they then baked hard by firing them in a kiln, or simply by drying them in the sun.

▲ **Ziggurat at Ur**
Mesopotamian ziggurats, like this one from the 14th-century BCE in present-day Iraq, were large buildings with external stairs. The steps led to high platforms on which the priests performed rituals in honor of the deities.

PRIESTS AND KINGS
Religious and political institutions overlapped in ancient Mesopotamia. Kingship was seen as a gift from heaven, so priests had a great deal of influence over political power, while rulers were also seen as sacred figures. In addition, the priests were highly literate, and soon they were inscribing religious and literary texts on clay tablets. The durable nature of these tablets has allowed many of them to survive with their inscriptions still intact and legible despite centuries of exposure to the elements, giving us ready access to an impressive group of early myths.

The first Mesopotamian cities were independent city-states, but some, such as Babylon and later Ashur, expanded in power to create great empires. They shared similar myths but with variations in language, so that gods and goddesses had different names in different parts of the region. Inanna, goddess of love, fertility, and warfare, became known in Babylon as Ishtar, while Utu, the sun god, became Shamash, and so on. The clay tablets that have survived from temple archives tell the stories and adventures of these deities, and of great heroes, who are semi-divine figures. The texts are often fragmentary because the archives have survived only in part. But those that have been pieced together yield many narratives that grip readers to this day, such as the famous epic of the great hero Gilgamesh.

MAJOR CENTERS
Babylon was the most powerful city of the Sumerian Empire, with two heydays, in the 18th and 6th centuries BCE. Under Nebuchadnezzar (605–562 BCE), Babylon was a flourishing city with a palace and "hanging gardens" that were one of the wonders of the world. Its temples, and the city gate dedicated to the goddess Ishtar, were impressive structures, indicative of the power of the city's religion. Hardly less powerful was the Assyrian Empire (c.880–c.610 BCE), based at Ashur. Assyrian scribes adopted and preserved many of the myths from neighboring cities.

There were other centers of early civilization and myth in West Asia. One was at Ugarit, in northern Syria, which flourished around 1500–1200 BCE. Another was in Turkey, where the Hittites founded a powerful empire around 1450 BCE. Both of these early cultures had rich collections of myths, which survive in a fragmentary but fascinating form, as well as prominent weather gods: the Ugaritic storm god Baal, and the Hittite weather god Teshub.

▶ **Babylonian boundary stone**
The Babylonians put up boundary stones to show who owned pieces of land. Carved on them were symbols of the deities protecting the boundaries: here, a crescent moon for the lunar god Sin.

ENUMA ELISH

The creation story of Babylon is called *Enuma Elish*, meaning "When on high," which is the first line of the epic. Inscribed on seven tablets, the myth describes the creation of the first deities from the coming together of the primal waters, and narrates how one god, Marduk, eventually became the ruler of the cosmos, ordering the creation of humans and the foundation of the first city, Babylon.

THE MYTH

In the beginning there were only Apsu, the god of the fresh waters, and Tiamat, the goddess of the salt waters, and everything was silent around them. The pair came together and produced several generations of deities, culminating in Anu, the god of the heavens, and Ea, a cunning and resourceful figure who eventually became the god of both the Earth and the waters.

WAR AMONG THE GODS

The new generation of young and lively deities annoyed Apsu and Tiamat, who longed for the silence that had existed at the beginning of time. Apsu suggested killing the young gods, but Tiamat could not bear the thought of putting to death what they had created. Nevertheless, Apsu decided to kill the other gods on his own. Ea saw what he

▶ Babylonian deity
Gula, the goddess of medicine, was the daughter of Anu. Believed to be the protector of boundaries, she was often depicted on boundary stones.

was about to do and killed him. Then he set himself up as the god of the waters.

MARDUK'S COMING

Ea and his consort, Damkina, produced a son, the mighty god Marduk. When Marduk was given the winds to play with, he caused storms in the waters of Tiamat. She was upset, and decided to avenge the death of her husband, Apsu. So she assembled a force of monsters and ordered the god Kingu to attack Marduk. Several of the gods, fearing a destructive war, tried to stop Tiamat, but she would not listen. Only Marduk was willing to fight her, provided the other gods gave him supreme authority over them all.

THE CREATION

Marduk gathered the four winds, commanded them to blow through Tiamat's mouth so she inflated like a balloon, and then sliced her body open with an arrow. Having defeated Tiamat, Marduk began to rule. He made the heavens from one half of Tiamat's body, creating rain clouds from her saliva. Then he used the other half of her body to create the Earth, so that her breasts became mountains, and the two rivers of Mesopotamia, the Tigris and the Euphrates, flowed from her eyes. He ordered the building of Babylon, and created the first man, Lullu, from the blood of Kingu. Lullu and his descendants dug canals to fertilize the land around Babylon to ensure that the human race could prosper.

▲ The Babylonians
The people of Babylon relied on agriculture for survival, and their creation myth tells how the first man, called Lullu, irrigated his fields so that the people could farm the dry land.

CITIES OF WORSHIP

As in all cultures, religion was crucial to the inhabitants of early Mesopotamian cities such as Babylon, because it offered them a way of understanding the cosmos. Each city was under the protection of a specific god—for example, Marduk in Babylon and the moon god Nanna in Ur—who was worshipped in a temple, usually the most impressive structure in the city. The priests tried to maintain good relations with the gods by making frequent offerings in the hope of good harvests. In addition, each temple owned much land and livestock, so the priests controlled the food supply and the economy of their city.

▲ **Making offerings**
A priest praying before the symbols of Marduk, the supreme Babylonian god, and Nabi, the god of wisdom.

KEY CHARACTERS

Like many creation myths, *Enuma Elish* begins with a pair of primal deities, Apsu and Tiamat, who create several generations of gods. These gods exist to breed, to fight, and, in the case of Tiamat and Kingu, to provide the raw materials of creation. Kingu becomes Tiamat's consort after Apsu's death, leading her army in the battle against Marduk. Some of the later generations also play many different roles, especially Marduk. He combines the jobs of dragon-slayer, warrior, king, and dispenser of justice—mostly roles that are highly relevant to the people of his city.

BABYLON

The renowned city of Babylon was one of the most powerful cities in Mesopotamia. It first came to prominence between c.1900–1550 BCE, and later became the center of a large empire. With its tall ziggurat, the city was always closely identified with the gods, but this link was emphasized by the magnificent city gateway, decorated with glazed bricks depicting beasts associated with the war goddess Ishtar.

Reconstruction of the Ishtar Gate

▲ **Tiamat**
The primordial mother, Tiamat, along with her consort, Apsu, symbolize the untamed chaos that existed before there was form and order.

◀ **Kingu**
A supporter of Tiamat, Kingu held the Tablet of Destiny, which gave him ultimate power over the cosmos. After killing Kingu, Marduk took the tablet from him.

MARDUK

The Babylonians regarded Marduk as the founder of their city and worshipped him as their supreme god. The creation myth describes how his link with the city began with its construction. When the god had won his battle with Tiamat, he glorified the heavens. He built his own dwelling directly above where Ea had lived and, from the bodies of the monsters that Tiamat had sent to fight him, made statues and placed them by the doorway of Ea's temple. Marduk then told the other gods to build a great city on Earth.

◀ **Godly ruler**
Often portrayed as a Babylonian warrior king accompanied by a mythical guardian beast, Marduk was said to have invented the idea of kingship.

HE WAS CLOTHED WITH TERROR, WITH OVERPOWERING BRIGHTNESS HIS HEAD WAS CROWNED. THEN HE SET OUT, HE TOOK HIS WAY, AND TOWARDS THE RAGING TIAMAT HE SET HIS FACE.

Enuma Elish

THE EPIC OF GILGAMESH

The story of Gilgamesh, the King of Uruk, is the oldest extended narrative to have come down from the ancient world. It survives in the form of an epic poem written on clay tablets in the 7th century BCE in Assyria, although the story dates back to the 3rd millennium BCE. Its themes of heroism, friendship, and the quest for immortality, together with the poem's exotic cast of characters, have proved fascinating for generations of readers.

THE MYTH

Gilgamesh was a ruthless and cruel ruler of Uruk. He forced the men to be his slaves and the women to be his mistresses. Helpless against the mighty Gilgamesh, the people prayed to the gods for help and they responded by sending a wild man named Enkidu to fight Gilgamesh and subdue him. Gilgamesh attempted to tame Enkidu by sending a temple prostitute to seduce him. The woman took Enkidu to Uruk to civilize him, but when they arrived at a wedding in the city, Enkidu saw Gilgamesh demanding to sleep with the bride, and challenged him to a fight. They were both strong and evenly matched, and realized after a long struggle that there could be no winner. Thus, they embraced and became friends.

THE TWO TYRANTS

Now there were two tyrants terrorizing the people of Uruk. This time the gods sent a creature called Humbaba, who was a fire-breathing monster. But Gilgamesh and Enkidu, who were supported by Shamash, the sun god, fought the monster and killed him. Next the gods tried to trick Gilgamesh by sending the attractive Inanna (known as Ishtar in Babylon)

◄ The Bull of Heaven
Killing supernatural monsters of great strength like the bull was common for the hero and antihero in ancient epic poetry.

► Gilgamesh
The main characteristics of Gilgamesh were his superhuman strength and great willpower – traits symbolized in this statue by the commanding way in which he holds the lion.

to seduce him, but he rejected her. Normally irresistible, she resented this rebuff and complained to the gods, who responded by sending another monster, the Bull of Heaven. But even this creature was killed by Enkidu and Gilgamesh. Now the gods decided that one of them must pay for killing Humbaba and the Bull of Heaven. They decreed that Enkidu would die.

THE SEARCH FOR IMMORTALITY

Enkidu's death forced Gilgamesh to consider his own mortality. He knew of a man named Utnapishtim who was the sole survivor of a great flood and had been granted immortality. So Gilgamesh visited Utnapishtim to find a way of attaining immortality. Utnapishtim told him that the gods had caused the flood because they were angry at the sins of humans. But Enki (Ea in Babylonian myth), the water god, had appeared in a dream to Utnapishtim and instructed him to build a boat.

Utnapishtim advised Gilgamesh to accept his fate as a mortal, but also told him of a plant growing at the bottom of a lake in the Underworld that gave everlasting youth to whomever ate from it. Gilgamesh went to the Underworld and found the plant, but on his way back, a snake stole the plant. Realizing the futility of his quest, Gilgamesh accepted his fate.

KEY CHARACTERS

Although the epic is set in a real place, a city-state called Uruk in the Mesopotamian region, most of its major characters are linked with the supernatural world. The creatures sent to challenge Gilgamesh are gigantic and terrifying because they come from heaven—the wild man Enkidu is created by Ninhursag, the goddess of the Earth, while the Bull of Heaven is sent by Anu, the god of the sky. Gilgamesh himself straddles both worlds. His parents are Ninsun, the goddess of the sky, and Ligulbanda, a semi-divine figure; his mixed parentage is why he is described as part-god and part-human.

◀ **The coming of Enkidu**
Gilgamesh had a dream about a star falling from heaven, which he and his friends could not lift. This star represented the coming of Enkidu.

DEITIES

The gods and goddesses play a major role in the epic, talking to the earthbound humans and acting directly in the decisive moments of the story. They also influence events in a subtler manner by sending dreams that predict the future—the killing of Humbaba and the death of Enkidu were both foreseen in dreams. Although they are extremely powerful, the deities are fallible—their schemes to defeat Gilgamesh with monsters do not work, and Inanna's plan to seduce Gilgamesh is also a failure.

▲ **Shamash**
Seen here dictating laws to a king, Shamash, the god of the sun and war, aided Gilgamesh in killing Humbaba.

▲ **Enlil**
The wind god Enlil (*right*) was widely worshipped. He ordered Enkidu's death after the latter had killed Humbaba, the protector of the forest.

▲ **Utnapishtim**
An old man by the time Gilgamesh met him, Utnapishtim told the king how he had gathered the animals of the world in his boat to save them from the flood.

▲ **Humbaba**
This forest-dwelling monster was much feared because of the deadly fire he breathed. Even Enkidu was initially reluctant to fight the beast.

➤ **Inanna**
The very beautiful Inanna was the goddess of sexuality. She was irresistible to most men, but Gilgamesh spurned her advances, infuriating her in the process.

▲ **Uruk**
The poem mentions the mud-brick temples and city walls of Uruk, the ruins of which survive near the River Euphrates in West Asia. Some of these date from the 4th millennium BCE.

▲ **Clay tablets**
Scholars have had to piece together fragments of Akkadian tablets in order to reconstruct epics like *Gilgamesh*.

VERSIONS OF THE MYTH

Several ancient texts tell stories about Gilgamesh, who was probably a real king who later gained mythical status. Most such texts are fragments that together tell Gilgamesh's story—one talks about the Bull of Heaven, another describes Enkidu's journey to the Underworld. At some point, these texts were recorded in Akkadian, a Semitic language that was widely used in Mesopotamia from the 3rd to the 1st millennium BCE. The best surviving copy of the epic —still fragmentary but more complete than the others—was preserved in the library of the Assyrian king, Ashurbanipal II (668–627 BCE), at Nineveh.

THE GREAT SKY GOD

The ancient Mongol and Turkic people were animists who believed in many spirits (*tengri*) that inhabited the natural world. Supreme among these spirits was a sky god called Mongke Tengri (or just Tengri), who was the creator of humanity and the world, and who protected humans from malevolent demons. Tengri also controlled the different elements and influenced the fertility of the land.

THE MYTH

The Mongol account of the Earth's creation involves the high-ranking *tengri* Qormusta, and Sakyamuni—the Buddha—who is also a member of the Mongol pantheon of gods. Qormusta gave Sakyamuni a handful of yellow earth that was composed of precious stones. Sakyamuni threw it into the eternal ocean, causing it to begin to coalesce into a vast continent. At this point, a tortoise emerged from the depths of the ocean and stole the Earth. Sakyamuni realized that only the death of the tortoise would free the Earth and let the ground form. As a monk and a lover of peace, he was hesitant about killing the tortoise, but the *tengri* assured him that it was the right thing to do, because many lives would eventually flourish on the Earth after the loss of one. Thus, Sakyamuni slew the tortoise and subsequently the world was formed.

THE FIRST HUMANS

When the Earth had taken shape, only animals lived on it, so Mongke Tengri created the first man and woman to populate the world. He perfected their physical forms over time, and then covered their bodies with soft hair. Once Tengri was satisfied with his creations, he decided to fetch water from the Spring of Immortality so that the first man and woman could live forever. Worried about their safety, Tengri

▶ **Mongke Tengri**
Tengri is a fierce sky god, and wields his weaponry to fight the demons and evil spirits that threaten human beings.

commanded a cat and a dog to guard the humans. But once he left for the Spring of Immortality, Erlik Khan, the Lord of the Underworld, tempted the cat away with a bowl of milk, and the dog with a piece of meat, and then defiled Tengri's creations by urinating all over them.

THE CAT AND THE DOG

When Tengri returned, he was enraged to find out that Erlik Khan had tainted his creations; he was especially angry with the cat and the dog because they had failed in their task of watching over and protecting the man and woman. Consequently, Tengri punished the animals by making the cat lick off all the body hair from the humans and stick it on the dog's skin. The cat licked off almost all the hair from their bodies, excluding that on their heads, which Erlik Khan had not polluted, and some on the lower parts of their bodies—which the cat avoided because they gave off a foul odor. Once the cat had finished the task, Tengri took the water of eternal life and poured it over his creations in an attempt to immortalize them, but he failed in this venture because the humans had been polluted by Erlik Khan's foul deed.

◀ **Burial stone**
The early Turkic people buried their dead in the Earth created by Tengri, and erected burial stones, such as this 6th-century one, to mark the graves.

Primal tortoise

THE TURKIC CREATION STORY

In the Turkic version of the creation story, Tengri flew across the sky as a white goose, over an enormous ocean symbolizing the endless flow of time. He heard a being called the White Mother asking him to create the world. Tengri made another being called Er Kishi, and together they made the Earth and its inhabitants. But Er Kishi was impure, and tried to seduce the people into leading a life of evil. So Tengri sent his sacred animals to Earth to make the shamans, or spirit guides, teach the people about living well and respecting their creator.

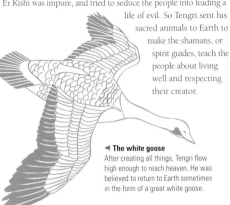

◄ **The white goose**
After creating all things, Tengri flew high enough to reach heaven. He was believed to return to Earth sometimes in the form of a great white goose.

TENGRISM

Tengrism is the modern term for the belief system of the Mongol and Turkic people of ancient times. Based on Mongke Tengri (representing the eternal blue sky), Eje (a female fertility figure and a Mother Earth goddess), and many other benign and malign nature spirits, it involved the practice of shamanism, or communication with spirits. Tengrism was promoted by later Turkic rulers such as Genghis Khan (reigned 1206–27) and his grandson, Batu Khan (reigned 1227–55). Its followers respected nature spirits and led a life of moral rectitude. If people lost their balance with the natural world due to their actions or the action of malign spirits, the shamans would intervene to restore it.

Turkic ruler Batu Khan

▲ **A simple life**
The early Turks and Mongols lived in harmony with nature. They settled in fertile areas near rivers, which were conducive not only to agriculture, but also provided suitable pastures for their cattle and horses.

TENGRI AND NATURE

The early Turkic and Mongol people attributed many of the strongest natural phenomena to Tengri and other gods and spirits. Thunder was supposed to symbolize Tengri's voice; lightning was a means of punishment and a display of Tengri's power. Tengri's storms were beneficial as well, because the plants grew and the crops flourished after the rain. These people considered all living beings —birds, animals, plants, and trees—to be inhabited by individual spirits. This meant that everything in nature was sacred.

Maize

▲ **Bolts of lightning**
Tengri was said to have lit the first fire with one of his lightning bolts. Lightning and fire had long been worshipped in West and Central Asia; they could not only cleanse the world, but ward off demons.

TENGRI IN THE EAST

Linguists have long noticed the similarity between the name Tengri and the Chinese word for sky, *tian*, which also means god. It is not known whether one word led to the other, but the two are related, just like the Chinese and Mongol cultures. The two terms appear together in the names of mountains, which are considered sacred places. In the Tian Shan (Sky Mountain) range on the border of Kazakhstan, the second highest peak is known as Khan Tengri (Lord of the Spirits).

"Tengri" in Orkhon (old Turkic script)

▲ **The birth of Rustum, from the _Shahnama_**

The epic poem the _Shahnama_ (Book of Kings) contains a series of legends and
is a key source of Persian mythical history. One central character is Rustum, a
brave hero who overcomes many enemies but tragically kills his own son.

CENTRAL ASIA AND ARABIA

These two regions of Asia, though now identified with Islam, have long been a melting pot of cultures and beliefs, with a number of mythological traditions flourishing through the long history of civilization in both areas.

Persia (modern-day Iran) was one of the most important crossroads of the ancient world, with traders and settlers arriving from almost all points of the compass over the centuries and contributing to the sophisticated culture of the region. One group, the Hittites, whose culture was a blend of Indian and Persian elements, left Persia for Turkey. But other groups—and especially those from the steppes of Central Asia—arrived and settled in Persia, bringing with them a variety of deities.

▲ Ahura Mazda, the Wise Lord
This gold earring from the 6th to the 4th century BCE depicts Ahura Mazda grasping a pair of antelope by the horns—an image that conveys his rulership over creation.

BULL RITUAL OF MITHRA

One of the most influential gods of the settlers was Mithra, a deity whose name appeared in documents beside early Indian gods such as Indra. Mithra then became popular throughout Persia and was worshipped as an all-knowing protector, a sun god very similar to the Mesopotamian sun god Shamash. Mithra was also a god of agreements and treaties—the very personification, in fact, of the idea of *mitra*, or contract.

The popularity of Mithra spread even further, and when the Romans expanded their empire into Asia, he was one of the deities they adopted. His central ritual was the slaying of a sacrificial bull. This ritual slaughter was the recreation of a rite first performed by Yima, the Persian primal man, and was seen as an act of renewal. By performing the rite, worshippers of Mithra believed they were recreating the ideal conditions that existed when Yima originally ruled the world.

AHURA MAZDA

The other influential deity of Persia was Ahura Mazda, the wise, all-seeing creator sky god. He was originally one of a large pantheon of ancient Persian deities that included, as in many pantheons, a number of gods of the elements, among

whom Tishtrya, god of rain, and Vayu, god of wind, were prominent. Anahita, a goddess of fertility and source of water on Earth, was another key figure; she and Tishtrya were clearly evidence of the precarious water supply in Persia.

MONOTHEISTIC BELIEF

In the 7th or 6th century BCE, change came with the work and vision of the prophet Zoroaster, who saw Ahura Mazda as absolute, the one god worthy of worship. With the rise of Zoroastrianism, Ahura Mazda overshadowed the other deities of ancient Persia. In a different way, the rise of Islam in the Arabian peninsula several centuries later eclipsed the "false gods" of the local people denounced by the prophet Muhammad. Yet the mythology of the Arabian peninsula is not so easily forgotten, and its stories of adventure and great heroism still enthral people around the world.

▲ The cult of Mithra
The young god Mithra prepares to slay the sacrificial bull in this dramatic Roman temple relief. Having adopted the Central Asian deity, the Romans made a mystery cult out of Mithra, with secret temples, often concealed underground.

THE FIGHT AGAINST EVIL

At the heart of Zoroastrianism lies a cosmic struggle between the kind god Ahura Mazda and his evil opponent Ahriman. The religion, which flourished in Central Asia until the 7th century, still has followers in Iran and among the Parsis in India. Although Zoroastrians consider Ahura Mazda to be the only god, their religion also features a rich body of traditions about other beings, from benevolent immortals to demons, who influence human life. In the struggle against evil, Zoroastrianism predicts that the forces of good will triumph in the end.

THE MYTH

The first god, Zurvan (Time), lived in the primal void that existed before creation. He longed for a son, but was doubtful of his power of creation. So he conceived two sons: Ahura Mazda (Wise Lord), who was born from his optimism, and Ahriman, who was born out of his uncertainty. Before they came into the world, Zurvan predicted that his first-born would rule the world. Ahriman heard what his father had said and forced himself into the world ahead of his brother, who was rightfully supposed to come first. Ahriman told Zurvan that he was Ahura Mazda, the first-born, but the god saw through his trickery. He knew that Ahura Mazda would be pale and sweet smelling, whereas Ahriman was dark and foul smelling.

◀ **Ahura Mazda**
This symbol from ancient Persia is believed to show Ahura Mazda raising one hand in blessing, with the ring of sovereignty in the other.

CREATION AND DEATH

After his birth, Ahura Mazda went to work to give the universe its form. He made the sun, moon, and stars, and all that represented good in the world. He also created six immortals, including Vohu Manah (Good Mind), to help govern his creation. Ahriman sent evil demons to attack Ahura Mazda, but the Wise Lord cast his brother out into the darkness. Then Ahura Mazda made Gayomart, the first man, and allowed the Good Mind to work within him. All seemed well at first, but Ahriman returned from the darkness and brought starvation, illness, pain, lust, and death with him. He dried up the lands, destroyed the crops, and defiled the Earth —and he poisoned Gayomart so that he would die.

THE HUMAN RACE

When Ahura Mazda saw that Gayomart was going to die, he took the man's seed and made Mashya and Mashyoi, the first human couple. Although they too were destined to die, their children went on to propagate future generations, ensuring the survival of humanity. Ahura Mazda could not defeat Ahriman, so he trapped the evil lord inside creation and gave humans the freedom to choose between good and evil. This struggle between the two forces will be resolved only at the end of time, when a new god called Saoshyant (the Savior) will come and, together with Ahura Mazda, destroy Ahriman and the evil he represents. The people themselves will become pure and good. The world will be created anew, after which all will be good, and the distinction between body and soul will cease to exist.

◀ **The dispute over the world**
Ahura Mazda and his wicked brother, Ahriman, fought to control the world, represented by the ring of sovereignty that they both tried to possess.

SIX IMMORTALS

The Amesha Spentas (Bounteous Immortals) are the children of Ahura Mazda, and second in importance only to that god. On one level, they are abstract entities and aspects of the divine nature of Ahura Mazda. On another level, they are seen as immortals, who sit on golden thrones and look after specific aspects of the natural world, ranging from fire to water. In doing so, they leave Ahura Mazda to concentrate on caring for humankind.

▲ **Vohu Manah**
The caretaker of domestic animals, Vohu Manah (Good Mind) is also the recorder of the good and bad deeds of humans.

▲ **Asha**
Meaning "Righteousness" or "Truth," Asha protects the element of fire and fights evil forces, such as disease and sorcery.

▲ **Armaiti**
Armaiti (Devotion) is the daughter of Ahura Mazda, the protector of the Earth. She is the embodiment of faith and worship.

▲ **Khshathra Vairya**
Personifying the power of Ahura Mazda, Khshathra (Dominion) protects the sky and metals, and fights Saura, a demon of anarchy.

▲ **Haurvatat**
Meaning both "Wholeness" and "Integrity," Haurvatat protects water and opposes thirst. She is closely associated with Ameretat.

▲ **Ameretat**
Ameretat (Immortality) sustains and protects plants, and hence, life and growth. She is the opponent of hunger.

THE FIRST HUMANS

The primal couple, Mashya and Mashyoi, were made from the seed of Gayomart, the first man, who Ahriman had doomed to die. Initially, the two grew together, entwined as a kind of tree, and the fruit they produced became the ten races of the Earth. They began in goodness, but Ahriman sent demons to corrupt them, and some of their actions became evil. But in spite of their corruption, deep down they kept their "heavenly self," which meant that they still had the power to make good decisions and choose a moral path through life.

▶ **Gayomart**
When the Wise Lord created the first man Gayomart, he was perfect in form and radiated his beauty like the sun.

▲ **The primal tree**
Because the first creation was in an ideal state, the original tree needed no bark to protect its branches and no thorns to defend its fruit.

THE SACRED FLAME

A prominent feature of Zoroastrian worship, the sacred flame burns continuously in the faith temples. The reverence accorded to these flames has led some to wrongly describe the religion as "fire worship." Zoroastrians worship Ahura Mazda, and the fire, which is described as the son of the god, stands for the place where people experience the god's presence. Although all fires are sacred, those set up with the correct ritual in temples are especially symbolic of his presence.

Fire burning in a Zoroastrian temple

ZOROASTER

The prophet of Zoroastrianism, Zoroaster (also known as Zarathustra) was born in Iran or Afghanistan some time in the 2nd millennium BCE. When he was 30 years old, he had a vision of Ahura Mazda, and subsequently began to propagate the worship of the god among his followers. Zoroaster insisted that there was only one true god, who was the source of goodness. He rejected the old religion of his homeland, insisting that some of its gods, who were warlike beings, were agents of Ahriman. Hymns said to be written by Zoroaster are collected in the sacred book of the faith, the *Avesta*.

Zoroaster, prophet of the faith

THE LEGEND OF RUSTUM AND SOHRAB

Rustum was the greatest hero of the early Persians: a brave warrior who defended himself and his people against the most fearsome and powerful foes. Rustum's bravery and skill, not to mention his mastery of the noble stallion Rakhsh, make him an exemplary character, but his life was marred by tragedy when he unwittingly killed his own son, Sohrab. The story of this event is a key episode in the Persian epic *Shahnama* (Book of Kings), and is also the subject of a famous poem by the British poet Matthew Arnold (1822–88).

THE MYTH

Out hunting one day, Rustum decided to take some rest. As he lay asleep, a group of men came across his horse, Rakhsh, and stole it. Rustum awoke to find his mount gone, and set off in search of the animal. When he reached the palace of Afrasiab, the ruler of a Central Asian kingdom, the king entertained Rustum and introduced him to his daughter, Tahmina. Rustum slept with her and, before leaving, gave her a clasp that he wore on his upper arm, asking her to give it to their child. The next day, his horse was found and Rustum went on his way.

YOUNG SOHRAB

Tahmina had a son whom she named Sohrab. He was an accomplished archer by the time he was five years old, and it became apparent that he would grow into a young man of great strength. When he asked about his father, Tahmina told him the truth, swearing him to secrecy.

Eventually, Sohrab became a great warrior and decided to launch an attack against Persia, hoping to meet his famous father in the course of the battle. His ultimate wish was to see Rustum as the Emperor of Persia, while he himself would take over his grandfather's throne. This plan pleased the devious Afrasiab, Sohrab's grandfather. He knew that if father and son came face to face,

one would be bound to kill the other. If Rustum were to die, Afrasiab could easily defeat the Emperor of Persia with Sohrab's help; if Sohrab were killed, Rustum would die of grief in any case, and Afrasiab could achieve the same objective.

THE FATAL FIGHT

The war began with Sohrab attacking a Persian castle. Its garrison, however, escaped and sent a message to their emperor that they were being attacked by a powerful leader, a man as mighty as Rustum. The Persian emperor knew that his only hope was to send his greatest warrior to the battlefront.

So Rustum joined the Persian camp. Sohrab proposed a duel and Rustum accepted the challenge, claiming that he was a slave. He did not reveal his identity, thinking that the enemy would be terrified if they found a mere Persian slave to be so strong. The two mighty warriors battled until they were exhausted, fighting with weapons and then with their bare hands. But there was still no victor as the pair was evenly matched. They resumed fighting the next day. This time Rustum, after long preparatory prayers, threw Sohrab and broke his back. As he lay dying, Sohrab showed Rustum the arm jewel and told him that his father would avenge his death. That was when Rustum realized that he had killed his own son. The anguished father built a golden tomb for Sohrab.

◀ **Rustum and Sohrab**
Even though they were exhausted, father and son refused to give up, wrestling one another to the ground and fighting on to the bitter end.

RUSTUM

Son of the legendary warrior Zal and a princess called Rudaba, Rustum was destined to be a warrior of great strength. While still in the womb, he grew so large that his mother almost died in childbirth. Both were saved because Zal knew how to perform a surgical operation to ensure a safe birth. Rustum was already very strong when he was born. As he grew up, he became skilled in arms, and his strength increased further. Over time, he became a champion of the early Persians, always ready to defend his people against fearsome enemies.

▲ The Simurgh
A mythical bird called the Simurgh taught Zal how to perform the surgical operation that enabled Rustum to be born.

▲ Rustum the warrior
Rustum's battles not only involved single combats and encounters on the battlefield, but also attacks on mighty castles.

◄ Rakhsh
Rustum picked Rakhsh from a herd of colts because of its size and strength. Famed for both power and loyalty, the horse was the envy of other warriors.

THE DEEDS OF RUSTUM

Rustum's story was largely one of war and battle. His heroic deeds involved defeating supernatural beasts, such as a dragon and a demon; strong animals, such as a lion; and opponents with the power of sorcery, such as a witch. Many of these encounters were part of a sequence, often called the "Seven Labors," which Rustum undertook in order to save his sovereign, the Emperor of Persia, who had been captured by demons.

▲ Rustum and the White Demon
One of Rustum's labors involved defeating a creature called the White Demon, together with another demon who was guarding the White Demon's castle.

▲ Rustum and the dragon
Rustum fought hard to kill the dragon—the third of his labors. He was joined by his horse, Rakhsh, who bit and tore at the flesh of the monster.

> # BEHOLD ME! I AM VAST, AND CLAD IN IRON, AND TRIED; AND I HAVE STOOD ON MANY A FIELD OF BLOOD, AND I HAVE FOUGHT WITH MANY A FOE.
>
> Matthew Arnold, *Sohrab and Rustum*, 1853

THE BOOK OF KINGS

Many of the ancient myths and legends of the Persian-speaking world are collected in the *Shahnama* (Book of Kings), an epic poem by the Persian poet Firdausi (c.935–1020). The poem, written in c.1000, consists of nearly 60,000 couplets, and recounts stories of Persia's glorious past from mythical times to the period when the region was conquered by the Arabs and Turks in the 7th century. These stories, which reflect Firdausi's unhappiness at the Islamic conquest, are frequently sad, involving defeats of noble warriors, attacks by demons, incompetent rulers, and people condemned by destiny.

◄ The Shahnama
A 16th-century manuscript of the *Shahnama* is beautifully illustrated with miniature paintings like this one depicting some of the most dramatic scenes of the Persian epic.

▲ Prince Isfandiyar
Isfandiyar, seen here in bonds and mounted on an elephant, was a legendary hero and heir to the Persian throne. He was destined to be slain by Rustum.

GODS OF WAR

Before going into battle, soldiers of old often called on their gods for protection. In most cultures there was a specific war deity they could invoke. This could be a figure who might reward them—such as the Norse god Odin—or else a god who was himself a brave warrior, perhaps having fought in a mythic war between supernatural races.

COSMIC WARRIORS

War gods naturally play a major role in great cosmic battles. They may lead armies of gods in wars for control of the cosmos, or heroically take on supernatural giants and demons that threaten the stability of the universe or the lives of humans. These struggles may involve much bloodshed, but cosmic warriors do the world a great service by ridding it of such monsters.

◄ Lugh
The Celtic war god Lugh was skilled in the arts, healing, and prophecy, as well as warfare. He led the Irish gods in battles against a monstrous race called the Formorians.

▲ Indra
The chief deity of the early Aryan invaders of India, Indra is the warrior king of the gods in the Vedas, defeating their demon foes.

◄ Kali
The fierce Hindu goddess Kali defeated the demon Raktabija, who could reproduce himself from his own blood.

PATRONS OF WARRIORS

One key role of war gods was to protect human warriors. They could do this either by intervening directly in human lives, as Odin liked to do, or by using their divine powers to change the course of a battle, as Greek and Roman war gods sometimes did. Warriors would encourage the support of their patrons by making offerings or sacrifices in their name.

◄ Mars
Worshipped more widely than the Greek war god Ares, the Roman god of war was patron not just of the Roman army but of the entire empire of Rome.

◄ Athena
Wise Athena was the protector of Greek heroes. Bearing the Gorgon's head, her shield turned people who looked at it to stone.

◄ Odin
Ruler of the Norse gods of Asgard, Odin was a friend of brave warriors, to whom he gave many weapons. Heroes killed in battle lived with him in his hall, Valhalla.

► Tu
The magical powers of the Maori war god Tu were so great that he controlled the weather and all the animals.

DEIFIED WARRIORS

Sometimes a hero's career is so remarkable that when he dies, he is allowed to join the ranks of the gods. Deification is reserved for the truly great heroes, usually people who demonstrate great bravery or supernatural strength on a number of occasions. It most often happens in cultures in which the way of the warrior is held in especially high regard—in parts of Africa, for example, and in Japan.

◄ Heracles
The exploits of this Greek hero were such that when he died, Zeus welcomed him to Mount Olympus, home of the gods.

◄ Shango
A king of the Yoruba people of West Africa, Shango displayed great success in war and outstanding magical abilities. After he died he became the god of thunder.

► Hachiman
The Japanese war god Hachiman began life as the 4th-century CE emperor, Ojin. As a god he was protector both of soldiers and of Japan as a whole.

WAR GODDESSES

Although some female figures actually fight in the battles of myth and legend, they are relatively few. But there are a surprising number of female goddesses of war. Some of these, such as the Egyptian goddess Sekhmet, are formidable fighters who are as aggressive as any male warrior, unleashing terrible violence on their enemies. But others take a less active part in war, influencing the real fighters or predicting that a battle is going to occur.

► The Morrigan
Along with her sisters, Badb and Macha, this Celtic goddess took the form of a crow who forecast the coming of war, and afterwards flew down to the battlefield to feast on the flesh of the fallen.

◄ Sekhmet
This lion-headed Egyptian goddess was usually calm, but when angry her power was awesome, with great arrows of fire shooting from her eyes.

◄ Meenakshi
Especially associated with southern India, this Hindu goddess set out to rule the universe, before accepting Shiva as her husband and lord.

▲ Nike
After helping the Greek gods in their war with the Titans, Nike became goddess of victory, bringing good luck to warriors

THE EPIC OF GESAR KHAN

Told by both the Tibetan and the Mongol peoples, the story of Gesar Khan is set in Ling, Tibet. The myth describes a time when the people were oppressed by warlords, treachery was rife, and famine was endemic. It is based on the life of a brave hero called Gesar, who came to the rescue of his people, battling with traitors and demons until the kingdom was finally made safe.

THE MYTH

Gesar was originally called Joru, and was the son of a dragon princess who had taken the form of a servant girl called Dzeden. When her pregnancy became apparent, the Queen of Ling threw her out of the castle because she believed that her husband, King Singlen, was the father of the unborn child.

When Joru was born, he seemed unremarkable. He was short and ugly, and very mischievous. Some disliked him, especially the king's brother, Todong, a power-hungry man who sensed that Joru was destined for greatness. He tried to have Joru killed but the boy escaped, and Dzeden took him to live in the woods, away from danger. He grew up into a handsome young man, skilled in shape-changing.

THE CONTEST FOR KINGSHIP

Gesar returned to the palace after receiving a message from a Buddhist monk, named Padmasambhava, that he was destined to become a savior of his people. On arriving, he found out that the king had left on a pilgrimage, and Todong was hoping to rule in his stead. In the guise of a prophetic raven, Gesar told Todong that he could rule Ling if he staged and won a horse race, in which anyone could participate. He could also marry Sechan Dugmo—a beautiful woman who led an unhappy life with her miserly father, but who was destined to become queen. An accomplished horseman, Todong organized the race because he was confident of his victory.

▶ **Gesar Khan**
A skilled rider, Gesar had a horse called Kyang Go Karkar, which was strong and resilient.

It was decreed that the winner of the race would become king and marry Sechan Dugmo. Gesar defeated Todong easily, and became the King of Ling, with Sechan Dugmo as his queen.

While Tibet prospered under Gesar's rule, Todong plotted to usurp his throne by allying with a monstrous demon called Lutzen. Gesar fought the demon, and chopped off its 12 heads. But Lutzen's wife, a stunning enchantress, seduced Gesar by giving him a cup of wine that made him forget everything but her. He forsook his kingdom, which fell into decline and was taken over by a demon king called Kurkar.

THE RETURN OF GESAR

Six years later, Gesar's brother found him and told him what had happened. Gesar returned to his kingdom disguised as a boy skilled in metalwork. He used his skill to distract and kill Kurkar, while his men destroyed the demon's army. After this, he had to defeat another demon called Shingti, who had a virtuous daughter. Despite his enmity with Todong, Gesar was fond of Todong's son, and arranged his marriage to Shingti's daughter. The couple became heirs to his throne, ending the conflict with Todong.

▲ **Padmasambhava**
A Buddhist monk named Padmasambhava spread Buddhism in Tibet in the 8th century. Revered by Tibetan Buddhists, he is seen as a second Buddha.

THE BIRTH OF GESAR

Dzeden was a shape-changer, who had transformed into a human girl when she inadvertently wandered far away from her home and took shelter in the kingdom of Ling. One night, she had a prophetic dream, in which a great lord told her that she would give birth to her country's savior. Nine months later, an egg popped out of her head. She nursed it, and her son hatched from the egg. Dzeden named him Joru, and he grew up to be a strong man.

◄ Dzeden
One version of the myth says that Dzeden, in her vision, drank nectar from a golden vase with an image of a lord on the side, and became pregnant.

► Ladakh
Home to people of Tibetan descent, Ladakh, a plateau between the Kunlun Mountains and Greater Himalayas in Kashmir, is believed by some to be the birthplace of Gesar Khan.

GESAR'S BATTLES

Tibetan and Mongol life centered on the horse, and warfare generally involved aggressive cavalry charges by armored warriors, who could be swift and ruthless. But Gesar found out that besides aggression, cleverness was also needed for victory. One of his enemies, Lutzen, had a castle guarded by three defensive rings, comprising gods, human soldiers, and demons. Gesar took over the castle by persuading the gods and humans to fight on his side and help him defeat the demons.

◄ Horseman's armor
Suits of plate armor and strong helmets helped protect Gesar's mounted warriors from the slashing sword blows of their enemies.

▼ Tibetan sword
Gesar succeeded in distracting Kurkar by posing as a metalworker who could forge fine weapons for the demon.

GESAR RESCUES HIS QUEEN

Gesar Khan rescued his wife, Sechan Dugmo, from a sorry fate on two separate occasions. By marrying her after the horse race, Gesar freed Sechan from a miserable life with her miserly father. He also saved her from the demon Kurkar, who had seized Gesar's kingdom and imprisoned his queen. Gesar's deep affection for his beloved queen equaled his love for his homeland, which he saved twice from tyrannical rule.

▲ The Kham region
From Mount Margyer Pongri in the Kham region of eastern Tibet, Gesar Khan and Sechan Dugmo bid farewell to their faithful and loving subjects, and disappeared forever.

▲ Racing horses
Gesar, a poor outcast, turned up in tattered rags for the race organized by Todong, but the other riders dressed up in fine clothes, as horse races were grand occasions.

GESAR'S PASSING

Todong's son married the daughter of the demon Shingti, and the pair became the new king and queen of Gesar's kingdom. In spite of their demonic parentage, they were virtuous rulers, and Gesar was convinced that the kingdom would be safe in their hands. So Gesar and Sechan Dugmo decided to retire. They went on a retreat to the side of a mountain in the Kham region, and disappeared the next day. It was believed that they had ascended either to the next world, or to the paradise of Shambala, the mythical home of the spirit kings.

THE GODDESS AL-LAT

The cultures of the Arabian Peninsula worshipped a number of deities before the coming of Islam in the 7th century. One of the most important was the goddess Al-Lat, now a shadowy figure, but whose image was once widely seen in West and Central Asia. Her cult was based near Mecca, the place where the Islamic faith was later revealed to the Prophet Muhammad.

THE MYTH

Al-Lat was a popular goddess in many regions of the Arab world before the spread of Islam. Apart from the Arabian Peninsula, she was also widely worshipped in the eastern Mediterranean region and parts of Iran. Essentially a moon goddess, she played a variety of other roles. As a bringer of fertility, she was a goddess of the Earth, and also a deity of love. Moreover, she was connected with the sun, and, although her main symbol was the crescent moon, it was sometimes shown with the disc of the sun resting in it.

THE NAME OF AL-LAT

Al-Lat's cult had a number of followers, especially in the city of Ta-if, near Mecca, Saudi Arabia. It was home to a tribe called the Thaqif, who considered her to be their patron deity. They possessed a stone cube that was held sacred to Al-Lat and two other goddesses, Manat and Al-Uzza—a triad known as the daughters of Allah. Many consider "Al-Lat" to be derived from an ancient Arabic word, *Al-Ilat* (the Goddess). According to another version, the word *lat* referred to the process of mixing or moistening. It was associated with a Jewish man at Ta-if who used to make a mixture of clarified butter and barley meal, which he served to pilgrims

◀ **Dhu Shara**
The Nabataeans of Petra, in Jordan, worshipped Dhu Shara, a high god and Lord of the Mountains, alongside Al-Lat.

▶ **Goddess Al-Lat**
Depictions of Al-Lat have been found on carved reliefs in many parts of the Arab world. Sometimes she is shown with a spear like the Greek Athena.

at the shrine of the goddess. The word was first attached to the shrine attendant, and after his death, to the rock that marked his burial place. Later, a statue of the goddess was placed on the rock, so "Al-Lat" became identified with the goddess herself. Thus, the goddess was initially linked closely to a specific place before her cult spread to other places in the Arab world. She was a popular figure, and people often named their daughters after her.

THE END OF THE CULT

After the Prophet Muhammad received the revelation of Islam, he gave up worshipping the three goddesses and other gods, claiming they were false deities. The people of the Arabian Peninsula—both the Quraysh, the prophet's own people, and other local tribes – renounced the goddess, and her shrine was destroyed. The cult of Al-Lat remained in other parts of the region for a while, but declined as Islam spread across West Asia. As a result, little is known about the goddess today. Some ancient Greek texts have compared her to Athena or to Aphrodite. They mention that Al-Lat was worshipped alongside a god, probably Dhu Shara, who resembled their wine god Dionysius.

THE DAUGHTERS OF ALLAH

Al-Lat, Al-Uzza, and Manat were often depicted together, and are sometimes confused with one another. Besides the crescent moon, the other symbols of Al-Lat were a sheaf of wheat and a pot of incense. Al-Uzza (the Strong One), a goddess of the morning and evening stars, represented love as well as war. She was similar to Inanna and was often shown with big cats, creatures that were sacred to her. She was an important deity of the Nabataeans (*see below*), who not only built a temple for her in Petra, but also worshipped her from rooftops and near acacia trees, which were sacred to her. Manat was the goddess of fate and death. People invoked her either to gain her protection, or to ask her to pursue their enemies. Her symbol was a waning moon, and she was often shown as an old woman, holding a cup of death.

Manat   Al-Uzza   Al-Lat

THE NABATAEANS

The ancient people of Jordan, Canaan, and parts of northern Arabia were known as the Nabataeans. Mainly traders, they controlled the oases and roads of the region, and charged merchants to travel across their lands. By the 3rd–1st centuries BCE, they had become so prosperous that they built the magnificent city of Petra, with numerous temples, tombs, and other buildings hewn directly out of cliffs. Although the Nabataeans left little in the way of writing, it is believed that they worshipped early Arabian deities, especially Dhu Shara and Al-Uzza. Their rule ended in 107 CE when the area was conquered by a Roman emperor, Trajan.

◀ **The Monastery at Petra, Jordan**
The Nabataeans imitated the Classical architecture of the Romans, with its columns and ornaments. However, many of the buildings in Petra were created by carving them directly out of the sandstone cliffs.

DEITIES OF THE SKY

In ancient times, the peoples of West and Central Asia looked to the skies for their most prominent deities. Their lives were ruled by the heat of the sun and by the infrequent rains, both of which were necessary to grow crops and ensure survival. They became skilled at predicting the weather and seasonal patterns, attributing both to the activities of the gods. Apart from the triple goddesses, the other sky deities worshipped by the ancient Semitic cultures were Samsu, a sun goddess, Warihu, a god of the moon, and Hadad, or Haddu, a god of storms.

◀ **Rising sun**
As in many other cultures, the ancient people of West Asia regarded sunrise as the return of a deity who had been absent during the night, and the event inspired celebration or worship.

PRE-ISLAMIC IDOLS

With the advent of Islam, most pre-Islamic cultures of the Arab world transformed rapidly—adopting a single god and giving up the practice of idol worship, as the new religion prohibited the veneration of statues. However, the *Kitab al-Asnam* (The Book of Idols), by the Iraqi historian Ibn al-Kalbi (born c.800), is a vital source of information about the early religious beliefs and practices of the region. It describes numerous deities from different cultures, such as Al-Lat, Al-Uzza, and Dhu Shara.

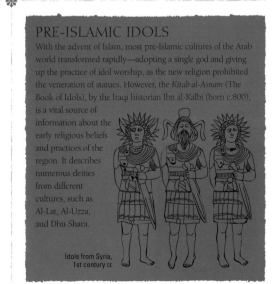

Idols from Syria, 1st century CE

SOUTH AND EAST ASIA

▲ **Vishnu riding on Garuda**
The great god Vishnu travels on the back of a giant bird—part eagle and part human
in form—called Garuda. This important animal god is said to mock the wind, so fast
does he fly, and such is his great size that he blocks out the sun.

SOUTH ASIA

The mythology of South Asia is dominated by Hinduism, a religion that has evolved over several millennia. With its thousands of gods and goddesses, Hinduism has one of the largest bodies of mythical narrative in the world.

Hinduism is highly diverse. It has no one sacred text, and no formal statement of belief. Probably the most ancient of the world's major religions, it has evolved steadily, producing countless stories of the cosmos and of the deities. This makes its traditions extremely complex, but at the heart of this complexity lies the belief that all the deities are aspects of a single, overarching reality.

VEDIC DEITIES

The earliest known texts about the gods and goddesses of India are the Vedas, four books whose stories probably date to the 2nd millennium BCE, though they were written down much later, in around 800 BCE. The oldest of them, the *Rig Veda*, comprises just over 1,000 hymns, each addressed to a deity. Many of these early Vedic gods and goddesses relate to specific aspects of the universe or the elements. Among the most prominent are Agni, god of fire, Surya, god of the sun, Vayu, god of the wind, Prithvi, goddess of the Earth, and Indra, chief of all the Vedic gods, who has a highly complex and powerful personality. The texts about these ancient deities still attract many readers, both for their poetry and for what they say about the beliefs of early people in South Asia.

HINDU DEITIES

In the centuries after the Vedas, another group of deities came to prominence. These, the central deities of Hinduism, include the prominent triad of Brahma the Creator, Shiva the Destroyer, and Vishnu the Preserver. Vishnu comes to Earth in a series of manifestations, or avatars, including two —Lord Rama and Krishna—who are worshipped as gods in their own right. Around these figures cluster dozens of other deities—from popular ones such as the elephant-headed Ganesh, Remover of Obstacles, to the various manifestations of the Great Goddess Devi—who play prominent parts in Hindu religion and mythology.

▲ Nandi, the bull
Shiva often travels on a white bull called Nandi, a symbol of strength, fertility, and religious duty. A statue of Nandi as Shiva's gatekeeper faces the main shrine in most temples of Shiva.

EPIC POEMS

The classic texts of Hindu literature are written in the ancient Sanskrit language. They are full of stories about all these deities, covering their various roles in the creation and history of the cosmos, as well as their appearances on Earth and relationships with humanity. Two major sources for these stories are the two great epic poems, the *Ramayana* and the *Mahabharata*, the latter of which is the longest poem in world literature. Although each of these poems has a narrative theme—the *Ramayana* is the story of Lord Rama's life on Earth, the *Mahabharata* the story of a rivalry between two families and of a great battle—they both contain much other material and are rich collections of tales of deities and people. These stories live on as part of a religion with millions of followers in India and elsewhere. They also form a mythology that continues to inspire poets, storytellers, and readers from outside the Hindu tradition, all over the world.

▼ Hindu temple at Bhubaneshwar, India
Large Hindu temples are often decorated with highly elaborate carvings. This stonework depicts episodes in the lives of the gods and goddesses and provides a rich record of the mythology of Hinduism.

THE VEDIC GODS

Some of India's earliest myths are derived from the Aryans, people of Central Asian origin who migrated to the region during the 2nd millennium BCE. Their myths were recorded in sacred texts known as the Vedas, which emphasized belief in gods that controlled the natural world and could influence human well-being. Chief among the Vedic deities were figures such as Indra, Agni, and Surya. These early deities were often known as the Adityas, or sons of Aditi, the goddess of space and mother of all creatures and deities.

INDRA

The god of thunder and rain, Indra was the chief of the Vedic gods and known for his strength and virility. He used his powerful *vajra* (thunderbolt) to attack demons who interfered with the process of creation, or threatened life. A popular myth tells how Indra gained his supremacy over the other gods. Once, Vritra (also known as Ahi, the serpent of drought) swallowed the cosmic waters and held back rains. Most gods ran away in fright, but Indra pierced the serpent's body with his *vajra*, allowing the vital waters to flow once again. Indra was worshipped as a provider of cattle and a deity who brought material wealth and wellbeing. The warrior classes especially grew to revere him because of his many successes in battle. His presence was usually signalled by a rainbow in the sky.

▶ Indra on Airawata
Indra is often depicted riding Airawata, a white elephant that emerged from the primal ocean. Here he holds an elephant goad and two thunderbolts (*vajras*).

◀ Giver of Life
Surya is sometimes shown holding lotus flowers in his hands, which represent the deity's life-giving powers. His attendants include two female figures who symbolize the two phases of the dawn.

▼ The sage Agastya
In the *Ramayana*, Agastya recites a hymn associated with Surya to Rama before his battle with the demon king, Ravana. It is believed that he introduced Vedic religion into southern India.

SURYA

Also known as *Savitar* (Giver of Life), Surya, the sun god, watched over the world by day, and was said to bring light, knowledge, and life itself to its inhabitants. He traveled across the sky in a chariot with a single wheel, signifying the cycle of the seasons. His charioteer, Aruna, the god of the morning, shielded the world from Surya's extreme heat. A myth tells how Sanjana, a goddess who married Surya, could not bear his brightness, so she turned herself into a mare and hid in the forest. When Surya found her, he changed into a stallion and fathered several children with her. He agreed to reduce his brilliance, and the pair returned to their palace in the heavens.

VAYU

Vayu was the god of the winds. One of the hymns of the *Rig Veda* portrays Vayu as either the breath of *Purusha*, the primal human, or as being created by *Purusha's* breath. According to a myth about Vayu, the god lost some of his power when he was expelled from Mount Meru, the home of the gods. Vayu attacked the mountain in retaliation, and despite resistance from Garuda, the king of the birds, he tore off the tip of the mountain and threw it into the ocean, where it became the island of Sri Lanka. Later myths have described Vayu as a servant of the god Vishnu and his consort, the goddess Lakshmi. He was a changeable character, at times stormy, but on other occasions gentle.

AGNI

The god Agni represented fire in all its aspects, such as lightning, the domestic fire, and fires used in rituals, which were all seen as his manifestations. As ritual fire, Agni took messages from humans to the gods, his smoke indicating where sacrifices were being made, while the fire lit at funeral pyres carried the souls to heaven. Agni, who was the son of Prithvi (Mother Earth) and Dyaus (Father Sky), was said to have been born three times: first from water, like the sun rising above the sea; then from the air, as lightning; and finally on Earth, in the form of fire that was kindled. He was so hungry that he ate his parents, and then grew tongues to lap the ghee (clarified butter) offered at altars.

VARUNA

The god of the sky, Varuna was the celestial lawgiver. He was the master of the rules that governed sacrifices and of the order that dictated the seasons and the annual round of sowing and harvesting. Some early myths describe him as a creator god, who formed the worlds of heaven, middle air, and Earth by his willpower alone. In another story, he was a ruler of the heavenly ocean, but after a war with the demons, the gods reallocated their powers and Varuna became the ruler of the western sky and of the earthly seas. His rule extended to the tides, and he was said to be the patron god of sailors and fishermen.

SOMA AND RITUALS

Like many early belief systems, Vedic religion involved the use of psychoactive substances, such as *soma*, a plant that could be identified with the herb ephedra. *Soma* was said to be the drink of the gods, and when mortals drank it, they made a connection with the deities. Accounts of its origin vary—some say Indra discovered *soma*, others that it was first produced from the primal ocean. Its use was quite popular among Vedic priests, who developed a special ritual for preparing the drink: first crushing the herb, and then mixing it with milk and water.

Ephedra

BRAHMA AND THE CREATION

Over their long history, the Vedic religion and Hinduism have produced a number of creation stories. Some involve a primal creator—Prajapati (Lord of Creatures) or the god Brahma— while other myths explain the creation of the various life forms, including humanity. They are told in the context of a cyclical notion of time, in which the universe will one day come to an end and a new era of creation will begin.

THE MYTH

In the beginning, the god Brahma, the Lord of Creation, spread his light around the universe and became the essence of all things. He also embodied time, presiding over a cycle of existence on a truly cosmic timescale. One day and night of his life was said to last 4,320 million human years, and when this period was over, the cycle of creation would come to an end as well.

DARK AND LIGHT

Brahma meditated, contemplating what the universe would be like, and created an image based on this vision. But he realized that since he was ignorant of what the universe would actually become once it came into existence, what he had created was merely an image of this ignorance. He discarded it, and it became Night. Soon Night began to produce dark children of its own, who became the first demons. When these creatures began to multiply, Brahma concentrated and started the process of creation once again.

As he meditated, he gave shape to a succession of beings, such as the sun and the stars, which began to emit light to balance the darkness of Night. According to some accounts, it was at this point that Brahma created the several thousand gods of the Hindu pantheon to balance the many demons that were the offspring of Night.

> **Brahma**
> Brahma's four heads symbolize the four Vedas, the four Hindu castes, and, as a reminder of Brahma's omniscience, the four points of the compass.

AN EVER-CHANGING FORM

One of the beings created by Brahma to bring light into the world was a beautiful creature called Vak (Word). According to some versions of this creation story, Brahma and Vak coupled, and while doing so, they changed their form continuously. As a result, they produced every kind of animal species that populate the Earth. However, other versions say that Vak, considered to be the creator's daughter, was unwilling to mate with him. When he persisted, she turned herself into a deer and fled. Although Brahma pursued and caught up with her, he was unable to impregnate her with his seed, which fell to the ground and became the first man and the first woman.

Since Brahma had changed his shape continuously to create different life forms, he was said to be present in all living beings. But despite his omnipresence, Brahma also had a home, the great citadel-palace of the gods on top of the sacred mountain, Meru. Mount Meru was at the very center of the Hindu cosmos; from its slopes, the sacred River Ganges flowed down in four streams, each of which ran towards one of the four cardinal points.

▲ **Lotus flower**
Some versions of the creation story describe how Brahma himself was born from a lotus flower that grew in the navel of a primal deity, Prajapati.

CREATORS

Different accounts of the creation story have often used the name Prajapati (Lord of Creatures) for the primal being. Some myths associate the deity Vishnu with Prajapati, and Brahma is said to have been born from the navel of Vishnu. The title "Prajapati" is also used for Brahma and his ten "mind-born" sons, who play a key role in creation by giving form to gods, humans, and animals. The Hindu pantheon includes other figures, such as Vishwakarma, who embodies creative power and wisdom, and is considered the architect of the cosmos.

▶ **Prajapati**
The primal deity wept at the emptiness about him; some of his tears became land masses in the primal sea, others became the stars and planets in the sky.

▲ **Vishwakarma**
The god Vishwakarma is usually shown surrounded by the tools that he used to create the universe. He is also considered to be an aspect of Brahma.

> THE GOD OF CREATION, BRAHMA [WAS] BORN OF THE GODHEAD THROUGH MEDITATION BEFORE THE WATERS OF LIFE WERE CREATED.
>
> *Katha Upanishad*

CREATION AND NATURE

The Hindus believe that the material or natural world is made up of five elements: earth, water, air, fire, and space or ether. These are personified by deities such as Prithvi, the Earth goddess, who is seen as the mother of all creatures. Water is vital in creation, and there are countless sacred lakes in India, as well as seven holy rivers, including the Ganges. The sea is also considered important; in some myths, the gods churned the primal sea in order to retrieve beneficial items from it, such as Kamadhenu (the Cow of Plenty).

▲ **Origin of the moon**
Some myths say that the moon emerged from the primal sea; others say it was created from the mind of Purusha (*see right*).

◀ **The fire of Agni**
Fire is personified by Agni. In Hindu myths, the smoke and flames of ritual fires helped carry messages to the gods.

THE PRIMAL HUMAN

An early creation myth mentions Purusha, the primal human, who split himself into a male and a female half that mated and gave birth to various life forms. In another version, told in the *Rig Veda*, Purusha created the Hindu castes from different parts of his body, with the Brahmins (priests) emerging from his head, the Kshatriyas (warriors) from his arms, the Vaishyas (farmers, artisans, and traders) from his thighs, and the Shudras (workers) from his feet. In yet another myth, the first human, called Manu, created a wife from one of his ribs and introduced a new era of creation.

MOUNT MERU

Mount Meru is accorded special reverence in Hinduism as the home of the gods. Known as the golden mountain, it is said to be in the Himalayas, and the Ganges flows from its top on its way to the Earth. The peak rests on a series of seven lower worlds, which some say are supported by a cosmic serpent, Sheshnag. Others believe the worlds rest on four elephants.

The snow-capped Himalayas

▲ **Page from the Rig Veda**
The *Rig Veda*, said to have been composed orally in the 2nd millenium BCE, is the first Hindu text to mention the divine creation of the different castes.

SHIVA

A member of the triad of great Hindu gods, Shiva (meaning "auspicious") represents the coming together of opposites—he is known as the destroyer, but also embodies great creative power. His complexity of character is reflected in his 1,008 titles, ranging from *Mahadeva* (Great God) to *Kaala* (Death). He is renowned for his profound knowledge, awesome strength, and his cosmic dance, which symbolizes both truth and destruction.

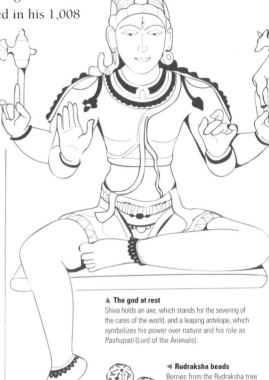

THE BIRTH OF SHIVA

One day, Brahma and Vishnu were having a discussion about who should be the supreme deity, the most powerful being in the cosmos. As the two gods were talking, a pillar of fire in the form of an enormous phallus appeared in front of them. It was so tall that its tip disappeared into the clouds and its base seemed to be buried deep in the ground. Mystified, Brahma transformed himself into a wild goose and flew up to find the top while Vishnu turned himself into a boar, burrowing deep down into the Underworld in search of its roots. But neither god could find what they were looking for. Just then an opening appeared in the phallus, and Shiva emerged. Immediately, Brahma and Vishnu recognized the power of Shiva, and agreed that the three of them should rule the universe together.

◄ Emergence of Shiva
Shiva appears out of a phallic column, or *linga*, in this carving depicting his birth. One of the god's titles is *Shiva Lingodbhava* (Lord of the Phallus).

▲ The god at rest
Shiva holds an axe, which stands for the severing of the cares of the world, and a leaping antelope, which symbolizes his power over nature and his role as *Pashupati* (Lord of the Animals).

◄ Rudraksha beads
Berries from the Rudraksha tree are used as prayer beads by devotees of Shiva, who believe the berries to be Shiva's tears.

► Shivalinga
Shiva is often worshipped as a phallic symbol or *linga*, rather than in his human form. These *lingas* can be found in temples dedicated to Shiva throughout India.

◄ Shiva's drum
Shiva usually carries a small, hourglass-shaped drum. According to the Hindus, its beat recalls the primal sound (*Aum*), with which creation began and with which it will end.

THE DANCE OF DEATH

When Shiva had an argument with Brahma and cut off one of his heads, a bitter feud developed between Shiva and Brahma's son, Daksha. So when Daksha held a betrothal feast in his palace to allow his daughter, Sati, to choose a husband, Shiva was not invited. He came to the feast anyway and claimed Sati's garland when she threw it into the air, and they were married. Later, Daksha held a holy sacrifice where he did not invite Shiva. Furious at this blatant insult, Sati threw herself onto the sacrificial fire and was burned to death. An enraged Shiva picked up Sati's body and began to dance with it, performing the dance of death that threatened to bring an end to all creation. To stop the dance, Vishnu intervened, bringing Sati back to life as the beautiful and benign goddess Parvati.

▲ **Shiva's three eyes**
The god's two eyes represent the sun and the moon. The third eye, usually closed, symbolizes wisdom. When it is opened, it has the power to destroy everything that is evil.

▶ **Lord of the Dance**
Sculptures of Shiva as *Nataraja* (Lord of the Dance) show him dancing, surrounded by a ring of fire. The figure crushed under his feet represents ignorance.

▶ **Shiva's bow**
The bow is one of several weapons associated with Shiva; he once used a single arrow to destroy three castles occupied by a group of demons.

◀ **Trident**
Shiva's trident is a weapon of great power. Its three prongs reflect the three *gunas*, or principles of the cosmos: purity, energy, and inertia. It is also believed to destroy ignorance.

SHIVA DEFEATS THE DEMONS

A group of demons persuaded Brahma to give them three castles that were so strong they could be destroyed only by a god—and the god had to attack them with a single arrow. Once installed in the castles, the demons began to launch attacks on heaven, and the gods realized that none of them had the strength to defeat these demons. So Shiva suggested that the other gods should combine their strength and lend him half of it. This, coupled with Shiva's already formidable strength—and the ability to control his power—was enough for him to defeat the demons with a single, all-powerful arrow. But when he had achieved his victory, Shiva refused to give back the strength he had borrowed from the other gods. And so Shiva remained the strongest deity of all.

SHIVA'S MOUNT

Shiva rides a white, humped bull called Nandi. As well as being a symbol of fertility, Nandi represents Shiva's strength and power, and is a formidable mount when the deity rides into battle. In Shiva's temples, the statue of Nandi always faces the shrine, symbolizing the soul's yearning for union with the divine. Nandi is also said to represent religious duty, or *dharma*, and has a role independent of Shiva as Nandikeshvara, when he is shown as a human figure with a bull's head and is a master of music and dance.

Nandi the bull

▶ **Shiva and Nandi**
Shiva and his consort Parvati ride the snow-white bull Nandi, who is garlanded and wears rich trappings of gold.

18th-century depiction of the ten avatars of Vishnu

THE TEN AVATARS OF VISHNU

Of the three great Hindu gods—Brahma, Vishnu, and Shiva—Vishnu has a special role as the preserver and sustainer of the world. He intervenes in human affairs by coming down to Earth in different forms known as avatars, meaning "descents." Vishnu appears at times of crisis: when demon kings rule the world or threaten to take it over, when natural disasters such as the great flood occur, or when the structure of society is out of balance. Devotees of Vishnu believe he has visited Earth innumerable times, but there are ten avatars that are especially important. So far, he has adopted nine of these forms, with a tenth still to come. Sometimes he takes heroic human shape, as he did when coming to Earth as Rama and Krishna, and sometimes he adopts the appearance of an animal.

Narasimha, the man-lion

1. Matsya
Vishnu first came to Earth as the fish Matsya, when a great flood covered the Earth. A demon snatched the sacred texts out of Brahma's hands, and Matsya helped Manu, the first man, get them back.

2. Kurma
Vishnu's second avatar was the tortoise Kurma, who supported Mount Meru on his back when the gods used it to churn the ocean and bring back precious objects and divine beings of benefit to humankind.

3. Varaha
As the boar Varaha, Vishnu rescued the Earth goddess Bhumidevi from the great flood. In many versions of the tale he lifted the Earth above the waves with his tusks.

4. Narasimha
Hiranyakashipu, an arrogant demon king, banned the worship of Vishnu, but his son disobeyed. When the king mockingly asked if Vishnu was in a pillar of their palace, Vishnu sprang out of the pillar as the man-lion Narasimha and killed him.

5. Vamana
Vishnu appeared as the dwarf Vamana to defeat the demon king Bali. Vamana asked Bali for as much land as he could cover in three strides. To Bali's horror he then grew into a giant and bestrode the whole Earth.

6. Parashurama
When the warrior, or Kshatriya, caste began to dominate the world, Vishnu was born into the Brahmin, or scholarly, caste as Parashurama, his sixth avatar, to slay the warriors with his axe.

7. Rama
Lord Rama, the seventh avatar of Vishnu, is worshipped as a deity in his own right. The adventures of this brave and virtuous character, who came to Earth to defeat the demon king Ravana, are described in the *Ramayana*.

8. Krishna
Vishnu appeared as Krishna to defeat evil King Kamsa. As told in the *Mahabharata*, Krishna was also pivotal in the war between the Pandavas and the Kauravas, encouraging the great archer Arjuna to fight with the words of the *Bhagavad Gita*. Krishna is also shown with his lover Radha in the central image.

9. The Buddha
A historical figure, the Buddha is seen in Hindu tradition as the ninth avatar of Vishnu. As such he defeated demons by encouraging them to turn away from the gods and the sacred texts.

10. Kalki
Vishnu's final avatar, Kalki, is predicted to come when the current era of the world ends. He will arrive riding a white horse, destroy the wicked, and renew the world.

Krishna and his lover, Radha

THE RAMAYANA

The *Ramayana* is one of the two great Indian epics written in the ancient Sanskrit language, and a seminal text in Hindu mythology. It tells the story of Rama, the Prince of Ayodhya and an incarnation of Vishnu, from his upbringing, through his exile, to the rescue of his wife, Sita, from the demon king Ravana's clutches. Through its depiction of the main characters, the epic extols the virtues of loyalty, kinship, devotion, and duty.

THE MYTH

Dasharatha, the King of Ayodhya, had three wives who bore him four sons: Rama, Lakshmana, Shatrughna, and Bharata. Rama was the eldest and the probable heir to the throne of Ayodhya. As a young man, he learned archery from the sage Vishwamitra. When Rama and Lakshmana were older, they were taken by Vishwamitra to the city of Mithila, where King Janaka had organized a competition to select a husband for his daughter, Sita. The competitors were required to string a great bow that had once belonged to Shiva. Rama, who had fallen in love with Sita, was the only one who was able to string the bow—he not only strung it, but broke it too. Rama won the contest and returned home with his wife.

RAMA'S EXILE

The time came when Dasharatha had to select an heir from among his sons. He wanted to choose his eldest son, Rama, who was an ideal prince in every way. But one of Rama's stepmothers, Kaikeyi, reminded Dasharatha of a boon he had

> ▶ **Prince Rama**
> Rama was famous as a skilful archer—his prowess with the bow enabled him to win the hand of Sita and, while in exile, to defeat the demons that upset the peace of the forest.

once promised her and demanded that he make her son, Bharata, the heir instead, and send Rama into exile so that he would not pose a threat to Bharata. Bound by his vow, the sad king banished his eldest son to the forest for 14 years. Rama obeyed his father unquestioningly. Sita and Lakshmana insisted on accompanying him.

Dasharatha died of grief soon after Rama's departure. Bharata, who had been absent from the palace during this time, was recalled to ascend to the throne of Ayodhya. Horrified by his mother's greed, he insisted that Rama was the rightful king, and traveled to the forest to bring Rama back. However, Rama refused to disobey his father's last wish, and Bharata had no option but to return home to be crowned as the next king. He devised an honorable compromise so that he could obey their father and show respect to Rama at the same time. Bharata took a pair of Rama's sandals back to Ayodhya and ritually enthroned them, to symbolize his rule as regent on behalf of his exiled stepbrother till the day that Rama returned.

Meanwhile, the exiles settled down, adapting to the hard life of the forest. Rama and Lakshmana frequently fought off demons who attacked the ascetics living in the woods and threatened their lives, or interrupted their prayers, rituals, and meditation. The ascetics were grateful to Rama and Lakshmana for their selfless deeds. Some of them realized that Rama was in fact a divine being.

▲ **Exiled in the forest**
When Rama, Sita, and Lakshmana arrived in the forest, they met the hermits who lived there, and had to adapt to their simple way of living, which was very different from the life of luxury that the royals knew.

»

RAMA AND SITA

In the epic, Rama and Sita are portrayed as the ideal couple. Rama wins his wife in a contest of strength, and fights fearlessly to rescue her when she is abducted. Similarly, Sita is considered the perfect devoted wife. However, Rama has been seen by some as a flawed hero who failed to appreciate Sita's goodness by doubting her chastity twice. Some accounts interpret Rama's actions as befitting a just ruler who has to place ideals of kingship above all personal bonds.

▶ **Rama's marriage**
Rama and Sita show their mutual devotion through their actions—she, by following him to his forest exile, and he, by rescuing her from the demon king, Ravana.

◀ **Plough**
Sita's name means "furrow." Her father found her in a furrow in the the soil while ploughing his fields.

THE IDEAL OF BROTHERHOOD

Brotherhood is thematically integral to the *Ramayana*. The ideal brother is Lakshmana—he accompanies Rama and Sita into exile, guards them, and aids Rama in his battles with the demons and in his rescue of Sita. Bharata, too, shows his love for Rama by overriding his kingly aspirations and placing Rama's sandals on the throne. Shatrughna is similarly devoted to Rama, and outraged at the injustice done to him.

Rama's slippers

▶ **Lakshmana**
When Ravana's sister tried to take revenge on Rama for spurning her advances, Lakshmana cut off her nose.

FROM THY FEET CAST FORTH THOSE SANDALS, THEY SHALL DECORATE THE THRONE.

Valmiki, *Ramayana*

THE EPIC

The *Ramayana*, one of the great works of world literature, is said to have been written by a sage, Valmiki, who plays a role in the epic, but may also have been a real person. Varying accounts place its date of compilation between 500 BCE and 200 CE. Valmiki probably did not write the entire poem; several passages were added after the work was originally composed. The epic primarily deals with the life of Rama, who belonged to the *Surya Vansha* (lineage of the sun god) or *Raghu Vansha* (lineage of his great-grandfather, Raghu, a great emperor).

The sun god

▶ **Sage Valmiki**
In the epic, Valmiki is a sage who lives in the forest, and is often visited by Rama and Sita during their exile. When the pair are estranged, Valmiki lets Sita stay in his hermitage.

THE RAMAYANA IN SOUTHEAST ASIA

Besides its popularity in India, the *Ramayana* is well known in Southeast Asia. The epic reached Indonesia during the early centuries of the Common Era. In Java, Malaya, and Thailand, local writers translated the Sanskrit text, and theatre companies adapted it. In Thai literature, the epic is called *Ramakien*. Episodes from it are presented in Thai *khon* (mask) plays and in such art forms as the Indonesian puppet and shadow theater.

Mask used in Thai *khon* plays

SURPANAKHA

One day, a female demon named Surpanakha lusted after Rama and Lakshmana, and made advances towards them. When the brothers rejected her, she tried to attack Sita, and Lakshmana retaliated by cutting off her nose. Surpanakha was infuriated at the way Rama and Lakshmana had treated her, so she went to her brother Ravana, the ten-headed demon ruler of Lanka, and incited him to abduct Sita in revenge. Ravana sent a demon disguised as a golden deer to distract Rama and Sita. When Sita wished to have the creature as a pet, Rama went off in pursuit of the deer. Ravana then tricked Lakshmana into following Rama and, having approached Sita disguised as a hermit, carried her off to Lanka.

RAMA AND HANUMAN

Rama and Lakshmana began their search for Sita. On their journey through the forest, they came across the monkey god Hanuman, who served Sugreeva, the monkey king. Sugreeva, like Rama, was also in exile. His brother Vali had taken his place as king. Hanuman asked for Rama's help in removing the usurper. Sugreeva challenged Vali to a duel, during which Rama killed Vali. His kingdom restored, Sugreeva agreed to aid Rama.

Hanuman decided to help in rescuing Sita. Parties of monkeys were sent out to search for her. After many adventures,

▲ **The final battle**
During the battle, whenever Rama cut off a head or arm of Ravana, a new one grew in its place. Finally, Rama used a celestial weapon given by Brahma.

Hanuman found Sita imprisoned on the island fortress of Lanka. Its location made Lanka difficult to attack, as did the fact that Ravana had an entire army of demons. Hanuman and his monkeys built a bridge over the sea so that they could attack Lanka. In a series of battles, Rama, Lakshmana, Hanuman, and the other monkeys killed the most fearsome demons. Finally, Rama slew Ravana and rescued Sita. Then Rama, Sita, and Lakshmana returned home.

Rama was unsure about accepting Sita as she had been a captive of Ravana. Hurt and distressed, Sita offered to walk through fire to prove her chastity. She emerged unscathed, but back in Ayodhya, a chance remark by a washerman prompted Rama to doubt Sita again. She sought refuge in the hermitage of the sage Valmiki, where she gave birth to twin boys. Years later, Rama recognized them as his sons and invited his wife to return after another trial by fire. Tired of constantly having to prove her chastity, Sita appealed to Mother Earth to take her back. On hearing her cry, the ground opened up and Sita disappeared into it.

◀ **The death of Jatayu**
When Ravana abducted Sita, an old vulture called Jatayu tried to save her. Jatayu attacked the demon king and destroyed his chariot, but Ravana cut off his wing, so killing him.

ALLIES

Rama's greatest allies in the rescue of Sita were Sugreeva, Hanuman, and their army of monkeys. Hanuman's great strength and powers of shape-changing and flight proved invaluable. He made two journeys to Lanka, the first to locate Sita, and the second to help Rama defeat Ravana and rescue his wife. Having found Sita on the first journey, he was discovered by Ravana's guards who set his long tail on fire, but he survived, setting Lanka ablaze as he escaped. During the final battle in Lanka, many of Rama's warriors, including Lakshmana, were killed. Hanuman fetched a magic herb from the Himalayas to revive them. He was rewarded with everlasting youth for his devotion to Rama.

▲ **Sugreeva fighting Vali**
Since Sugreeva and Vali looked alike, Rama told Sugreeva to wear a garland so that Rama could identify him.

▲ **Hanuman carrying the mountain**
Hanuman was unsure which herb would revive Lakshmana, so returned to Rama carrying the entire mountain of herbs.

ADVERSARIES

In the *Ramayana*, Rama's enemies are referred to as *rakshasas*, or demons. Traditionally, they were malign beings who attacked women and children or possessed people at night, driving them insane. Prominent among the demons helping Ravana were his brother, Kumbhakarna, a giant who spent most of his life sleeping, and Ravana's son, Meghnath, who had defeated Indra and was said to be unbeatable in battle. These demons posed such a great threat that Vishnu had to come to Earth as his avatar, Rama, in order to defeat them for good.

▶ Meghnath
Meghnath's magical serpent arrows vanquished many of the enemy warriors, including Lakshmana.

▲ Kumbhakarna
The giant Kumbhakarna had been given a boon whereby he could sleep for six months at a stretch. When he finally awoke to fight for Ravana, he devastated Rama's army before being killed by the prince himself.

RAVANA

The king of the *rakshasas*, Ravana was a fearsome figure with 10 heads and 20 arms. He was a scholar and an authority on the Vedas. He pleased Brahma with his rigorous austerities and arrogantly sought invulnerability against gods and demons, believing no human could harm him. He also appeased Shiva, who gave him a sword. He is seen as either a wicked counterpart to the virtuous Rama, or as a tragic figure who had potential for good but was destined to become evil.

▲ Ravana moving Kailash
Once Ravana angered Shiva by moving his abode at Mount Kailash, and was punished.

▶ Ravana's sword
Ravana attacked Rama with the *Chandrahas* (moon blade), which he had been given by Shiva.

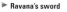

> # FOR THIS DEED OF INSULT, RAVANA, IN THY HEEDLESS FOLLY DONE, DEATH OF ALL THY RACE AND KINDRED THOU SHALT REAP FROM RAGHU'S SON!
>
> Valmiki, *Ramayana*

HINDU FESTIVALS

There are some popular Hindu festivals associated with Rama. He is believed to have worshipped the goddess Durga before setting off to fight Ravana. So during the nine nights of the festival of *Navaratri*, episodes from the epic are enacted, with a climax on the tenth day, *Dussehra*, when Rama slew Ravana. On this day, effigies of Ravana, his brother, Kumbhakarna, and his son, Meghnath, are ritually burned to symbolize the victory of good over evil. Rama also has a role in the festival of Diwali. On Diwali, people light lamps to commemorate the return of Rama to Ayodhya after his long exile.

Diwali, the festival of lights

地文官祖

德配天地

代帝王師

天地

EAST ASIA

Both China and Japan have complex mythologies involving many thousands of gods, goddesses, and spirits. For centuries these beings have played a central role in the lives of the people and their rulers.

China has been a melting pot of religion and mythology for thousands of years. The great richness and variety of its belief systems comes from several sources. First, the country developed many traditional deities over the thousands of years during which its great civilization was formed. Later, in the 6th and 5th centuries BCE, three major belief systems further shaped Chinese thought and mythology: Confucianism, a philosophy that emphasizes ritual, social order, and duty; Daoism, which stresses harmony with nature; and Buddhism, which embraces ways of avoiding the suffering of the world through following the teachings of the Buddha himself to attain inner peace.

PANTHEON OF IMMORTALS
Of the three traditional Chinese belief systems, Confucianism did not involve the worship of gods and spirits, although Confucius himself was revered as an immortal and became a figure about whom various myths were told. Daoism, on the other hand, involved a belief in thousands of "immortals": deified heroes, scholars, emperors, priests, and sages, who had lived a good life and joined the gods in heaven after their time on Earth. Buddhism was not in its original form a religion of gods and goddesses, but in the form in which it reached China it developed a vast pantheon of Buddhas and Bodhisattvas, saintly beings who had reached the threshold of enlightenment but held themselves back in order to help others attain the same goal. The Bodhisattvas of Buddhism, the Daoist immortals, and a host of traditional deities and

▲ **The goddess Luo Shen**
Me Fei, daughter of the legendary Chinese emperor Fu Xi, drowned in the River Luo and emerged as the beautiful goddess Luo Shen.

spirits surviving from earlier religions, were amalgamated in Chinese mythology into one vast pantheon of immortals. Many of them are the subjects of elaborate stories about how they became deified or what their powers in heaven encompassed. They are said to assist those who pray to them or make offerings at their temples.

JAPANESE MYTHOLOGY
In Japan, mythology developed differently, although there, as in China, the influence of the various deities and Bodhisattvas of Buddhism was also strong. More central to Japanese mythology, though, are the thousands of spirits, or kami, who are said to inhabit the land. Virtually everything, whether animate or inanimate—every place, rock, lake, tree, creature—has its kami, a kind of spirit that has influence over human life and that must be respected and not offended in any way.

In addition, Japan has a number of prominent gods and goddesses whose lives form a national mythology, from the creation of the world onwards. Foremost among these deities are the sun goddess, Amaterasu, and her descendants. Amaterasu's family was said to have been responsible for uniting Japan, and the imperial family that ruled the country until the middle of the 20th century was said to be descended from her. Although Japan's imperial family no longer claims to be descended from the gods, the people of Japan still accord these ancient deities deep respect.

◀ **Confucius and attendants**
The great Chinese scholar and teacher Confucius, who lived from 551–479 BCE, had a huge influence on Chinese thought, teaching respect for authority, social harmony, and regard for one's parents. After he died, many people believed that he had become one of the immortals, and some people worshipped him as a god.

▶ **Stone altar at Qingxiling**
At altars inside and outside Chinese temples, devotees make offerings to the deities—and burn incense—to petition their assistance.

PAN GU CREATES THE UNIVERSE

The Chinese creation myths describe how the primal god Pan Gu beat chaos into order to make the world. After this, a gentler, more nurturing creator deity appeared, the goddess Nü Wa, who formed the first people out of clay. The origin of the many other gods and goddesses is told elsewhere in Chinese myth.

THE MYTH

In the beginning there was only chaos, and amid this disorder slept the lone creator deity Pan Gu. He was in a state of deep slumber, building up his strength for the monumental task of creation. After an immeasurable period of time, Pan Gu awoke. Looking around he saw only disorder and was angered by the sight. He brought his arms crashing through the chaos, his hands hitting the swirling elements with a great echoing bang.

THE CREATION OF THE ELEMENTS

The impact of Pan Gu's blows caused the elements of chaos to move off in different directions. He struck the chaos once again, and the elements started to become more ordered, until the heavier ones began to sink and the lighter ones floated upwards. This process created the Earth and the sky, both of which then began to expand as the elements continued to separate. Pan Gu stood between the two domains, his feet pressed down on the Earth and his hands holding up the sky,

◀ Nü Wa
The name Nü Wa means "Snail Maiden," and the goddess is often portrayed with the body of a snake or a snail and the head of a woman.

▶ Pan Gu
The creator god is usually depicted wearing a skirt of leaves. He holds in his hands the sky that emerged after the separation of the elements of chaos.

to prevent them from coming together. He grew progressively taller as the two moved further apart. Once the two were permanently separated, the creator lay down to sleep.

As he slept, Pan Gu himself began to transform. His eyes became the sun and the moon. The strands of hair in his beard broke into pieces that became the stars. Some parts of his body turned into the mountains and the rest of his flesh turned into the soil. Soon, the hair on his head became the plants and trees that took root in the Earth. They were nourished by his blood, which formed the lakes and rivers.

THE FIRST PEOPLE

A goddess called Nü Wa appeared when Pan Gu had finished creating the world. She looked at the cosmos that had grown out of Pan Gu's body and considered it beautiful. But after a while she felt lonely, and decided to create human beings who could live on this landscape. She took some clay and molded it into the first people, and kept making more when she saw that they were happy together. However, she also noticed that after some time they began to age and die. Weary at the prospect of molding people out of clay indefinitely, Nü Wa gave her creations the ability to procreate; now there would always be people to populate the Earth. Nü Wa stood back, and was pleased with what she had made.

THE DARK LADY

Certain versions of the myth say that the goddess Jiu Tian Xuannü (the Dark Lady) created the human race once again, after the first people were wiped out in a great flood. Some accounts consider her to be the sister and wife of Fu Xi, although others say he was married to Nü Wa. Fu Xi and the Dark Lady married in order to have children and revive humanity. Some say that she also brought the flood to an end by mending a hole in the heavens. Jiu Tian Xuannü was also thought to be a teacher, who taught many tenets of Daoism, an ancient Chinese philosophy, to Huangdi (the Yellow Emperor), an ancestor of the mortal rulers of China.

◄ Jiu Tian Xuannü
Early accounts of the Dark Lady depicted her with a serpent's body, confusing her with Nü Wa. Later, she was shown as a beautiful woman (shown seated on the right).

▲ The Yellow Emperor
Huangdi, the Yellow Emperor, was a legendary ruler who taught the arts of civilization to the people of China. He was later deified for his achievements.

► Lantern festival
Celebrating the New Year, this festival marks the Full Moon on the 15th day of the first lunar month. Deities worshipped include the three primeval emperors.

▼ The three emperors
These primordial rulers were revered in ancient China as deities who brought happiness and had the power to forgive sins and heal.

Tian Guan   Di Guan   Shui Guan

THE PRIMORDIAL EMPERORS

After the human race was created and the first people began to multiply, the Jade Emperor sent three great primordial emperors to rule them. The first, Tian Guan (the ruler of heaven), was the bringer of happiness, freedom, and wealth. Extremely powerful, he was second only to the Jade Emperor himself. The second, Di Guan (the ruler of Earth), was known as a great judge of humans and their actions. The third, Shui Guan (ruler of water), controlled the floods and took away disease and sickness. This trio of rulers was worshipped all over China.

GODS OR MORTALS

Two of the true founders of Chinese culture and philosophy were Laoze (born 604 BCE) and Kong zi, or Confucius (551–479 BCE), who helped people make sense of the natural world and their everyday existence. They were hugely influential and attracted many followers. These men became so popular that myths about them began to spread, and they came to be accepted as gods. Laoze was believed to be an immortal, who was born as a human to teach his followers and write the philosophical masterpiece, the *Daode jing*, which later formed the basis of Daoism. Confucius, although a real person too, came to be seen as a semi-mythical figure and was worshipped as a deity in temples.

► Laoze
According to Laoze's philosophy, human beings should try to achieve a state of equilibrium within themselves. Since they are a part of nature, they should live in harmony with nature, not violate the natural world.

◄ Yin and Yang symbol
Chinese philosophy states that a fundamental duality exists in the universe between the feminine principle, Yin, and the masculine principle, Yang.

◄ Confucius
The philosophy of Confucius was summed up in his belief in the eight virtues: filial piety, brotherly love, loyalty, honesty, righteousness, politeness, integrity, and chastity.

THE COURT OF THE JADE EMPEROR

According to Daoist myths, the vast and complex court of the Chinese emperor was mirrored in a celestial court of immortals who served his heavenly counterpart, the Jade Emperor. Even the deities of other religions such as Buddhism were seen as a part of this huge organization of gods and goddesses. By making offerings, believers sought the blessings and help of these deities.

▶ **Yühuang**
The Jade Emperor is usually portrayed as a bearded man wearing the regalia of a mortal emperor, and clasping to his chest a tablet of jade.

THE MYTH

The emperor of heaven was popularly known as Yühuang (the Jade Emperor) but was also often referred to as Shang Di (Lord of Heaven). He was a supreme deity but, like Confucius, he was originally a mortal. Yühuang was the child of a king, Ching Teh, and his queen, Pao Yüeh. For many years, the royal couple could not have children. Pao Yüeh asked the priests to pray for her to have a child and the next night she dreamed that Laoze, the deified father of Daoism, visited her carrying a baby. Soon after, she became pregnant. She gave birth to a son who grew up to be a kind and wise ruler, but after ensuring prosperity for his subjects, he left his throne to follow a life of prayer and meditation. When his perfect life was over, he was deified as the Jade Emperor and became the ruler of the immortals.

THE CELESTIAL BUREAUCRACY

The Jade Emperor lived in a celestial palace and ruled heaven with the help of a huge retinue of other deities, each of whom controlled a particular department of the heavenly civil service. This was a vast bureaucracy that resembled in size and complexity the organization of the civil service that worked for the Chinese emperor on Earth.

▶ **The immortals**
Many ministers and judges assisted the Jade Emperor in the day-to-day running of the heavenly court. Devotees of Chinese popular religion placed statues of these immortals in temples and made offerings to them.

At the emperor's side sat Xi Wangmu (Queen Mother of the West), the empress of heaven. A powerful goddess, she had her own palace, built of gold and surrounded by a garden with trees that bore the magical Peaches of Immortality. The fruit took a thousand years to ripen, but when they were ready to eat, they gave eternal life to the eater.

PROTECTORS OF CHINA

The Jade Emperor's court included many gods who looked after different aspects of life on Earth, helping people in their daily lives. Longwang, known as the dragon king, took care of the waters, especially the seas and rivers, and was also considered to be the god of rain. Yue Lao took the form of an old man who lived on the moon, and cared for couples when they got married. However, the most important god to humans was Zao Jun, known as the Kitchen God. People kept his image above the stove in their kitchen. Every year they would put up a new picture of the god and burn the old one. As the smoke rose heavenwards, it took a message to the Jade Emperor, reporting how the members of the household had behaved during the year.

BUDDHIST IMMORTALS

For many Buddhists, the spiritual leader of their faith, the Buddha, is seen as a great human teacher, not as a god. But, in some forms of Buddhism, a multitude of figures (including the Buddha himself, and other Buddhas and Bodhisattvas) attract devotion and worship. In Chinese popular religion, these figures join the ranks of the Daoist immortals and are worshipped in temples. Among the most popular are: Omitofu, Buddha of the Western Paradise; Da Shi Zhi, the Lord of Strength and Success; Mile Fu, the Buddha of the Future; Pilu, the god of wisdom and embodiment of Buddhist law; and Guan Yin, the goddess of mercy.

▲ The Buddha
A prince who renounced the world to achieve ultimate wisdom, the Buddha is revered by the Chinese as one of the greatest of all spiritual teachers.

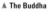

▶ Guan Yin
The goddess Guan Yin is known as the one who watches and listens. She responds whenever her devotees call upon her for help.

THE QUEEN OF HEAVEN

Known as the Golden Mother or the Queen Mother of the West, Xi Wangmu was one of the most powerful immortals. She heard the reports of the other immortals after they returned from visits to Earth. She ruled the mortal world too, and was able to bring death, or to grant eternal life to a person by allowing them to eat one of the Peaches of Immortality from her garden. Devotees prayed to her for a long life, and women called on her for good fortune when they were about to be married.

▶ Xi Wangmu
As the controller of life and death, the mother goddess Xi Wangmu is often shown holding one of the Peaches of Immortality.

THE EIGHT IMMORTALS

The Ba Xian, or Eight Immortals, were Daoist scholars and heroes who achieved immortality due to their devotion to Daoism. They figure in numerous myths along with the Jade Emperor, flying across clouds, fighting dragon kings, or defeating evildoers, and also in comic adventures, such as getting drunk, or setting fire to the sea. Some, like Han Hsiang Tzun, whose flute was said to give life, were patrons to musicians; some helped the sick, like Ho Hsien Ku, a female immortal who carried objects associated with immortality in her ladle. Chung Li Chuan's fan could revive the dead, and Chang Kuo's castanets prolonged life.

Chung Li Chuan

Chang Kuo

Ho Hsien Ku

Han Hsiang Tzun

THE IMPERIAL COURT

China had one of the largest and most complex systems of government in the ancient world. Hundreds of officials, each with a clearly defined job, worked for the emperor, and these people were chosen by a competitive examination system. There was a rigorous hierarchy, with only key advisers allowed direct access to the emperor, who would meet them, as well as foreign officials, in one of the audience halls in his palace. In Chinese mythology, a similar government existed in heaven.

Audience hall in the Forbidden City, Beijing

THE ADVENTURES OF MONKEY

One of the best-loved of all Chinese myths is the story of a mischievous character named Monkey. It tells how Monkey runs amok, upsetting all the gods, and causes still more mischief when he is punished. Finally, he is made to join a Buddhist pilgrim on an expedition and reforms himself. Involving Daoist, Buddhist, and ancient Chinese deities, the story appeals to all with its lively plot and likeable, albeit roguish, central figure.

THE MYTH

Monkey was the most intelligent of all his species. When he was young he went to study with a Daoist master, but unable to resist playing pranks on other students, he was sent to the forest. There the other monkeys revered him for his wisdom and skill and made him their king. A feast was held for him, and Monkey, having drunk too much, fell asleep, whereupon the King of the Underworld kidnapped him and took him to hell. There Monkey was confined to keep him out of mischief.

FROM HELL TO HEAVEN

In hell, Monkey broke free and went to look at the register of judgements, which contained the destiny of every living being. When he read that he would die when he was 342 years old, he crossed out his name so that he could live for ever. When the Jade Emperor was told about Monkey's impudent behavior, he decided to summon the irrepressible creature to heaven. He tried to keep him in check by giving him the vital

► **The monkey king**
Monkey's desire for immortality at all costs is comic, but also a reflection of a common human trait.

responsibility of looking after the heavenly peach garden, where the Peaches of Immortality grew. Monkey was very happy in heaven until the gods threw a party for Xi Wangmu. They forgot to invite Monkey, and in revenge, he stole and ate all the Peaches of Immortality, reaffirming that he was now actually one of the immortals.

MONKEY AND THE BUDDHA

After he had stolen the peaches, Monkey ate some pills belonging to the sage Laoze that were made from the Peaches of Immortality. Assured for a third time of eternal life, he began to plan to take over heaven. The baffled emperor appealed to the Buddha, the greatest sage of all. When the Buddha asked Monkey why he wanted to rule heaven, he replied that he deserved to be king as he was the most powerful creature in the universe, and could leap thousands of miles in one jump. Holding Monkey in his hand, the Buddha asked him to demonstrate his power. But when Monkey obliged, the Buddha showed him that he had only jumped across the sage's enormous palm—the mountains where he had landed were the Buddha's fingers. The astounded Monkey was imprisoned inside a magic mountain, and was released when he had truly repented. He was ordered to accompany the monk Xuanzang, who was going on a westward journey to India to find Buddhist scriptures and bring them back to China.

◄ **In the Buddha's palm**
After Monkey discovered that he had merely traversed the breadth of the Buddha's palm, he realized that his powers were, after all, limited.

MONKEY'S JOURNEY

The most popular aspects of Monkey's story deal with episodes of his mischief-making, and his meeting with the Buddha. But the tale concludes with his journey to India with Xuanzang and his disciples, Zhu Wuneng (also known as Pigsy) and Sha Wujing. They travel through an imaginary landscape populated by dragons, demons, volcanoes, and other dangers, and Xuanzang's companions do their best to protect him so that he can fulfill his quest for the scriptures. In the end they return to China, and Monkey and Xuanzang are rewarded by being bestowed with the status of Buddhas.

▶ Xuanzang
The Buddha told Monkey to accompany Xuanzang because the monk was too gentle to defend himself.

◀ The Jade Emperor
The emperor of heaven found Monkey hard to deal with, and happily complied with the Buddha's solution to send him with Xuanzang.

▼ Sha Wujing
Sha was a powerful heavenly general who was exiled to Earth because he broke a goblet in the peach garden.

◀ Zhu Wuneng
A heavenly marshal, Zhu was banished to Earth in the form of a pig because he got drunk and flirted with the moon goddess.

THE HEAVENLY PEACH GARDEN

The heavenly garden, where the Peaches of Immortality grew, belonged to Xi Wangmu (Queen Mother of the West). It was a place of great beauty but also power, because eating the fruit made a person immortal. Monkey abused his position in the garden by eating the peaches, which were not only powerful, but very scarce, because the trees rarely bore fruit. Moreover, Xi Wangmu's banquet was held only once every 3,000 years. Eating the peaches was just one of the three ways in which Monkey made himself immortal—each time he was challenging the power of the deities to confer immortality upon him.

▼ The paradise garden
Chinese painters depicted the heavenly peach garden as an elegant Chinese garden, crossed with streams and featuring pavilions where one could rest.

Peaches

THE JAPANESE CREATION

Japanese myths about the origin of the universe tell how, after six generations of primal deities, the seventh generation, comprising the brother and sister duo of Izanagi and Izanami, set the process of creation in motion. Their union produced some of the most popular deities of Japan, such as the sun goddess Amaterasu and the storm god Susano-O. However, because Izanami erred during the first marriage ceremony, she was condemned to give birth to monsters as well as to gods.

THE MYTH

At the beginning of time, there existed three invisible deities. These mysterious gods were known as the Heavenly Center Lord, the High Generative Force, and the Divine Generative Force. Together, they contained all the potential for life and creation. They were followed by several generations of deities, until the time was ripe for the creation of the universe.

THE CREATORS

Creation was started by the seventh generation of deities: the creator god Izanagi (He Who Invites), and the creator goddess Izanami (She Who Invites). These deities represented the two balancing principles of creation, the masculine and the feminine. They stood on the rainbow bridge of heaven, and churned the chaos beneath them with a spear until an island was formed. The two deities descended to this island and decided to marry. The wedding ceremony required Izanagi and Izanami to circle a ceremonial pillar in opposite directions, with the bridegroom reciting the marriage vows first. However, Izanami spoke first, which was considered improper by the other gods. So their union was flawed and it produced Hiruko, the leech-child, who was sent out to sea.

The ceremony was repeated, and this time, Izanagi spoke first. This union was happy and fruitful, and Izanami gave birth to a whole new generation of deities—the gods of the oceans, rivers, winds, trees, mountains, and lowlands. She also gave birth to all the islands of Japan. But Izanami was

▲ **Izanagi and Izanami**
The first two deities to descend to Earth from heaven, Izanagi and Izanami became the parents of deities such as Amaterasu, the sun goddess, and Tsuki-yomi, the moon god.

destined to perish because her final child was the fire god Kagutsuchi, who consumed her in his flames. The goddess died and left for Yomi, the Japanese Underworld.

THE FLIGHT FROM THE UNDERWORLD

Izanagi mourned the loss of Izanami, and traveled to the Underworld to retrieve her, but Izanami's body had already begun to decay. It seemed that he was too late to save her, and he fled from the Underworld, with Izanami following him. The warriors of the Underworld pursued Izanagi, and so he threw some rocks at them, which magically turned into food, delaying the warriors. Izanagi failed to notice Izanami trailing him on his way to Earth. To prevent the warriors from catching up with him, Izanagi placed a vast stone over the entrance to the Underworld, trapping Izanami inside forever.

◀ **The jeweled spear**
The creation myth tells how Izanagi and Izanami stood on the bridge of heaven and churned the water with the heavenly jeweled spear to stir the first land mass into existence.

▲ Shinto shrine
Followers of the Japanese Shinto religion believe in invoking the blessings of the kami. They are worshipped in shrines or in all buildings and homes where their presence is felt.

THE KAMI

The Japanese believe that thousands of gods, goddesses, spirits, and deified ancestors, known as kami, exist across the cosmos, on Earth or in heaven. They are said to reside in natural phenomena such as rocks, rivers, and lakes. They range from popular deities such as Amaterasu, to local and family deities known to only a small number of people. Mostly comprising Shinto deities, the kami also include Buddhist deities, as well as some derived from Hinduism, such as Benten, the Japanese version of the Hindu goddess Saraswati.

▶ Shinto spirit
Spirits in the Shinto religion are variously depicted in either human form or in the shape of animals or birds, such as this winged kami, known as a *tengu*, a monster spirit that resembles a bird of prey.

AMATERASU

One of the most prominent of all Japanese Shinto deities, the sun goddess Amaterasu was the eldest daughter of Izanagi and Izanami. When she was born, she was so bright that her parents sent her up to heaven, from where she shone down on the Earth. Her clothes were studded with jewels and her necklace of light formed the Milky Way. Later, having warmed the Earth with her rays and made conditions suitable for living things to grow, Amaterasu came down to Earth. She taught the people of Japan how to grow rice and wheat, and how to keep silk worms, harvest their thread, and weave cloth. According to a popular myth, Amaterasu was angered when her brother, Susano-O, damaged her rice crops and tarnished her home. She shut herself in a cave, plunging the world into darkness as a result.

▶ Illuminating the world
The gods tricked Amaterasu into coming out of the cave by showing her a mirror with her own reflection. Having never seen herself, she thought it was a new goddess and stepped out, bringing light back to the world.

▲ Sun symbol
Amaterasu's emergence from the cave is a powerful image of the rising sun, which was featured on the Japanese flag for many years.

YOMI

The Japanese land of the dead, Yomi, or Yomitsukumi, was believed to be a place of darkness, full of demons and sinister deities who attacked or pursued whoever arrived there. The ruler of this dismal place was Emma-O, a judge of the dead, who lived in a subterranean castle made of the metals and jewels that could be mined underground. When evil people died and went to Yomi, they were made to wear plaques around their necks. These carried lists of their sins, according to which they were tormented physically before their flesh rotted away, to become a breeding ground for maggots, that would turn into demons.

▶ Demon of Yomi
In Yomi there were 80,000 demons; their job was to carry the dead to their land, present them before Emma-O, and then torture them as ordered by Emma-O.

▶ Emma-O
The ruler of Yomi passed judgement on the deceased who were presented before him. He punished the guilty souls and sent the innocent ones to the upper world to be reborn.

SUSANO-O AND HIS DESCENDANTS

Many Japanese myths deal with the storm god Susano-O, who, like Amaterasu, was conceived by the creator god Izanagi himself. Susano-O's early years were tumultuous, but he later reformed and settled down with a princess in the Izumo region. His son, Okuninushi—the god of abundance, medicine, sorcery, and happy marriages—became a powerful ruler and the most important Shinto deity after Amaterasu.

THE MYTH

When Izanagi returned from his trip to the Underworld, he felt dirty and so he washed himself in a river. The goddess Amaterasu and the moon god Tsuki-yomi were created when Izanagi cleansed his eyes, while Susano-O appeared when he washed out his nose. Susano-O wanted to see his mother, Izanami, so he decided to go to the Underworld. He went to bid farewell to Amaterasu, but troubled her so much that she hid in a cave.

SLAYING A DRAGON

The gods punished Susano-O by cutting off his beard and fingernails, and banishing him from heaven. While wandering the Earth, he came across a dragon attacking Kusa-nada-pime, the Princess of the Rice Paddies. Turning the princess into a comb and hiding her in his hair, Susano-O sliced the dragon to pieces with his sword. Then, when all was safe, he turned the princess back into a human, and married her. They settled down in Izumo and had a number of children, known as the Earthly Gods, who later became very powerful rulers.

OKUNINUSHI'S ORDEALS

One of Susano-O's sons, Okuninushi, had set his heart on his half sister, Suseri-hime, but the storm god wanted to make sure his son was worthy of the match. So he set Okuninushi a series of difficult tasks to prove himself.

> ▶ **Susano-O**
> A valiant but cunning deity, Susano-O lured the dragon with bowls filled with rice wine before hacking it to pieces with his sword.

He asked his son to spend a night in a room full of poisonous snakes. Although it was a dangerous task, Suseri-hime gave Okuninushi a magic scarf, which he used to protect himself. Next, he was sent into a room full of wasps and hornets. Again, the scarf came to his rescue. Then Okuninushi was ordered to go to a field and retrieve an object buried there. When he got towards the middle of the field, the storm god set it on fire. Okuninushi asked a field mouse to show him a way out, and it led him to a tunnel where he hid until the fire subsided.

THE ELOPEMENT

Even after his son got through the ordeals, Susano-O did not agree to the marriage. So one night, while the storm god was asleep, Okuninushi quietly crept up on him and tied his long hair to the roof beams. Then he picked up his father's weapons and a musical instrument called a *koto*, and ran away with Suseri-hime. When Susano-O awoke he had to tear down the beams before he could give chase. Having finally caught up with them, he surprised the couple by forgiving them and consenting to their marriage.

◀ **Kusa-nagi**
After killing the dragon, Susano-O found a sword called Kusa-nagi (Grass Cutter) hidden in the remains of the beast's tail. He offered it to Amaterasu to make peace with her.

➤ **Okuninushi and the rabbit**
The story of Okuninushi and the rabbit illustrates the traditional Japanese belief that even the humblest of living things have spirits and that they may, in fact, be powerful deities in disguise.

OTHER JAPANESE DEITIES

Many of the Japanese deities linked to weather and the cosmos belong to the family of Susano-O and Amaterasu. Tsuki-yomi, the moon god, was Amaterasu's husband, while Wakahiru-me, the sun goddess's sister, was the goddess of the rising sun. Takami-musubi, a deity from an earlier generation of gods, became the messenger of Amaterasu. Two wind deities, Shina-tso-hiko and Shina-to-be, were born from Izanagi's breath. Five mountain gods were created when Izanagi chopped the fire god Kagutsuchi into pieces for burning to death his beloved Izanami.

▲ **Kagutsuchi**
The fire god was severed to create the mountain gods. But fire can rekindle itself, and so the god returned, burning atop the volcanoes.

OKUNINUSHI'S BRIDE

Once, Okuninushi and his 80 brothers wanted to marry a beautiful princess called Ya-gami-hime, so they went to woo her. On the way, they met a god in the guise of a rabbit that had been skinned alive by a crocodile and was in severe pain. Okuninushi's wicked brothers wanted the rabbit to suffer further, so they advised it to bathe in salt water to restore its fur. But the kind-hearted Okuninushi told the creature to bathe in fresh water and then roll in the pollen of kama grass. The rabbit did as Okuninushi had suggested and re-grew its fur, and being a deity, granted Okuninushi his wish of marrying the princess. Jealous of Okuninushi's success, the brothers killed him twice, but the gods revived him both times.

▲ **Hachiman**
Originally a fertility god, Hachiman's martial character turned him into a war god, and he was seen in this role as a protector of Japan.

▲ **Inari**
A god of smiths and craftsmen, Inari was married to Ukemochi, the goddess of food, and thus also became the god of rice and the bringer of prosperity.

SHRINE IN IZUMO

An important Shinto shrine, located in the Izumo province, is dedicated to Okuninushi, the deity of happy marriages. Some say that all the kami congregate here in October to discuss issues of love and marriage. This month is known in Izumo as *kamiari tsuki* (the month when the kami are present), elsewhere it is called *kanna zuki* (the month when the kami are absent).

Okuninushi's shrine at Izumo, Japan

CHRONICLES OF THE GODS

Two important texts, the *Nihongi* (Chronicles of Japan) and the *Kojiki* (Records of Ancient Matters), talk about the myths of the kami and describe the early, mythical history of Japan and the role played by the kami in shaping the country. The *Kojiki* also devotes space to a mythical "Age of Men," in which semi-mythical ancestors of the imperial family are described. These books, which date back to the 8th century, have become very important in Japan, giving the country a strong connection to its own mythology and history.

▲ **The Kojiki**
Containing a mixture of myths and history, the *Kojiki* has played a vital role in the development of the Shinto religion. It is considered to be the oldest surviving book in Japan.

AFRICA

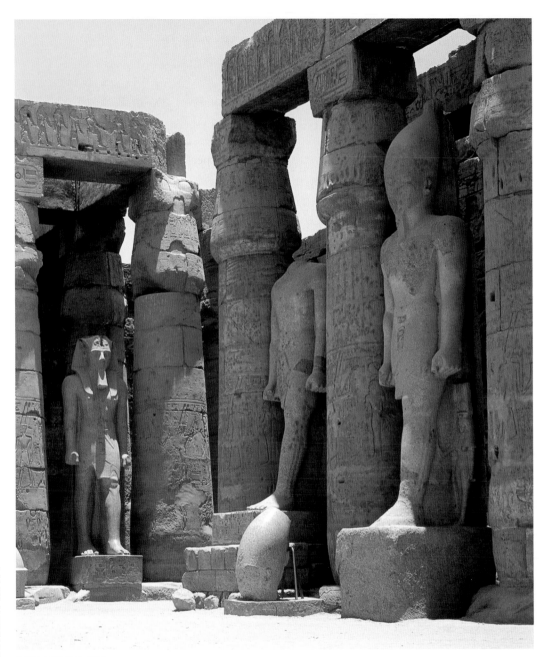

▲ **Shrine to the Theban Triad**
Some Egyptian temples were vast, state-run edifices, the centers of which only priests or pharaohs
could enter. This temple at Luxor (modern-day Thebes) is dedicated to the supreme god Amun, his
consort, Mut, and their offspring, Khons. It dates from the reign of Ramesses II (13th century BCE).

ANCIENT EGYPT

Although covering only a small area—the delta and banks of the River Nile—
the civilization of ancient Egypt lasted for some 3,000 years. It produced a
complex mythology that pervaded every aspect of people's lives.

The ancient Egyptians worshipped numerous gods and goddesses who were said to influence the whole of life, from the creation of the universe to the annual flooding of the River Nile, from a person's birth to a person's death. Goddesses such as Hathor watched over women when they gave birth, while the great god of mummification, Anubis, looked on when a body was ritually prepared for the afterlife. There were also more local deities: Horus, the god of the sky, was the great god of Lower Egypt, while Set, the god of chaos, was the ruling deity of Upper Egypt.

ANIMAL GODS

Many of the gods and goddesses of ancient Egypt took animal form. Hathor took the form of a cow; Bastet, goddess of sexuality, had the body of a cat; Sobek, who embodied the power of the Egyptian pharaohs, was a crocodile; and Thoth, the god of wisdom, had the head of an ibis. These animal forms gave the deities a strong sense of identity. Priests at their temples raised real animals, then sacrificed and mummified them in honor of the temple deity. So a pilgrim to a temple of Bastet, for example, could pay to have a cat mummified so that the animal would speak up for humanity in the next world. Over the years, archaeologists have found the mummified remains of thousands of cats, crocodiles, and other creatures that were ritually

▲ Decorative scarab beetle brooch
Tutankhamun (14th century BCE) was identified closely with Ra, whom he expected to join in the sky when he died. Many items in his tomb, like this one, were adorned with symbols of Ra.

sacrificed and preserved in temples. Certain animal forms—such as Sobek's crocodile, or the hippopotamus form taken by the birth goddess Taweret—were especially relevant to the daily lives of a great many ordinary Egyptians who frequently came face to face with these often extremely dangerous animals when working on the banks of the Nile, especially when the river was in flood.

CHANGING DEITIES

The animal forms taken by the gods and goddesses of ancient Egypt were not constant, however. Ancient Egyptian deities existed in a state of flux, and some of them could take many different forms at different times. Anubis, for example, was often portrayed as a jackal, but he could also take the form of a snake or a falcon.

The deities themselves could also take the form of multiple gods. The sun god Ra, for instance, took several forms, each with the identity of a separate deity: he could be the beetle Khepri, rolling the sun across the sky as a scarab beetle rolls its ball of dung across the ground; he could be Ra-Harakhty, the hawk that soars across the sky; or he could be Amun-Ra, the king of the gods. In this last form he was identified closely with Egypt's pharaohs, whom he supposedly protected when they led their armies on the field of battle.

THE AFTERLIFE

One area in which ancient Egyptian deities were especially important was that of death and the afterlife. The ancient Egyptians saw life on Earth as preparation for the life to come, so they evolved a whole system of mummification and entombment rituals. Accompanying these were many myths involving Osiris, the god of the Underworld, and the deities who presided over the rituals and assessed the worthiness of the dead person's soul to enter the next world.

◀ Symbols of Ra
This bronze from around 590 BCE shows two of the symbols of the ancient Egyptian sun god Ra: the head and beak of the falcon Horus, and the solar disc that he carried across the sky.

THE BEGINNING OF
THE WORLD

The creation stories of Egyptian mythology describe how order and life emerged out of the primal chaos. Ra, the sun god, is featured as the main creator deity in many of these myths. He is aided in the task of creation by deities such as his children, Shu and Tefnut, and grandchildren, Geb and Nut. Ra and his creation exist in the light; the darkness that remains is personified by a serpent, Apep, who constantly threatens to swallow the light.

THE MYTH

The creator deity Ra rose out of Nun, the primal ocean of non-being. When Ra sneezed, Shu, the god of dry air, emerged from his nostrils. Then he spat and Tefnut, the goddess of moist air, appeared from his mouth. Ra sent the two gods on a journey across the ocean. Then, using his powers of creation and perception, he called the primal elements into being, speaking their names and watching them appear. At this time, he also created Ma'at, the goddess of universal harmony, who was tasked with bringing order to his creation.

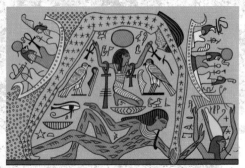

◀ **Nut, Geb, and Shu**
Shu held up in his hands the sky goddess Nut, whose body curved high above the Earth to make the arch of the heavens. Geb, the earth god, lay below Shu's feet.

THE CREATURES OF THE EARTH

Ra needed a dry place to stand on while carrying out his task, so he made Nun recede, which revealed a rocky island or mound, known as the Benben stone. The god stood on the stone and envisioned everything he was about to create. From the primal ocean, he summoned forth the plants, animals, and birds of the Earth; he spoke their names and they appeared before him. Next, Ra told his eye, the goddess Hathor, to look for Shu and Tefnut. After returning with the two deities, Hathor saw that another eye had replaced her on Ra's face. She wept at being supplanted in this way, and the first people were born from her tears. Ra returned Hathor to his brow, but this time she took the form of a cobra, staying there to help Ra rule over the world he had created.

THE GREAT GODS

Shu and Tefnut had two children, Geb, the Earth, and Nut, the sky, who lay together and gave birth to the stars. Jealous of the pair, Shu separated them and forbade Nut from giving birth on any day of the month. But Nut won five extra days while gambling with the god Thoth. On these days, she gave birth to Osiris, Set, Nephthys, and Isis, Egypt's greatest deities.

▶ **Ma'at**
Ma'at represented truth, and gave order to Ra's creation. She also judged the dead in the Underworld, where souls were weighed against one of her feathers.

PTAH

In an alternative creation story, the central creator is the god Ptah, a craftsman deity. This myth describes how Ptah began the task of creation by imagining and then naming the different gods, bringing them into being. He then used his skills as a sculptor to produce the other beings of the cosmos. He carved and chiseled some of them from stone, and made the others out of metal, having invented the technology of metalworking for this purpose. Ptah founded several cities, as well as shrines where he could be worshipped, creating each one by thinking about it and then pronouncing its name. Ptah's cult was especially important at Memphis, ancient Egypt's administrative capital.

◀ **Heart-shaped amulet**
In the myths of Ptah, the heart is very important, because the gods and other beings are said to have been created in his heart. The Egyptians believed that the intellect resided in the heart.

▶ **The sculptor god**
Although sometimes portrayed as a craftsman, Ptah was often depicted as a kingly figure in more formal temple art.

KARNAK

At Karnak, near the River Nile, stands a huge complex of ancient Egyptian temples, the most important of which is dedicated to the god Amun. He was originally one of the forces of chaos (some accounts portray the god as a primal snake living in the water), but his name and character became linked to that of Ra to form Amun-Ra, who was known as one of the greatest creator deities and was attributed with all the creative powers of the sun god. The temple of Amun stands in a large precinct, and contains massive columns that are topped with carvings resembling lotus blossoms. The walls of the temple enclose many smaller temples and a sacred lake.

◀ **Temple of Amun**
Stone statues and columns carved with religious inscriptions in hieroglyphic script form the principal remains of this temple's structure.

▼ **Pyramids**
The pyramids of Giza, constructed during the Fourth dynasty (c. 2575–c.2465 BCE), were the largest structures of the ancient world, and paramount symbols of the power of the pharaohs.

THE PHARAOHS

Ancient Egypt's rulers were seen as not just kings but gods. During a pharaoh's lifetime, he was supremely powerful, and it was believed that after death, he would spend eternity with the gods. The pyramid-shaped tombs of the early pharaohs were originally designed to resemble stairways, up which the souls of the deceased kings could climb to join the sun god in the sky. The shape also resembled the Benben stone, the primal mound on which the sun god stood when he began to create the world. The sight of the pyramids silhouetted against the sky was a permanent reminder to the people of the link between their kings and the mighty sun god.

THE BENU BIRD

A heron-like creature present at the beginning of creation, the Benu bird was thought to be a form of the sun god. Some versions of the myth said that the bird flew over the ocean to find the Benben stone. On landing on it, the bird began calling out loudly, breaking the eternal silence and signaling the birth of sound, light, and life. The priests at Karnak would release a duck to fly across the sacred lake each morning to commemorate this flight.

The Benu bird

BOOK OF THE DEAD

This painting on the Papyrus of Anhai is part of the Egyptian *Book of the Dead* written in the 13th-century BCE for Anhai, a priestess of Ra, the sun god. It shows several different aspects of Ra as he travels across the sky in his solar boat. Ra was one of the most important Egyptian deities—he was depicted and worshipped in several forms, including Amun-Ra, king of the gods. As the rising sun he took the form of Khepri, the scarab beetle; at midday he was seen as a glowing disc moving across the sky; and as the setting sun he was Atum, who took on the identity of an old man. As king of the gods, Ra was also linked to the kings of Egypt. The pharaohs were seen as earthly embodiments of the sun god—the sons of Ra— and they built temples in his honor.

1. Solar disc
This disc is one of the most familiar images of the sun god. In this depiction, the sky goddess Nut is shown raising her son, Osiris, king of the Underworld, towards the disc, ready for the sun god to begin his journey into the night, when Osiris and the sun will become one.

2. Scarab beetle
Just as a scarab beetle rolls a ball of dung along the ground, so the sun god in the form of the beetle, Khepri, rolls the sun disc across the sky. This repeated daily movement made the scarab beetle an icon of self-generation and renewal for the Egyptians.

3. The menace of Uraeus
Uraeus, the cobra, is another symbol of the sun god Ra. It is also the emblem of the pharaoh, and in paintings, the creature's menacing hood often appears on the forehead of the pharaoh. It is believed that the cobra was given to the pharaohs as a symbol of kingship by Geb, the god of the Earth. When the pharaoh became associated with the sun god, he wore a headdress in the form of a cobra, which was said to spit deadly fire at his enemies.

4. The power of Horus
Horus, one of the most powerful Egyptian gods, was the son of Isis and Osiris. Here, he is shown with a falcon's head, emphasizing his role as a god of the sky. His right eye was the sun and his left eye the moon. In the fluid mythology of ancient Egypt, he merges with Ra to become another incarnation of the sun god, known as Ra-Harakhty. As well as being a sky god, Horus is also the god of war.

5. Boat of the sun
The vessel in which the sun god travels across the sky, carried by Nun, is shaped like an Egyptian Nile boat with a large steering oar at the stern. Ra is accompanied on his journey by seven other gods, with Horus at the helm.

6. Nothing but Nun
According to Egyptian myth, in the beginning, before creation began, there was nothing but the endless ocean of Nun. He was also the god of the primal floods. Both he and Ra were vital to the Egyptians' survival, because Ra, as the sun god, ripened their food crops, and the floods brought by Nun deposited rich layers of silt on the Nile's banks, making the fields fertile. So in this myth the two gods move together in harmony. Nun is depicted here holding up the solar boat of Ra.

Papyrus of Anhai, c.1250 BCE

A KING'S MURDER

A popular myth from ancient Egypt narrates the story of a tragic rivalry for the throne of Egypt between two divine brothers, the virtuous Osiris and the wicked Set, and the subsequent dispute between Set and Horus, the son of Osiris. The myth was well known because it dealt with the rule of Egypt, and also because the story of the death and revival of Osiris gave people hope of an afterlife.

▲ **Horus fights Set**
This stone relief from the Temple of Horus at Edfu, Egypt, depicts a scene from the battle Horus fought against Set, with the goddess Isis at the helm of the boat.

THE MYTH

The first king of Egypt was the god Osiris; like some rulers of Egypt after him, he took his sister, Isis, as his wife. He was a good king, much liked by his people, and Isis was a popular queen. But Osiris had a wicked and violent brother, Set, who was jealous of Osiris's power and lusted after Isis. To get rid of Osiris, Set tricked the king into climbing into a wooden chest, which he then sealed and threw into the Nile. Osiris was dead by the time Isis found the box, but she retrieved the king's body. Set discovered what Isis had done so he hacked Osiris's body into many pieces. Although it was supposedly impossible to destroy the body of a god, Set had all but done so.

REVIVING OSIRIS

Isis decided to salvage Osiris's body. With the help of her sister, Nephthys, who was the wife of Set, she gathered the fragments of Osiris's body, joined them together, and bound them tightly to make the first mummy. Then, transforming herself into a bird of prey—a kite—she hovered over the body, beating her wings to infuse it with the breath of life. Osiris breathed for long enough to impregnate Isis. Later, Osiris departed for the Underworld. Isis then fled from Set, taking with her a guard of seven scorpions.

While she was fleeing, Isis was treated inhospitably by a rich woman, and one of the scorpions bit the woman's child. Isis took pity on the child and used her magic

▲ **Hippopotamus**
The hippopotamus was a much-feared creature of the Nile, capable of overturning a craft sailing on the river, as Set did when he took the form of the beast to capsize Horus's boat.

to cure the infant. But later, when she gave birth to her own son, Horus, he, in turn, was bitten by a scorpion and Isis, who had used up her power, could not cure him. Fortunately, Ra, the sun god, saw Isis in distress, took pity on her, and sent the moon god Thoth to cure Horus.

HORUS AND SET

Meanwhile, Set had usurped the kingship of Egypt. When Horus grew up, he challenged his uncle for the throne, and the two fought many times. On one occasion, Set blinded a sleeping Horus. When Isis found her son blinded, she nursed him and restored his sight. Then Set tried to rape Horus, and told the other gods that the young man was unworthy to be king because he had slept with Set. But the gods found out that Set was lying.

Finally, Set challenged Horus to a boat race, insisting that the vessels used in the race should be made of stone. Horus tricked his uncle by using a wooden boat he had plastered to look like stone. Set's boat sank, and in his anger, he turned himself into a hippopotamus and capsized Horus's vessel. But the gods at last saw that Horus was truly worthy and made him king, while Set was exiled.

KEY CHARACTERS

The characters in the tragic story of the murder of Osiris have a number of roles in other aspects of Egyptian mythology. After being killed by Set, Osiris became the ruler of the Underworld, a very important position in the Egyptian cosmos, which meant that he was widely worshipped. Isis was a very prominent deity too, worshipped as the goddess of magic and guardian of the dead. She won great devotion as a mother goddess, on account of the way she cared for both Osiris and Horus. Horus became a sky god who took the form of a falcon, and his eyes were said to be the sun and moon. The eye of Horus, or the Wadjet Eye, became the most popular of all Egyptian amulets. Set, on the other hand, was a sinister figure, a god of chaos and the desert.

▲ Osiris
Wearing a crown of ostrich feathers, Osiris is depicted as a mummy with the king's symbols, the crook and flail.

▲ Set
Set is seen as a mythical beast with a long, curved muzzle, a two-tufted head, and a straight tail.

▲ Isis
Isis wears a throne-shaped crown, which indicates that she originally personified the throne of the pharaohs.

▲ Horus
Horus is often depicted as a falcon or a humanoid figure with a falcon's head, or as a child in human form.

▲ Writing tools
The Egyptians used reed pens to write with, dipping them into ink and making marks on papyrus, a material also made from reeds. The shape of the reed pen was associated with Thoth's narrow beak.

THOTH

The ibis-headed Thoth was the god of time, knowledge, writing, and the moon. His curving beak resembled the crescent moon, and his black and white feathers denoted the moon's waxing and waning. Certain accounts of his origin say that he was the son of Ra, the sun god, and that he either inherited his wisdom from his father or found it in books belonging to the sun god. Thoth was said to have invented a range of intellectual pursuits, including astronomy, law, music, and—most relevant in the myth of Osiris and Horus—medicine. He was also the inventor of the Egyptian hieroglyphic writing system, and since he was also a god of magic, hieroglyphs were said to have magical powers.

Thoth

THE CULT OF OSIRIS

Osiris was revered by the Egyptians because his myth gave hope of a life after death. He presided over the Underworld, and along with other deities, such as Anubis and Serket, he oversaw a series of rituals through which the souls of the dead passed into the afterlife. His cult originated at Abydos, an important city in ancient Egypt, where a festival was often held, re-enacting the story of the god's murder. The temple at Abydos also held secret rituals that were not disclosed to those outside Osiris's priesthood. By the 1st millennium BCE, other temples began to celebrate the god's death and rebirth, linking them with winter and the spring.

Serket

▲ Temple of Osiris
The sanctuary of Osiris at the temple at Abydos is decorated with inscriptions and murals illustrating various scenes from the life story of this ancient Egyptian god.

JOURNEY TO THE LAND OF THE DEAD

Death was considered by the ancient Egyptians to be the potential beginning of a new life. After a person died, the body was carefully preserved as a mummy because it was believed that the deceased began a journey through the Underworld to the next life, where their souls would need to take up residence in their bodies once again. This belief in the migration of the soul to the Underworld was widespread and the journey was described in great detail in a complex myth.

THE MYTH

The Egyptians believed that many spiritual aspects of a person's being survived death and, if they were correctly cared for, could re-inhabit the person's body in the afterlife. Foremost of these was the *ka*, the person's life force, and the *ba*, the soul. If all went well after death, the *ka* and *ba* would unite to form a spirit that would live again inside the body. To achieve this, the dead body had to be preserved appropriately through mummification, which was a reenactment of what happened to the god Osiris's body after he died. The process involved a series of 75 rituals, in which parts of the body would be touched with special instruments to be reanimated—as a result, the body would become a fitting vehicle for the person's *ka*. This process also identified the deceased with the god Osiris, ensuring that they would set out on the journey to everlasting life.

▲ **Osiris**
Osiris presided over the process in which the deceased traveled from this life to the afterlife.

JOURNEY THROUGH DUAT

The deceased then began their journey through a realm known as Duat or the Underworld, which was full of many horrors and perils. Here, they had to contend with dangers such as fiery lakes and venomous snakes. There were many special spells that could be recited to protect the voyagers on the way. These spells were written down in a *Book of the Dead*, a compilation of important texts that was often buried with the mummies so that the deceased had access to the right spells on their journey through the dark realm.

JUDGING THE SOULS

The souls of the deceased were judged at a place near the end of the journey, the Hall of the Two Truths. The souls were put through a test and if they passed, the deceased would declare their innocence and then be judged by Osiris and 42 assessor gods. Osiris was assisted in his task by judges who included Ra, Shu, Tefnut, Geb, Nut, Isis, Nephthys, Horus, and Hathor. Each god judged a particular aspect of the soul. Three possible fates awaited the soul after the assessment. The truly wicked characters were condemned to a second and final death devoid of mummification and with no chance of passing unharmed through Duat. The ordinary souls were sent to serve Osiris eternally, and the virtuous souls were allowed to move on to a happy and free eternal life.

▲ **Assessor gods**
The assessor gods had names such as Bone-breaker and Blood-drinker, and looked on eagerly when the souls protested their innocence. They drank the blood of the deceased if there was any proof of guilt.

PREPARING FOR DUAT

The preparatory rituals for the afterlife were complex. First, the embalmers took the deceased person's body to their workshop (known as the Beautiful House), where they removed the liver, lungs, intestines, and stomach, placing each organ in canopic jars. Then the body was covered completely with a chemical mixture of salts called natron, packed with dry material such as sawdust, and wrapped in linen bandages, with labels and amulets attached to identify and protect the body. The mummy was then placed in a coffin for secure storage.

An Egyptian mummy

▲ Anubis
The ancient Egyptians believed that the jackal-god Anubis had invented the art of mummification.

◄ Canopic jar
Jars capped with the heads of Underworld gods, such as Anubis or Osiris, were used to preserve the organs of the deceased person.

THE HALL OF THE TWO TRUTHS

Souls were judged in the Hall of the Two Truths, which contained a balance in which the heart—the only vital organ not removed from the mummified body—was weighed. The feather of Ma'at, goddess of truth and justice, was placed against the heart on the scales. If the heart outweighed the feather, it would be deemed full of sin, and Ammut, the Devourer of the Dead, would feast on it. If the heart was lighter, the soul moved on to the next stage of judgement.

► Thoth
The god of wisdom and scribe to the gods, Thoth was tasked with waiting in the hall to record the judgement passed on the souls of the deceased.

▼ Weighing the heart
The god Amun presided over the weighing of every heart, an organ believed to contain a record of a person's former deeds.

DEITIES OF THE UNDERWORLD

Besides Osiris, Anubis, and the ferocious assessor gods, several other deities were associated with the Egyptian Underworld. Some of these were sinister, shadowy beings with the heads of rams, tortoises, or hippopotamuses. Others included the serpent-god Apep, or Apophis, who constantly waged war on Ra, the sun god. Among the less intimidating deities was the goddess Nephthys, sister of Isis, who led the pharaohs through the Underworld and also cared for the stored organs of the deceased.

Ma'at

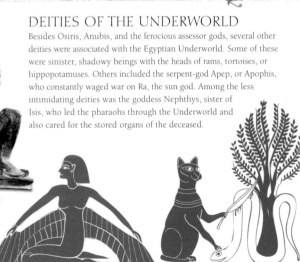

▲ Nephthys
Often seen as gentle and caring, Nephthys also had an affair with Osiris, which led to the birth of the deity Anubis.

▲ Ra and Apep
The sun god Ra transformed himself into a cat to defeat the serpent Apep, one of the most feared and vilest creatures in the Underworld.

BODY AND SOUL

The *ba*, or soul, was imagined to be a winged being with the head of the deceased and the body and wings of a hawk that flew free of the body at the time of death. Each night, it had to be reunited with the dead person's body; this could only happen if the corpse had been mummified correctly. A person's shadow and name were also thought to have an independent existence that could be perpetuated by mummification.

Winged *ba*

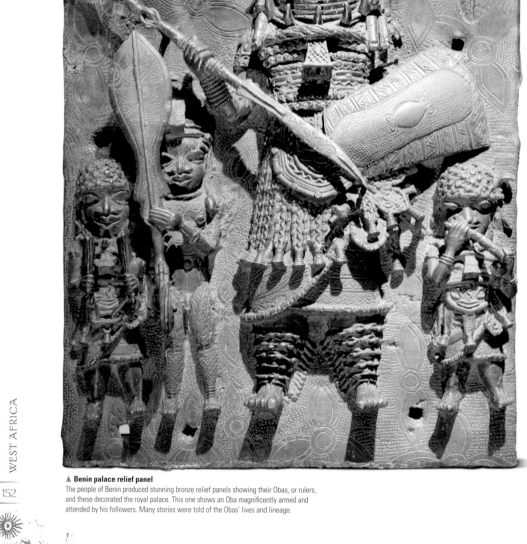

▲ **Benin palace relief panel**
The people of Benin produced stunning bronze relief panels showing their Obas, or rulers, and these decorated the royal palace. This one shows an Oba magnificently armed and attended by his followers. Many stories were told of the Obas' lives and lineage.

WEST AFRICA

The sophisticated cultures of West Africa produced mythologies in which a variety of different deities are responsible for the entire range of natural phenomena, from the creation of the universe to the weather.

West Africa—stretching southwards from the southern edge of the Sahara to the coast of present-day Ghana and its neighbors—has a long history of civilization. From around 500 BCE, empires and large city-states came and went, each developing its own sophisticated arts and crafts—especially metalwork—that allowed them to trade with peoples from far beyond their own borders. The bronze work of Benin and the gold jewellery of the empire of Ashanti, which flourished in the 18th and 19th centuries along the coast between Ghana and Côte d'Ivoire, are particularly well-known examples.

SURVIVING TRADITIONS

Trade brought with it many contacts from outside the region, from North African Berber merchants crossing the Sahara to European slave-traders arriving by sea. Despite these foreign influences, and the legacy of European colonization in the 19th and 20th centuries, many local traditions and beliefs have survived, and some in turn have influenced the religion and mythology of the Caribbean. Traditions that have been particularly well preserved include those of the Fon of Benin and the Yoruba of Benin and Nigeria.

In the mythology of the Fon, the prominent deities are Lisa and his wife, Mawu, who are sometimes combined as a composite deity. They created the world and all the plants, animals, and humans. They also had a number of children, formed from their faeces, including Dan, a snake god whose thousands of coils support the world. Another son, Gu, is the patron of craftsmen and warriors. He is said to use his skills to make the world a better place for people to live in. Weather gods, including various thunder deities, also abound in the Fon pantheon.

▲ West African elephant pendant
West Africa has a tradition of highly skilled metalworking. Craftsmen from Ghana cast this pendant depicting two elephants, creatures familiar in mythology for their great strength.

The Yoruba have a supreme being known as Olorun or Olodumare. In addition they have numerous Orishas, or spirits, that are manifestations of this high god. Believers appeal to one or more of the Orishas as a way of communicating with the supreme being. There are countless Orishas, but some are particularly popular. Shango, a powerful sky god and god of thunder, and his consort, Oshun, benevolent goddess of love, are among the most important.

ABIDING THEMES

The role of the hero is a prominent theme in West African mythology. Sometimes he is a culture hero who brings the gifts of craft skills and technology. At other times he is a wonder-child, a being of such power that he has the strength and skills of an adult as soon as he is born. West Africa also has some entertaining trickster myths. The best-known trickster is the spider Ananse, who gets the better of everyone from gods and humans to the most powerful of all creatures on Earth, the elephant. Amusing stories of Ananse's tricks have a wide appeal, and are enjoyed by adults and children alike.

▼ An Oba's ceremonial arm ornament
The ceremonial jewellery of the Obas, or rulers, of Benin included arm ornaments such as this one depicting a leopard. The creature's attributes—its speed, strength, and prowess as a hunter—were traits that any ruler would wish to be associated with.

AFRICAN ORIGINS

The peoples of Africa have different stories that explain the creation of the Earth, the origin of the sun, moon, and stars, and the ancestry of each tribe. Sometimes humans emerge from a hole in the ground, sometimes they are molded by a creator deity. Most of these stories revolve around the activities of one supreme being, although in the creation myth of Dahomey, this deity is helped by a cosmic serpent in the task of creation.

THE MYTH

The story of creation, as narrated by the Fon people of Dahomey, begins with two primal beings the eternal male serpent Aido-Hwedo, and the female creator deity Mawu. First, Mawu gave birth to the gods and goddesses. She had many children, too many to name, but they formed various groups according to their powers and dwelling places. They included the Earth deities, ruled by Mawu's first son, Da Zodji; thunder deities, ruled by Mawu's second son, Sogbo; and sea deities, ruled by Mawu's third son, Agbe. Once she had made all the gods and goddesses, Mawu turned her attention to the human race, which she made out of clay.

▶ **Primal serpent**
Early African sculpture often depicts the creation myth in the form of a serpent coiled around a human figure.

MAKING THE EARTH

Mawu realized that the human beings needed somewhere to live, so she decided to make the Earth. She rode in the mouth of the cosmic serpent Aido-Hwedo, and as the pair traveled they shaped the Earth like a huge calabash. The world was defined by Aido-Hwedo's turning, serpentine motion; as Aido-Hwedo snaked his way along, his path created winding rivers and valleys with steep sloping land on either side. His sinuous course shaped the Earth's high and low places, the curving hillsides, and the round-bottomed valleys. Because of this meandering, the landscape was not even; everything in it was curved and undulating like the track of the serpent.

▲ **Snake track**
The notion of Aido-Hwedo's sinuous track carving out the landscape is grounded in nature because some snakes create a winding track as they slide across sand.

After each of their creative journeys, Mawu and Aido-Hwedo stopped to rest. When they paused, the serpent's excrement built up, creating the higher mountains. As time went by, this waste material solidified to become hard rock, hiding inside it all the precious metals that Aido-Hwedo expelled from his body. So the primal serpent became the source of all the rich mineral resources that are hidden deep in the ground.

SUPPORTING THE EARTH

The Earth that Mawu and Aido-Hwedo had made together floated on a vast sea contained in an enormous calabash. But its wealth of rocks and resources, together with the weight of all the people and animals Mawu had created, made it too heavy. Mawu saw that it must be supported, otherwise it would sink. She told Aido-Hwedo to coil himself all the way around the Earth, holding it up so that it would not sink into the water. Aido-Hwedo was content to lie in the cool sea water because he did not like the heat of the Earth. Mostly he lay still, but now and then he would shift into a more comfortable position, making the ground shake violently and causing an earthquake.

KEY CHARACTERS

The main characters in the Fon creation story are the snake Aido-Hwedo, who helps in the creation, and the more complex creator goddess Mawu. Mawu is actually half of a composite deity—her other half is the god Lisa, and when encountered together they are referred to as Mawu-Lisa, a deity with two faces. Whereas Mawu is the goddess of the Earth and the moon, Lisa is the god of the sky and the sun.

▲ **Aido-Hwedo**
The cosmic serpent supports the Earth. In some accounts he also holds up the sky, and is visible as the colorful rainbow.

▲ **Mawu**
The goddess Mawu is said to live in the sky. Her eyes shine with a pale light and are said to create the light of the moon.

ONE DAY AIDO-HWEDO WILL EAT HIS OWN TAIL, AND THE WORLD WILL FALL INTO THE SEA.

KOM ORIGINS

For the Kom people of northwest Cameroon, the snake is an ancestor figure rather than a creator. Once, their chief was mortally wounded in a war with the neighboring Fon. He told his people to move to new territory, following the track of a python. Soon after the chief died, a python appeared and the people followed its winding track. Finally, the snake stopped and the Kom made their new home at this place.

▼ **Brass plaque of python**
For the Kom, the python was closely linked to the origins of the tribe and their native homeland.

IMAGES OF THE COSMOS

West African peoples, such as the Dogon tribe of Mali, visualized the world and the sky as an egg. Another conception of the universe was in the form of a calabash. To the Fon, for example, the two halves of the calabash represented the sky (also housing the sun and moon) and the water vessel in which the Earth floated. It was the task of the serpent Aido-Hwedo to hold the two halves of the cosmic calabash apart.

Egg

Calabash

YORUBA CREATION

The Yoruba of Nigeria describe how the sky god Olodumare sent his son, Obatala, down to create the Earth. He gave him a bag of earth and a hen, and lowered a palm tree down with him. Obatala took brown earth from the bag and sprinkled it on the water, where it formed land. Then he put the hen on the Earth and she scratched about, scattering the soil to form the continent of Africa. Later, Obatala created humans out of clay.

▶ **Palm tree**
The palm tree was a precious gift from Olodumare. Its juice, oil, and nuts became useful resources for the Yoruba tribe.

▲ **Obatala**
According to some accounts, Obatala (king of the white cloth) was the founder of the first Yoruba city, Ife. He was associated with purity, honesty, and peace.

▲ **White Hen**
Olodumare sent a white hen with five toes to help Obatala create the Earth. The scratching of the hen created hills and valleys on the ground.

ANANSE

The spider Ananse is a trickster and also a culture hero in West Africa, especially among the Ashanti people of Ghana. Besides his tricks, Ananse is well known for using his intellect to outwit creatures much stronger than himself—stories about these pranks are commonly told both for amusement and to highlight the fact that brains are as important as muscles. In some myths, the trickster acts as an intermediary between human beings and the sky god Nyame. Some even believe that it was Ananse who persuaded Nyame to create the sun and moon so that people on Earth could benefit from having night and day.

MESSENGER TO THE SKY GOD

Nyame, the sky god, was the creator of all things, but he sat aloof from his creations. Down below on the Earth, people worked constantly in the fields—there was no time for them to rest. Ananse heard their complaints, and spun a thread up to Nyame to ask for help. So Nyame created night, when everyone could sleep. But the humans were frightened of the darkness, so Nyame set the moon in the sky to provide light at night. Then the people shivered because it was always cold, so yet again, Ananse went to tell Nyame, and he put the sun in the sky to give warmth. This time, the scorching heat was too much for the mere mortals, and once more, Ananse climbed up his thread to ask for help on behalf of the people. This time, Nyame sent great rains to cool everyone, but his rains were so heavy that they caused floods and people drowned. Nyame made the floods recede and, finally, everybody was content.

▲ **Ananse beaker**
Embossed with the relief work of a large spider in its web, this bronze vessel from Nigeria points to the popularity of the trickster Ananse in West African myths.

▲ **Ananse weeding grass**
One story talks about how Ananse won the hand of Nyame's daughter by clearing a field full of itchy weeds without scratching himself.

▲ **African sun and moon masks**
Masks representing the sun and the moon are common in West Africa. As the markers of day and night, the sun and the moon are very important, and Ananse was credited with enabling their creation.

MASTER OF STORIES

Nyame owned all the stories in the world. Ananse wanted to buy the stories from him, and as payment, Nyame asked Ananse to bring him some hornets, a python, and a leopard. Ananse tricked the hornets into a calabash. He then went to the python carrying a long staff and declared that he was unclear about which was longer, the snake or the staff. The python lay by the staff, and Ananse quickly tied it to the staff, thus trapping it. Next the spider dug a pit for the leopard and covered it with branches. The unsuspecting leopard fell into it and was caught. Ananse delivered the animals to Nyame and, for fulfilling all the conditions, won the stories of the world.

◄ **Leopard**
Renowned for its speed and hunting prowess, the leopard should have posed an impossible challenge for the spider.

▼ **Python**
The python generally kills its prey by constriction, so Ananse tricked the snake into being tied up so that it could not attack.

TRICKING THE ELEPHANT

One day, an elephant was bored and challenged the other animals to a head-butting competition. Fearing the elephant's strength, none of the animals rose to the challenge, except for Ananse. It was decided that the contest would take place over 14 nights, with the elephant having the first seven butts over the first seven nights. Ananse tricked an antelope into coming to Ananse's house at night to receive some food. Since it was a time of famine, the antelope agreed. That night, the elephant butted the antelope in the dark and killed it. Over the next six days, Ananse tricked more animals in the same way. When it was his turn to butt the elephant, the spider took a hammer and wedge, and aimed with great care at the creature's head. He killed the elephant with a single blow, outsmarting it in this uneven contest.

► **Elephant**
In one version of the story, after the first attack with the hammer, the elephant merely complained of a headache, but on the second night, Ananse refined his aim and killed the elephant.

THE ORIGINS OF ARGUMENT

Once, there was a man who argued with everyone, and killed several animals because they disagreed with him. Ananse decided to meet the man. When the man began to tell Ananse fantastic stories, Ananse invited him to his house. On his arrival, the man could not find the spider, but Ananse's children fed him the hottest of chilies, which burned his mouth. He asked for water, but Ananse's children explained that the water at the top of a pot belonged to their father and they were afraid of mixing it with the water below when pouring from the pot. The man argued with this preposterous story, and when Ananse returned, the spider declared that the man must die since he continued to argue. So the spiders killed the man, tore his body to pieces, and threw the bits everywhere. In this way, argument spread around the world.

▼ **Popular folklore ingredient**
Although American in origin, chilies became such a popular ingredient for flavoring in West African food that they found their way into the region's folklore, such as the myth about Ananse and the man.

► **African cooking pot**
Metal cooking pots are widely used to boil food over an open fire. Such a vessel can also be used to store water, as in this story of Ananse.

MYTHICAL HEROES

World mythology is full of heroes, men who often have one mortal and one divine parent. Their parentage gives them such outstanding qualities as superhuman strength, bravery, intelligence, or the ability to travel to dangerous places like the Underworld. They lead their peoples, found nations or empires, play decisive roles in battles, kill monsters, and right wrongs. Their bravery can also lead them to a heroic death.

◄ **Ninigi**
Grandson of Amaterasu, the Japanese sun goddess, Ninigi was a kind ruler of the Earth who introduced rice growing, and bequeathed royal regalia to the emperors.

▲ **Nezha**
A hero and brave warrior of Chinese legend, Nezha was born from a ball of flesh, had superhuman strength even as a child, and also had the power to grow extra limbs.

▲ **Arjuna**
Arjuna was a great archer in the *Mahabharata*, the Hindu epic. When unwilling to fight, Krishna persuaded him his destiny was to be a warrior.

◄ **Hayk**
Hayk is a legendary hero of folklore from Armenia in West Asia. A skilled archer, he slew a wicked giant called Bel before going on to found the Armenian nation.

▲ **Moshanyana**
A mythical warrior hero and chief of the Basuto people of Southern Africa, Moshanyana was born fully armed and killed a monster.

▲ **Aswatama**
A warrior of the *Mahabharata*, Aswatthama was the son of Drona, teacher of the Pandavas and Kauravas. He was one of the few survivors of the Kaurava army after the great war.

MYTHICAL HEROES

Gawain
One of the bravest of Arthur's knights, Sir Gawain accepted a challenge to behead a green giant and then risk having his own head chopped off.

◀ Glooscap
A shapeshifting trickster-hero of many Native American forest peoples, Glooscap bound the wings of a mountain-top eagle whose flapping caused terrible storms.

▲ Wolfdietrich
A hero of Germanic legend—and often identified with the hero Dietrich—Wolfdietrich was abandoned by his father, the emperor, but after a long exile returned to fight for and claim his throne.

◀ Neoptolemus
The son of Achilles and Princess Deidamia, Neoptolemus was a Greek hero who fought bravely in the Trojan War, but was said by some ancient sources to be a bloodthirsty killer.

▼ Hector
King Priam's son Hector (*left*) led the army of Troy in the Trojan War. None defeated him until he faced Achilles (*right*), who chased him three times around the walls of Troy before killing him.

▲ Orestes
The Greek hero Orestes was Agamemnon's son. When his mother, Clytemnestra, and her lover, Aegisthus, murdered his father on his return from the Trojan War, Orestes killed them.

◀ Kintu
In the mythology of the Buganda people of Uganda in East Africa, Kintu was the first man on Earth. At first he lived alone with his cow, before marrying the creator's daughter, Nambi.

▲ **The face of a culture hero**
Intricately decorated with cowrie shells and hand-carved red, white, and blue beads,
this mask from the Democratic Republic of Congo was made by the Kuba Bushongo
people and represents their founder and culture hero, Woot.

CENTRAL AFRICA

Central Africa is dominated by the vast and densely rainforested basin of the River Congo, one of the world's longest rivers. Many of the myths originating in the region reflect this rich and vibrant tropical landscape.

Much of Central Africa is home to people who, like many of the inhabitants of southern Africa, speak languages from the Bantu group. The myths of Central African Bantu-speakers share some of the features of those myths found among Bantu-speakers further south, including tales of heroes. These heroes frequently encounter and defeat monsters and evil beings and are often rewarded with power and kingship. Other peoples in the region have mythologies with many deities who embrace specific functions in the cosmos.

CREATION STORIES

One indication of the diversity of the myths in Central Africa is the great variety of creation stories. Among the Bushongo people of the Democratic Republic of Congo, for example, the supreme god brings the cosmos into being simply by vomiting it up. In turn he vomits up the sun, the moon, and the stars, then he vomits up all the animals and, finally, the first human beings. For the Fang people, who live in Gabon, the Democratic Republic of Congo, and the Central African Republic, creation takes places in two stages, not one. First, a primal creator deity makes a world egg by mixing his underarm hair with a pebble and part of his brain. He then anoints this egg with his seed, following which three gods hatch out of the egg, including a secondary creator who goes on to make both the land and the people. Other peoples, such as the Efe and Mbuti of the Democratic Republic of Congo, tell a story about how the creator deity, with the help of the moon, makes the human race from clay, adding a skin, and pouring blood into the skin to give people life.

▶ **Protector of the home**
Statuettes called *bitegues*—like this one from the Bateke people of the Democratic Republic of Congo—are designed to be placed by the head of the family in a corner of the home facing the entrance, to protect the whole household from evil.

▶ **Protecting the dead**
The Kota people of Central Africa traditionally attach protective metalwork figures called *mbulu-ngulus* to containers of bones and other important relics of their ancestors.

MYTH AND REALITY

In the vast and dense tropical rainforest that makes up much of Central Africa, the close relevance of myths to everyday life is often clear. The Pygmy people, for example, see their supreme deity not only as their creator but also as the god of the hunt. In their mythology he lowered the first human beings from the sky and communicates with his creations through certain animals: often an elephant—known as the Thunderer—or a chameleon. As the god of hunters, he created all the animals as food for the human race, and gives the sustaining light of the sun new life every day by gathering light from the stars to add to its brilliance in the morning.

HEROES AND TRICKSTERS

Whereas the Pygmies' supreme deity is also a helper of humanity, in many Central African cultures there are also culture heroes who bring with them specific skills. The Fjort people of the Democratic Republic of Congo, for example, have a mythical blacksmith called Funzi who receives the gift of fire from a deity and teaches the people how to work copper and iron. Sometimes the task of culture hero is combined with that of trickster, as in Ture, the trickster of the Zande people of the Democratic Republic of Congo, who brings the people fire. Characters like these ensure that the myths of Central Africa have remained vividly relevant to the lives of native people for many thousands of years.

LONKUNDO

The founder and culture hero of the Mongo-Nkundo people of the Congo basin was called Lonkundo. He is primarily known for teaching his people how to hunt, but there are also myths about other aspects of his life, particularly his relationship with his wives.

They tell of how Lonkundo set up house in the forest, and how he caught his favorite wife, Ilankaka, in one of his animal traps. These myths, which continue with tales of Lonkundo's descendants, reflect the dangerous and unpredictable world of the forest hunter.

THE FIRST HUNTER

The first people did not know how to hunt, and having little in the way of survival skills, they wondered how they would survive. One night, the spirit of Lonkundo's father came to him in a dream. Lonkundo's father told his son to look for animal paw prints in the soil, and to follow the tracks to find the creature's regular habitat. He should then construct a trap for it using raffia fibers and twigs. When he awoke, Lonkundo followed his father's instructions and set a trap in the path of one of the creatures he had tracked. The trap was successful, and Lonkundo then traveled widely, tracking beasts and setting traps, and providing food for his people. He also taught them how to set their own traps for animals, and they were never short of food again.

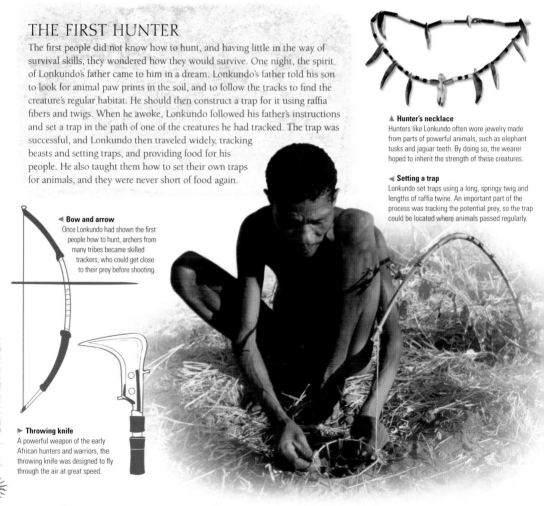

▲ Hunter's necklace
Hunters like Lonkundo often wore jewelry made from parts of powerful animals, such as elephant tusks and jaguar teeth. By doing so, the wearer hoped to inherit the strength of these creatures.

◀ Setting a trap
Lonkundo set traps using a long, springy twig and lengths of raffia twine. An important part of the process was tracking the potential prey, so the trap could be located where animals passed regularly.

◀ Bow and arrow
Once Lonkundo had shown the first people how to hunt, archers from many tribes became skilled trackers, who could get close to their prey before shooting.

▶ Throwing knife
A powerful weapon of the early African hunters and warriors, the throwing knife was designed to fly through the air at great speed.

CATCHING A WIFE

One night, Lonkundo dreamed that he had caught the sun in one of his animal traps. When he awoke, he went to inspect his traps as usual and was amazed to see a bright light coming from one of the traps he had set. He went over and found a beautiful woman, called Ilankaka, caught by the raffia noose of the trap. When he released her, Lonkundo, entranced by her beauty, asked her to become his wife. She accepted on one condition: he must never boast that he had caught her in a trap. He agreed and the two settled down. Later, Lonkundo took other wives, and the extended family became prosperous. When other families became jealous of their success, Lonkundo and his wives decided to move to the forest to start a new life.

◄ **Parrot**
The parrot's bright plumage and ability to mimic sounds and voices meant the bird was thought to be able to foretell the future or bring good omens.

► **Palm nuts**
The oil palm is valued both for its oil and for its nuts, which are a source of food for birds such as parrots.

LOSING A WIFE

In the forest, Lonkundo and his wives traveled to find a new home. After a while they heard the screeching cry of parrots, which was considered a good omen, so they stopped where they were to make their home. They cut down trees to build huts and, as was customary at that time, made a human sacrifice. But one of Lonkundo's wives, Nsombe, quarreled with her husband about her hut, which she thought was too small, and she left the village with her son, Yonjwa. Lonkundo's wife Ilankaka was pleased, believing that Lonkundo loved her best. Ilankaka planted palm trees and harvested the nuts, but when Lonkundo demanded more nuts from the trees, the couple argued. Lonkundo, forgetting he had promised not to boast of catching his wife, exclaimed, "Remember, I caught you in my trap," and Ilankaka disappeared.

ITONDE AND LIANJA

The most famous of Lonkundo's descendants was his grandson Itonde. He was the son of Yonjwa and the grandson of Nsombe, the wife who had left Lonkundo after a quarrel. Itonde was a notable explorer who traveled through the forest and the lands around them, naming all the beasts he found. One day he met a woman called Mbombe among the trees, and the pair were married. When Mbombe became pregnant she had a craving for a strange nut dropped by a bird. Itonde went to search for more of these nuts, but was attacked by rivals and killed. Mbombe, however, went on to give birth to several children, who became the ancestors of the Mongo-speaking tribes of Central Africa. One of these sons, Lianja, became a hero, who avenged the death of his father.

▲ **Mongo brass knife**
A beautifully made knife was a prized possession among the hunters of the Mongo, and was a sign of great status.

▼ **Naming the animals**
As the person who named the animals, Itonde was seen to have an intimate knowledge of the animal world and the power to influence its creatures.

THE WISE KING

A myth of the Bushongo people of the southeastern Congo region describes the achievements of their greatest ruler, Shamba Bolongongo, who is seen both as a king and a culture hero. Shamba, who was wise and just, is said to have been a real king who reigned in the 17th century, a time when many tribes united to create large and powerful political factions. He was revered not only for his great wisdom, but also because he avoided violence and war, preferring to use his intelligence to forge alliances or resolve disputes.

THE MYTH

Shamba Bolongongo, a prince of the Bushongo people, was very inquisitive and loved learning. As heir to the throne, he realized that he would be able to rule over his subjects more efficiently if he knew more about them, their way of living, and their needs. So when he was still young, Shamba set out to journey far and wide. On his many travels, he found out all that he could about the different peoples who lived in his kingdom and in the lands beyond his own. The prince learned many things that he believed would eventually help his own people to prosper and to live peacefully and happily.

THE CULTURE HERO

When Shamba returned from his long journey and became the king of his people, he taught them many new skills that have been used ever since among the Bushongo. The king showed them the technique of making textiles out of raffia fibers, and how to turn these textiles into clothes. He taught them how to prepare the nourishing cassava root properly, ensuring that it was cooked well enough to remove the poison that could be left behind in the plant. Shamba also planted palm trees and used them for making oil. And he introduced the Bushongo to tobacco smoking.

◄ **Shamba Bolongongo**
This carved wooden scepter depicts the king sitting on his throne, chewing on a medicinal root. His crossed legs and ritual nudity are typical of the Bushongo people.

THE MAN OF PEACE

The Bushongo were a warlike people, skilled in the use of weapons. But Shamba hated violence and killing, and wanted to introduce his people to the ways of peace. Soon after ascending the throne, he issued an order banning the use of bows and arrows, as well as the shongo, a type of throwing knife, in battle. At first the people thought that criminals would thrive under a king who did not allow the use of weapons, but they were proved wrong. Shamba tried harder than any king before him to hunt down criminals and punish them harshly. But he was not very keen on handing out the death penalty, and would only do so as a last resort in the case of the most hardened of offenders.

The people saw that Shamba respected all his subjects. He was especially mindful of women and children, and severely punished anyone who tried to harm them. Whenever people approached him with a problem or a dispute, he would give good advice or offer a fair judgement. Ever since that time, Shamba has been held up as the ideal ruler, an example that every Bushongo king has attempted to follow—even though not all of them have been as successful or as wise. His period of rule is often said to have been a golden age by the Bushongo people.

◄ **Wooden dagger**
Shamba's symbol of office was a dagger, though this was merely a ceremonial weapon, as the king disliked violence so intensely he would have used it only in extreme situations.

▲ **Raffia fabric**
The fibrous leaves and branches of the raffia palm are useful for making ropes, roof coverings, and other items, but are most commonly seen in boldly patterned fabric.

▶ **Cassava**
Once introduced, this plant quickly spread across Africa, becoming a staple food. The right way of cooking the plant, by detoxifying it, was said to be one of Shamba's gifts.

THE CULTURE HERO'S GIFTS

Shamba was credited with introducing a number of skills into the lives of his people that later proved beneficial. It is uncertain if these innovations were introduced by the actual 17th-century king on whom the story is based. Items like cassava and tobacco came from the Americas in the 16th century, so the story could well be based on fact. Raffia, however, is native to Africa, and the historical Shamba may have pioneered its use in making textiles.

▲ **Tobacco plant**
European merchants shipped tobacco from America to West Africa in the 1560s, after which it may have been promoted by local rulers such as Shamba.

THE BUSHONGO

The Bushongo, dominant among the Kuba people of Central Africa, have existed as a federation of tribes since the 16th century. They have a rich mythology, centered on many spirits of nature and past kings. Their creation myth narrates how Bumba, the supreme deity, vomited up the sun, moon, and stars, followed by animals and the first human, Woot. He then handed over the world to the human race. During ritual ceremonies, every king wears a Moshambwooy mask, representing Woot, the primary ancestor.

Moshambwooy mask

THE PEOPLE'S GAME

Another innovation popularized by Shamba was a game called Lele or Mancala. Shamba devised it because he found out that his people were addicted to gambling. Wishing to encourage them to take up a safer amusement, he introduced Lele. Claimed by some to be the world's oldest board game, Lele, in fact, originated in the Arab world and made its way across Africa. It is played using a board with small depressions (about 32 in number), in which the players put small counters, nuts, or stones, which need to be accumulated during the game.

KILL NEITHER MAN, WOMAN, NOR CHILD. ARE THEY NOT THE CHILDREN OF CHEMBE [GOD], AND HAVE THEY NOT THE RIGHT TO LIVE?

Shamba Bolongongo

◀ **Shongo**
Banning the shongo, or throwing knife, a traditional Bushongo weapon, was crucial in ushering in an era of peace among the peoples of the region.

PEACE AND JUSTICE

In traditional West African societies, arguments or disputes between two people or families were resolved by the head of the village. Similarly, disputes on a larger scale would be resolved by the king. People looked up to these leaders because of the authority that their status gave them, an authority that was often enhanced by the belief that the leaders were linked to ancestors and gods. Subjects used to obey their rulers because the ruler had the power to enforce his will, but when a king had a personal reputation for wisdom, his judgements were respected all the more.

▲ **Playing Lele**
The game of lele is played by two people. Different boards have different numbers of depressions, but the objective remains constant—to win more counters than an opponent.

▲ **Kikuyu ceremonial shield**
Shields like this one have been used for centuries by the Kikuyu people, who
live in Kenya. This example was made for use in dances following circumcision
ceremonies that mark a boy's passage from childhood to the world of the adult.

EAST AFRICA

Supreme deities who bring the necessities of life, from rain to cattle, dominate the mythology of East Africa. Side by side with these gods exist thousands of spirits who often have a direct and personal influence on people's lives.

This region covers the eastern parts of Africa from Ethiopia in the north, south through Kenya and Tanzania to the northern areas of Zambia and Malawi. Humans have lived in this part of the world for longer than in any other. The earliest human remains, together with the remains of hominids who are related to our species—some of which date from four million years ago—have been found at sites such as Koobi Fora in Kenya and the Olduvai Gorge in Tanzania. This long history of human habitation produced cultures well adapted to the varied local conditions, which are generally quite cool and dry in the many uplands, and more hot and humid towards the coasts. Among the many cultures of the region, a number, such as the Masai of Kenya and Tanzania and the Tumbuka of Malawi, have outstanding mythologies.

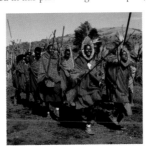

▲ **Masai men dancing**
Ceremonially armed with spears, Masai men perform a ritual dance in Tanzania. Such dances traditionally accompany preparations for war, rites of passage, and welcoming guests.

CATTLE MYTHS OF THE MASAI HERDERS

The Masai traditionally live by herding cattle, so their most important deity is Enkai, a creator god who in some of their myths gave them the first cattle. These myths also explain the role of other peoples who live by hunting and gathering or by farming. The rich Masai pantheon also includes Enkai's consort, Olapa, goddess of the

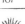

◄ **Lucky charm**
Amulets or lucky charms made from materials such as bone and worn around the neck, wrist, or leg—or simply carried on one's person—are believed to have special power in many cultures around the world. This lucky charm from Ethiopia is said to ensure that cattle breed successfully.

moon. The role of cattle as sustainers of life is also seen in the Masai myths of death and the next world. Each person has a guardian spirit, who looks after them from the day they are born. When the time comes for the person to die, the guardian spirit also acts as judge of the deceased. The spirits of people who led good lives on Earth are taken to a land where there are abundant cattle; the spirits of those who are less worthy go to a place where there is neither water nor cattle.

SPIRITS AND ANIMALS

In addition to a supreme deity, many cultures have a host of other spirits. Sometimes these spirits take the form of animals about whom amusing or moral stories are traditionally told—stories that in some cases have become familiar and well-loved around the world. For example, the Tumbuka, a people of Malawi, have a supreme god called Chiuta. Chiuta is the Tumbuka creator, an almighty being who, as well as creating the universe, is a fertility god and a bringer of life-giving rain. But in addition to myths about Chiuta, the Tumbuka tell stories about three animals: the wise tortoise, the trickster hare, and the wicked hyena. In these it takes the wisdom of the tortoise to defeat the devious tricks of the hare or the villainous behaviour of the hyena.

RITES OF PASSAGE

In addition to this body of myths and moral tales, East Africa, like the rest of Africa, has a rich heritage of ceremony and ritual. Special music and dances accompany the rites of passage that mark the key stages of a person's life, especially the initiation rites for when a young person comes of age. These ceremonies survive intact to this day—in spite of a long period of contact with cultures from outside Africa, both during the colonial period and more recently—so keeping traditional beliefs and stories alive.

THE FIRST CATTLE

The Masai, a cattle-herding people who live in Kenya, have several myths about how they came to own cattle. Other herding tribes in Africa have similar stories, which are testimony to the important role of cattle in their prosperity. In one myth, a Masai tribesman is contrasted with a man from one of the hunter-gatherer tribes of Kenya and Tanzania, who are widely referred to by the herding people as the Dorobo (the ones without cattle).

THE MYTH

Long ago there lived a Dorobo man who shared his land with an elephant and a snake. One day, the elephant had a calf. When the Dorobo approached the mother elephant, she attacked him to protect her young, and the man killed her in self-defence. The snake was lurking nearby and he slew that too. The alarmed elephant calf ran away, fearing for its life, and the Dorobo was left alone.

A MESSAGE FROM THE GODS

The baby elephant ran until it met a Masai tribesman called Le-eyo and told him what had happened to its mother and the snake. Intrigued by the tale, Le-eyo traveled to the place where the Dorobo lived, and peered through the bush to see what was going on. He was amazed to see Naiteru-kop, the messenger of the gods, talking to the Dorobo. Naiteru-kop told the Dorobo to meet him the next morning at a clearing in the forest, where he would be given a great gift. Le-eyo decided that he would get to the meeting place early, before the Dorobo arrived. When the next day dawned, Le-eyo hurried off to the meeting place while the Dorobo was still fast asleep. When Le-eyo reached the clearing, Naiteru-kop spoke to him, thinking he was the

▲ Masai house
Le-eyo hid in his hut while the sky god lowered the cattle to Earth. The walls of traditional Masai houses are plastered with cow dung, which dries hard in the sun.

Dorobo. The messenger told him to go home and build a fence around his hut, then kill and skin a wild animal, and put the meat inside the skin. After doing this he was to stay inside his hut and wait. Naiteru-kop insisted that he must stay indoors, even if he heard a great thundering sound outside, and Le-eyo said that he would be sure to obey.

THE COMING OF THE CATTLE

So Le-eyo went home, and did everything as instructed. Soon there was a thundering sound outside. At first, Le-eyo stayed inside, as the sound was so great that he trembled with fear. But eventually he went out to investigate. To his astonishment, he saw that Enkai, the sky god, had lowered a strip of hide from the sky and a huge herd of cattle had come down on it. As he watched, the strip of hide disappeared into the sky. Le-eyo now had plenty of cattle, but the sky god told him that he would have had even more if only he had done as he was told. From then on the Masai became the owners of all the world's cattle while the Dorobo were forced to carry on with their former way of life as hunters.

▲ Making fire
The Masai use friction generated by rotating a fire stick to make fire. Some accounts say the cattle of the Masai came down to Earth on a fire stick.

CATTLE AND THE MASAI

The Masai believed they had been entrusted with the responsibility of safeguarding all the world's cattle. In a traditional Masai settlement, everyone took part in caring for the cattle, the men herding and the women milking. The meat and milk of the cow was the staple diet of the people, its hide was used to make clothes, and its horns and bones were made into utensils. People even drew blood from a cow if there was nothing else to drink. So the number of cows kept by a family was an indication of their wealth and their status in society. Even today, cattle may be used as currency when Masai people are buying and selling other goods.

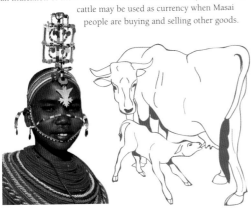

▲ Masai bride
When a Masai man marries, his family traditionally has to pay a bride-price to the woman's family, and this payment is usually made in cattle.

▲ Status symbol
Masai families own around 15 head of cattle each, sufficient for a regular supply of milk and meat, with enough left over to breed and to exchange in transactions.

ORIGINS OF POLYGAMY

The Kikuyu farming people of Kenya have a history of intermarriage with the Masai. Kikuyu clans carry women's names and yet the men are allowed to take more than one wife. Their mythology says that the opposite arrangement once prevailed, with each woman taking several husbands. The men rebelled, changing the custom when all the women were pregnant and powerless to defend their rights. So the men gained the power to have several wives, but the women insisted that the clan names stay with the female line, threatening to kill their boy children if the men tried to impose male clan names.

► Kikuyu man with his wife
This Kikuyu couple are wearing their traditional tribal dress. The shield and spear are generally used today in ceremonial dances.

ENKAI THE CREATOR

In many Masai myths, the creator god Enkai is a central character. Enkai is the sky god who represents both the sun and the rains, and lives in the sky with his wife, Olapa, the moon. Once, Enkai told the people to leave their *kraals* (enclosures) open at night, but not everyone obeyed. Those who did discovered in the morning that Enkai had given them cows, sheep, and goats. These people became the Masai. The Dorobo became hunters and the Kikuyu took up farming for their livelihood.

► Masai herders
The Masai myth about ownership of livestock is often used to justify their right to raid others' cattle.

◄ Dorobo hunter
When the Dorobo ignored the creator's generosity, they were left without livestock and so had to continue being hunters. But nowadays most of them live as cattle-herders.

▼ Kikuyu farmers
The Kikuyu are Kenya's prominent farmers. They claim the supreme god placed their ancestors on the fertile soil of Mount Kenya.

▲ **Southern African ceremonial masks**

Masks are used in ceremonies in many parts of Southern Africa. Masks such as these ones in a museum in Angola completely disguise the wearer, allowing him to assume the identity of the spirit depicted by the face of the mask for the duration of the ceremony.

SOUTHERN AFRICA

The myths of Southern Africa—an area that has traditionally been home to both hunters and farmers—form two distinct traditions of gods, heroes, and spirits that are still important to the cultural identities of people there today.

Southern Africa encompasses Angola, Zambia, and the countries to their south, and is a culturally diverse region. The area was originally inhabited by peoples commonly known outside Africa as "bushmen": peoples such as the Khoikhoi, San, and !Kung—the exclamation mark expresses one of the clicks in their language—who lived by hunting wild game and gathering wild plant produce. But at some point in the past, groups of farming peoples began to move into the area. These farmers, who spoke languages of the Bantu group, such as Xhosa and Zulu, slowly but surely colonized the land, gradually displacing the various hunter-gatherers to its more remote regions.

▲ **San hunting aids**
The San have traditional divination ceremonies to establish where best to hunt. Finely carved antelope bones and antlers help provide the answer.

beings. The Khoikhoi of South Africa, for example, call their supreme deity Gamab or Gauna. He is a sky god, but also the god of death, and is said to end people's lives by shooting his arrows into them from the heavens. Other important Khoikhoi deities include Gunab, the god of evil, and Tsui, a rain god and patron of sorcerers who had the power to bring himself back to life after death. The range of malign creatures in the Khoikhoi mythological canon includes the man-eating Aigamuxa, who is human in form but has his eyes in his feet, not his head, and Ga-gorib, a spotted creature resembling a leopard who silently and patiently lies in wait for his unfortunate victims in the bottom of a pit.

THE MYTHS OF THE HUNTER-GATHERERS
The cultural heritage of Southern Africa therefore became a mixture of two diverse sets of peoples. The hunter-gatherers, or "bushmen," of Southern Africa have complex mythologies involving deities, heroes, and a host of monster-like malign

THE MYTHS OF THE BANTU-SPEAKERS
Among the Bantu-speakers, Xhosa mythology has a similar mix of deities, ancestral figures, and other spirits. At the head of the deities is the supreme god uThixo. People traditionally communicate with uThixo through ancestor spirits, and special reverence is given to the primal ancestor, Tashawe, from whom all Xhosa believe they are descended. It is the job of the *imbongi*, or praise singer, to accompany the chief on important occasions and to sing songs praising both him and the ancestors, and as a result cement the link between the ruler and the illustrious heroes who have gone before him.

Southern African mythology also features familiar spirits who cause mischief, disease, or even death. A noted example is the *tokoloshe*, a dwarf-like spirit of the Xhosa and Zulu peoples. He is said to strangle people in their beds, so it is traditional to raise one's bed up on bricks, out of his reach.

Despite a history of European colonization, traditional myths survive widely in Southern Africa. Their popularity, connection with important ceremonies, links to essential aspects of life, and long history, sustain the indigenous peoples' cultures and their sense of belonging to the land.

▲ **Cave paintings of the "bushmen"**
African artists have been drawing on rocks for millennia. Hunter-gatherer artists depicted scenes of hunting—like this one on the walls of caves in the Matobo Hills of Zimbabwe from 2,000 years or so ago—giving us an insight into their ancient belief systems.

MYTHS OF THE SAN

Part of a group often known as "bushmen," the San are a hunting people who live mainly in Botswana, Namibia, and South Africa. Their mythology includes stories about how the first people of their tribes were created, as well as accounts of events important to them, such as the beginning of hunting. Some key characters in their stories are the bee, which, as the maker of honey, is a symbol of ingenuity and wisdom; the mantis, a primal spirit involved in the creation of humanity; and the eland, a type of antelope and a popular quarry for hunters.

THE FIRST HUMANS

At the beginning of time, a honey bee carried a praying mantis over the dark waters of a river. But the waters stretched far and wide, and as the bee looked for a solid patch of ground on which he could land, he became tired of flying with the weight of the mantis on his back. The mantis seemed to grow heavier and heavier, and the bee flew lower and lower until, quite exhausted, he began skimming on the surface of the water. As he floated, he saw a large white flower that was half open, waiting for morning to come so that the sun's rays could help it bloom. The bee set the mantis down on the flower, planting within the mantis the seed of the first human before dying. When the sun rose, the flower opened wide. As the air warmed, the mantis awoke and the seed germinated to create the first San.

▲ **South African landscape**
The San live in the Kalahari Desert of Southern Africa, a region where water is scarce, unlike at the time of the creation. Water is thus a precious commodity that is, for them, a symbol of life.

▲ **San rock art**
The San are outstanding painters, creating images using natural pigments on the rock of cliffs and caves. The subjects of San artists include the hunt and the animals of the Kalahari Desert, both part of their mythology.

THE FIRST HUNT

The mantis made an eland, the first of its kind, and nurtured it on honey. One day, a young man saw it at a water hole and went to tell his father, the ancestor Kwammang-a, who took his bow and shot the eland dead. The mantis had gone to gather food, and when he returned, he saw the creature dead and Kwammang-a's followers dividing up the meat. He was enraged, and tried to shoot the hunters, but all his shots missed. Then he took the creature's gall bladder and split it open, so that all the world was flooded with darkness as the gall flowed out. Later, he threw the bladder into the sky, where it became the moon. Since then, it has given people light as they hunt by night.

▲ **Eland**
Although San hunters pursue wildebeest or smaller creatures, the eland is a popular subject in their mythology, because it is a symbol of strength.

SOUTHERN AFRICA

HLAKANYANA

A trickster figure belonging to myths of the Xhosa and Zulu peoples of South Africa, Hlakanyana was a "wonder-child" who could talk even before he emerged from his mother's womb, and who clamored to be let out. He could walk as soon as he was born, and immediately headed for the cattle enclosure, intent on satisfying his hunger—not with his mother's milk, but with some roasted meat. When Hlakanyana grew up, he had a series of adventures, most of which involved tricking people or animals out of food.

HLAKANYANA'S POT

One night, Hlakanyana crept out, took a number of birds caught in traps set by some other boys in the village, and gave the birds to his mother to cook. She left them in the pot to cook overnight. The following morning, Hlakanyana got up very early and ate all the meat except for the birds' heads. Then he filled the pot with cattle dung, put the heads on top, and went back to bed, pretending to be asleep. When his mother awoke, Hlakanyana got up from his bed as if he too had just woken up. He complained that she was late and had probably let the food spoil. He told her that the meat would have turned to cattle dung because she had not taken the birds out of the pot soon enough. His mother scorned the idea, but when she went to check on the food, she found the pot full of cattle dung, just as her son had predicted. He then ate the birds' heads, saying she did not deserve any.

► **Cooking pot**
Food is an integral part of many myths associated with Hlakanyana. In yet another myth, he is himself caught and put into a cooking pot by an old woman, but manages to trick his way out.

◄ **Leopard cub**
The leopard is one of the most efficient hunting mammals of Africa, and Hlakanyana needed to use his wits in order to deceive the leopardess and eat her offspring.

HLAKANYANA AND THE LEOPARD CUBS

Hlakanyana once came across four leopard cubs without their mother. When the leopardess returned, she made to attack Hlakanyana. The trickster talked his way out, offering to guard the cubs while she went hunting, and saying he would build a hut for the family too. After she left, Hlakanyana built a hut with a narrow entrance, and then ate one of the cubs. When the mother returned, he brought out the remaining cubs to be suckled one at a time, and tricked her into thinking all four were safe. Over the next two days he played the same trick, and on the fourth day, he brought the single remaining cub out four times to fool her. When she grew suspicious, he escaped from the back door while the leopardess tried to squeeze her way in.

► **Antelope**
Large antelope were often taken by big cats and were also a more likely quarry for huntsmen than leopard cubs.

THE AMERICAS

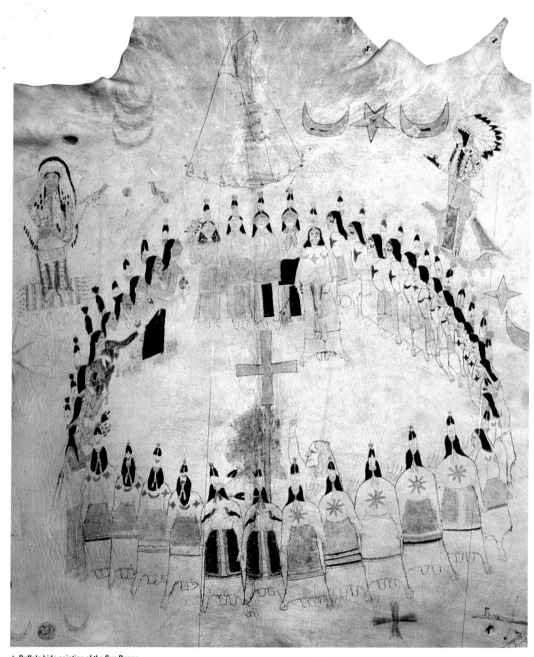

▲ **Buffalo hide painting of the Sun Dance**
The Sun Dance was an annual ceremony performed by various Native American peoples
of the Great Plains to confirm their beliefs and ensure their continued wellbeing. The
presence of Europeans on this 19th-century occasion is indicated by the Christian cross.

NORTH AMERICA

The varied myths of the native peoples of North America are a vital part
of their national and cultural identity to this day. Many of the stories told
are at the very heart of their diverse belief systems and ceremonies.

After the first people arrived in
North America, they spread out
far and wide across the continent,
settling in scattered communities
and adapting to the wide range of local
conditions. As a result, the Native
Americans formed a multitude of separate
peoples or nations, and the cultures of
these different groups vary a great deal.
Their rich mythologies, which still play an
integral role in their lives, are equally diverse.

▲ **Shaman's mask**
A shaman's spirit can make a
voyage while his body remains
in a trance. The symbols on this
mask represent such a journey.

VARIED CULTURES

Although the lives and myths of Native Americans
are highly varied, there are some similarities from
one group to another, and these often reflect
region and environment. People in the northwest,
for example, traditionally lived in settled villages of wooden
houses. Families told stories of their clan founders, the people
who originally created these settlements and who took the
form of mythical animals, represented on intricately carved
totem poles. There were similar settlements in the southwest
—though here the architecture was more likely to be in
mud-brick, not wood—and large pueblos housing many
families were commonplace. The myths of the southwest
describe the origins of the people of the area, with an
emphasis on "emergence" stories and the beginnings of
agriculture. Rituals in which people put on elaborate masks
and imitate or "become" spirits are also important in the area.

The central Great Plains form another quite distinctive area,
traditionally being home to nomadic peoples who hunted
buffalo and used every part of the animal, from meat to hide,
in their daily lives. Animal myths abound here, as do deities
who control the elements. Important ceremonies include
those involving smoking a sacred pipe. In the eastern United
States, meanwhile, spirits of woods, lakes, and rivers are
prevalent, reflecting the local geography. Further north, there
are yet more distinctive cultures, such as those of the Arctic,
where the myths involve many stories of
animals, such as seals or fish, who are the
hunter-fisher's quarry, but are respected as
being creatures with souls, like people.

MYTH AND LIFE

For Native Americans, myth has always been
closely related to daily life. The ancestors who
gave the tribes of the northwest their identity,
the weather gods of the Great Plains, the animals
of the Arctic—all have long been seen as having
a real impact on real people. Often, such myths
explained thunder and other mysterious natural
phenomena, which could affect the farmer's crop
or the hunter's quarry, thereby influencing the
people's very survival. Many myths were closely
tied to special occasions; these were only to be
told as part of a ceremony, often one performed at a set time
by a priest or shaman. All were stories of power, told for
generations, and of crucial worth to their people. They retain
their power for Native Americans still.

▲ **Alaskan clan house decoration**
The traditional wooden clan houses of Alaska were decorated with colorful symbols
and figures to indicate the owner's lineage. Both human figures and those representing
animal ancestor figures, such as the Raven visible here, are typical features.

NAVAJO EMERGENCE

The myths of the Navajo people of southwest North America focus on the Emergence, a myth also recorded in the legends of other southwester n tribes such as the Pueblo. It tells how the first people travel upwards through a series of different worlds before arriving in this world, which is widely described as the fourth world. Other related myths talk about Changing Woman, the Earth goddess; her children, the warrior twins; and various other figures who are injured or lost and approach the gods to be healed.

THE MYTH

In the beginning, the First World, or the Black World, existed. It was black and had four corners; standing over each corner was a column of colored cloud—black, white, blue, and yellow. The black and white clouds joined at the northeast corner to form First Man. At the southwest corner, the blue and yellow clouds merged to create First Woman. A white wind, blowing over two ears of corn, entered First Man and First Woman, breathing life into them. The descendants of First Man and First Woman were known the Air People, and had no clear shape or form initially. They began to quarrel among themselves and, becoming dissatisfied with their world, climbed upwards, until they reached the Second World.

◀ **Coyote**
An important figure in the Navajo stories of the First People, Coyote is considered to be the bringer of death.

WORLDS OF DISCONTENT

When these First People reached the Second World, or the Blue World, they were as unhappy as they had been before. Everyone quarreled and there was widespread discontent. First Man decided that they should leave this world too, and move on to the next. He took an abalone, a white shell, turquoise, and jet, and made a wand that carried the people up to the Third World, or the Yellow World. This too was an unhappy place. The people lived sinfully and their unnatural ways brought them misery. Then a great flood came to destroy the world. First Man realized that the people needed high ground to escape the flood, and built a tall mountain. Then he planted a cedar tree, a pine tree, and a male reed, but none of these were tall enough to reach up into the next world. So he planted a female reed, and this was sufficient for the people to climb into the Fourth, or Glittering, World.

THE FOURTH WORLD

When the First People arrived in the Fourth World, they performed a Blessingway ceremony (*see opposite*), and built the first sweat lodge for meditation and healing. They brought up soil from the Third World and built sacred mountains. First Man constructed houses for his people, and put the sun and the moon high up in the sky to create day and night. He was helped by Black God and Coyote; deities from the First World. Black God tried to carefully arrange the stars in the sky, but Coyote became impatient with his slowness and scattered them hastily across the sky. Finally, the people could live happily and prosper.

◀ **Sacred mountains**
The Navajo Indian reservation areas in the US have many mountains that are considered sacred by the Navajo. Some mountains are believed to be female, and some male; together, they symbolize the balance of nature.

CHANGING WOMAN

One of the most important female deities of the Navajo is Changing Woman, who represents the Earth and the stability of the cosmos. Some accounts say that she was created by First Man, and that she later produced the Navajo ancestors from her body. However, others mention her to be either the daughter of the sky and the Earth, or the offspring of First Boy (denoting thought) and First Girl (speech). Changing Woman got her name because she could change from one stage of life to the next (baby, girl, woman, and old woman) rapidly and endlessly. When she reached puberty in four days, people performed a puberty ceremony. This later became a necessity for all Navajo girls on the verge of womanhood.

◀ **People and corn**
This blanket, bearing a design based on a Navajo sand painting, shows First Man and First Woman standing on either side of a corn plant. It underlines the importance of corn for the Navajo people.

◀ **Cycle of change**
Changing Woman represented the cyclical changing of the seasons. She would put on a dress of a different color for each season to signal its arrival.

FIRST PEOPLE

The First People are central to the origin myths of the Navajo. They directed the journey of the Navajo ancestors through the first three worlds to the final one. First Man and First Woman were the ones who planned for the birth of Changing Woman. The accounts of the First People, the Emergence, and Changing Woman, form the core of the important Navajo ceremony known in English as "Blessingway." Changing Woman passed on the knowledge of this rite to the Navajo; the ceremony is a ritualistic blessing of a person to ensure general health and wellbeing. Blessingway rituals are performed on many occasions, such as births, weddings, and puberty ceremonies for girls. So the First People are remembered at key events in Navajo life.

THE WARRIOR TWINS

Changing Woman had two sons. One of her sons, fathered by the sun, was called Killer of Enemies. The other boy, called Child of Water, was the offspring of water. Although their fathers were different, the boys were born together and were therefore always considered to be twins. Eventually, even the sun accepted Child of Water as his own son. The boys grew up as rapidly as their mother, and one day decided to visit the sun to ask for his help in defeating the evil spirits and monsters that roamed the land. When they reached the sun's house, he gave them powerful arrows and the knowledge to slay the evil spirits. Together, the warrior twins rid their land of evil by defeating a number of creatures, including a man-eating antelope called Teelget, gigantic and fearsome birds of prey called the Tsenhale, and a scaly monster known as Yeitso.

◀ **Spider Woman**
The warrior twins were said to have a wise grandmother called Spider Woman. She gave them advice that helped them on their missions to outwit and destroy evil.

SAND PAINTINGS

A number of Native American peoples—the Navajo, Apache, Cheyenne, and Pueblo—make sand paintings, in which dry materials such as sand, corn pollen, and crushed flower petals are used to create patterns on the ground or floor. These paintings are created as part of ceremonial healing rituals and depict scenes from the various myths. There are, in fact, hundreds of different ceremonies, each associated with its own specific painting design. The images are made during the ritual and swept away afterwards.

A Navajo sand painting

JOURNEY TO THE SKY

The native cultures of North America have long been fascinated with the sky, using the movements of heavenly bodies to time key rituals and predict the changing seasons. Some of the most popular myths deal with the sun, moon, and stars, and some—like the Blackfoot sun dance tale—also narrate the journeys of ancestors to the sky. Besides explaining the role and movement of these heavenly bodies, these stories account for the apparently random arrangement of the stars, said to be the result of someone scattering them across the sky.

THE SUN DANCE

A popular Blackfoot myth tells of Morning Star, the young son of the moon and the sun, who fell in love with a girl called White Feather. She returned his love, and the couple traveled to the sky on a spider's thread. They lived there happily with Morning Star's parents, and had a boy named Star Boy. One day, White Feather was told to harvest the root crop, but to leave one large turnip alone. She became curious and pulled up the turnip, revealing a hole in the sky. As punishment for having disobeyed orders, White Feather was told to return to the Earth with her son. After her death, Star Boy visited his grandparents by ascending to the sky on one of the shafts of light that appeared at sunset. Star Boy learned the sun dance from the sun, who said that he would heal all the sick if the Blackfoot performed a festival in the sun's honor. This is how the sun dance ritual originated.

▶ **White Feather**
Morning Star's parting gift to White Feather when she returned to the Earth was an elk-skin robe, which he said could only be worn by a pure woman.

◀ **Sun dance headdress**
This headdress was worn during the sun dance by a sacred woman who had pledged allegiance to the sun. The components of the headdress represents aspects of the myth.

▼ **Sun dance**
Elements common to the sun dance ritual performed by the different native cultures included singing, dancing, and self-torture.

STAR POWER

The Pawnee performed the sun dance too, to show their gratitude to the sun, and to ask him for protection, fertility, and the renewal of the seasons. However, according to their mythology, the dance originated when it came to a young man in a vision. Keen observers of the sky, the Pawnee aligned their lodges to the four points of the compass, and built them with smoke holes to give views of certain groups of stars. Their ceremonies, such as those heralding the beginning of spring and those performed before hunting, were timed by observing the movements of the stars. The Pawnee believed that if they carried out their rituals according to the stars, the universe would continue to function and the people would thrive.

▲ **Star charts**
The Pawnee recorded their observations on star charts, maps of the night sky that were often painted on buckskin and wrapped in sacred bundles, indicating their importance.

◀ **The Pawnee**
The knowledge of the stars and their movement across the night sky helped the Pawnee find their way while traveling across the plains.

▶ **Kotcimanyako**
The story of Kotcimanyako follows a very common mythological theme. It is that of a person entrusted with something that must not be examined, but the individual cannot resist taking a look.

SPILLED STARS

The Cóchiti Pueblo people tell a story of how there was once a great flood, and the people moved north to escape the waters. When the land began to dry, Iatiku, the mother of the people, told them that it was safe for them to travel southwards to their homeland. She gave a girl called Kotcimanyako (Blue Feather) a bag to carry and forbade her from opening it. But Kotcimanyako was a very curious girl and could not resist opening the bag. As soon as she untied the bag, thousands of stars spilled out, flying around in all directions until they finally settled in the sky. The girl quickly tied the bag up again but only a few stars were left inside. When the Cóchiti Pueblo reached their homeland, Kotcimanyako showed Iatiku what she had done, and they carefully put the remaining stars in their rightful places in the sky. These were the stars whose names are known to the people.

THE ORIGIN OF THE MILKY WAY

A number of Native American myths describe the origin of the Milky Way, such as the Navajo creation story featuring Black God and Coyote. Once, Black God, the deity considered to be the creator of fire, was carefully arranging the stars in the sky. This was a slow process as the stars had to be set in the correct patterns, and Black God took great care to get it right. He was observed by the trickster Coyote who was annoyed with Black God's slow progress. After watching for a while, Coyote grabbed the bag with the remaining stars and threw them all into the sky at once, creating the Milky Way.

▶ **Milky Way**
For many peoples, the Milky Way was a pathway across the sky, and also the route along which the souls of the dead traveled.

◀ **Coyote**
Coyote appears in a number of Native American myths as a trickster or culture hero, and as a very impatient character in the Navajo story of the Milky Way.

▶ **Relief carving, Yaxchilan**
A series of carvings from the
Mayan city of Yaxchilan in the
state of Chiapas, Mexico depict
rituals that took place when a
ruler called Shield Jaguar took
the throne in 681. His name
is recorded in the glyphs at
the top of the stone relief.

MESOAMERICA

The civilizations of Mesoamerica worshipped a varied and vivid group of gods at their imposing pyramid-shaped temples. Rituals of blood sacrifice played a key part in both the mythology and worship of these deities.

Mesoamerica is the name now given to an area made up of Mexico and parts of the neighboring countries—mainly Belize, Guatemala, and Honduras—where there developed a highly sophisticated urban civilization before the arrival of the European conquerors in the 16th century. Several cultures built this civilization. The first, the Olmecs (c.1500–400 BCE), lived in southern Mexico, at sites such as La Venta. The Zapotecs (c.300–600 CE) built cities at Mitla and Monte Alban, also in southern Mexico. The Maya (c.300–900) were based in the Yucatan Peninsula, at sites such as Uxmal and Tikal. The Toltecs (c.900–1180) had their home city at Tula, north of Lake Texcoco. Finally the Aztecs (c.1300–1521), the last of the great Mesoamerican cultures, built their base at Tenochtitlan, the site of present-day Mexico City.

COMMON ACHIEVEMENTS

The Zapotecs, Maya, Toltecs, and Aztecs had several things in common. All developed a system of writing using picture symbols called glyphs. All were skilled astronomers who used two parallel calendars: a solar one similar to the modern calendar, and a religious one based on a 260-day ritual year. And all had complex mythologies with numerous deities, many of whom governed areas such as the weather and farming, which Mesoamericans depended on for survival. Some of these deities had several identities, partly because they were handed down from one culture to the next and partly because of their varied roles. The Aztec deity Tezcatlipoca was Yaotl when he was god of war and Yoalli Ehecatl when he was god of the wind. Another Aztec high god, the plumed serpent Quetzalcoatl, also took on the role of wind god, as Ehecatl.

The temples in which these deities were worshipped were also broadly similar. Set on tall, stepped pyramids, often in large plazas, they dominated the early Mesoamerican cities.

◀ **A page from the Codex Fejervary-Mayer**
Details of the Aztecs' rulers, deities, and sophisticated calendars are recorded in the glyphic writing of a number of books called codices. Not all of these texts have been fully deciphered, puzzling experts to this day.

Many still stand, impressive testimonies both to the skill of their builders and to the great resources the Mesoamericans poured into their religious worship.

BLOOD SACRIFICE

Another aspect common to most Mesoamerican cultures was the practice of blood sacrifice. The Aztecs and their predecessors believed that the deities needed to be nurtured with human blood, partly because they had spent their own blood in creating humanity, who therefore owed the gods a debt. The Toltecs and Aztecs, especially, sacrificed people—often prisoners of war. Much Mesoamerican ritual art, including carvings of skulls, images of priests wearing victims' flayed skins, and statues holding dishes for victims' hearts, reflects this religious practice.

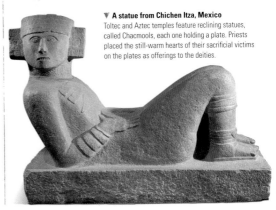

▼ **A statue from Chichen Itza, Mexico**
Toltec and Aztec temples feature reclining statues, called Chacmools, each one holding a plate. Priests placed the still-warm hearts of their sacrificial victims on the plates as offerings to the deities.

POPOL VUH

The creation story and other myths of the Quiché Maya, a native people belonging to the highlands of Guatemala, are told in a book called the *Popol Vuh* (Council Book). This text was written down in the mid-16th century, after the Spanish conquest of the area, and was copied from an earlier version in Maya glyphic writing. It records myths dating back many centuries; one important section of the narrative concerns the adventures of a pair of Hero Twins, who travel to the Mayan Underworld, Xibalba.

THE MYTH

In the beginning, the sea god Gucumatz and the sky god Heart of Sky decided to create a human race to populate the Earth and do honor to the gods. But their first creations were a failure: they could not say the names of the gods and were only able to howl and chatter, so they became the first animals. The creators took some clay and tried to make another race, but these turned out limp and twisted; they were unable to speak, and dissolved in water. Frustrated by these failures, the two gods went to see the diviners Xpiyacoc and Xmucane, wise beings who were even older than the gods. The diviners told the creators to make men from wood and women from reeds. But these creatures did not please the gods either, as they refused to worship them, so Heart of Sky sent a flood to overwhelm them. It became clear that other events had to take place before humans could be successfully created.

World tree
The Mayan world tree is a symbol of their conception of the cosmos. Its roots are in Xibalba, the Underworld, its topmost branches the heavens.

THE UNDERWORLD

The diviners had two sons, the twins Hun Hunahpu and Vucub Hunahpu. They spent all their time gambling and playing ball. While playing, they made a terrible noise that annoyed the lords of Xibalba (the Underworld), who sent messengers to challenge them to a ball game. When the brothers went down to Xibalba, the lords of the Underworld began to play cruel tricks on them. First they told the brothers to sit down on a bench, but it

▲ **Hun Hunahpu and Xquic**
When the maiden Xquic reached out to pick a tempting fruit from the gourd tree the head of Hun Hunahpu in the tree spat at her, making her pregnant.

was so hot that they jumped up at once. Then the twins were sent to stay in a section of the Underworld called the Dark House for the night, with only a torch and two cigars for light. In the morning, the lords of Xibalba came back to claim their torch and cigars and, on finding they were burned up, proclaimed that the brothers would be punished with death. So the two brothers were killed at the sacrificial ball court, and the head of Hun Hunahpu was sliced off and displayed on a tree. The tree's fruit took the form of the first gourds.

THE BIRTH OF THE HERO TWINS

A girl from Xibalba called Xquic went to look at the gourd tree. When she tried to pick a fruit, Hun Hunahpu spat at her. This made Xquic pregnant, and her angry father ordered her to be put to death. She escaped and went to live with Hun Hunahpu's mother. Later, she gave birth to the Hero Twins, Hunahpu and Xbalanque.

Like Hun Hunahpu and Vucub Hunahpu, the Hero Twins loved to play ball. When they learned that their father and uncle had been killed by the lords of Xibalba, they decided to avenge their death. One day, they began playing ball, making a lot of noise. The lords of Xibalba challenged them to a game, and they accepted. »

PRIMAL DEITIES

Mayan deities were often known by alternative names, and certain gods became important at different points in their history. Itzamna was a high god of the early Maya, although by the time of the Quiché Maya, he was more of an abstract force. For the Quiché Maya, the gods occupied two separate realms, the sea and the sky, each of which had a ruler—the gods Gucumatz and Heart of Sky respectively. There were also malign deities like Vucub Caquix (Seven Macaw), the Underworld god who falsely claimed to be the sun. He was attacked by the Hero Twins, who eventually tricked and defeated him.

▼ **Hunahpu shooting Vucub Caquix**
Vucub Caquix was an arrogant bird-god who ruled the world after the primeval flood. Although one of the Hero Twins, Hunahpu, shot at him with his blowpipe, he escaped.

◄ **Itzamna**
An early sky-dwelling creator god, Itzamna was also said to be the god of medicine and inventor of writing. He is sometimes portrayed as a human, occasionally as a lizard.

◄ **Gucumatz**
One of the creators of humanity, Gucumatz was a feathered serpent, and the Quiché Maya equivalent of the supreme Aztec deity Quetzalcoatl.

HEART-OF-SKY ONLY SAYS THE WORD, "EARTH" AND THE EARTH RISES LIKE A MIST FROM THE SEA.

Popol Vuh

THE HERO TWINS

Like many cultures around the world, the Maya saw twins as magical beings with a special role in their history, and they sometimes claimed that the Hero Twins, Hunahpu and Xbalanque, were the ancestors of their rulers. The twins used ingenuity and courage to outwit and defeat the lords of Xibalba, as well as to fight their jealous half-brothers—the Howler-Monkey Gods—and the tyrannical Vucub Caquix. At the end of the story they reigned supreme in the sky as sun and moon deities. They were also often pictured with the Mayan Maize God, who, in some accounts, is seen as a resurrected form of their father, Hun Hunahpu.

▲ **Rabbit scribe**
A rabbit helped the Hero Twins during the ball game, and sometimes is depicted on Mayan vases as a scribe.

▲ **Hunahpu and Xbalanque**
The heroic exploits of the twins cleared the universe of evil and made way for the successful creation of the human race.

FIRST CREATURES

The jaguar, deer, and serpent were among the first creatures created by Gucumatz and Heart of Sky. All were powerfully symbolic, the jaguar as a hunter, the deer as a sacred creature eaten at feasts honoring the gods, and the serpent as a symbol of the sky because of the similarity between the words for "snake" and "sky" in the Mayan language.

Deer

Serpent

Jaguar

SURVIVING IN XIBALBA

When the Hero Twins reached Xibalba, they were subjected to a series of deadly tests. They were made to stay each night in a different house fraught with peril. They survived the Dark House, the Razor House, the Cold House, the Jaguar House, the Fire House, and the House of Bats. They spent a night in each one of these houses and on each of the following days, they played the ball game against the lords of Xibalba. Every night they survived by using their wits—in the Dark House they avoided the trap their father and uncle had fallen into, by using fireflies to stop their cigars from going out. Then on the final night they hid inside their blowpipes to avoid the vicious bats, but Hunahpu put his head out and a bat bit it off and rolled it to the ball court.

When Hunahpu lost his head, Xbalanque carved a new one for his brother and the pair went to the ball court once more. At first they used Hunahpu's head as the ball. Xbalanque

hit it right out of the court and a rabbit brought it quietly back to him. While the lords of Xibalba searched for it, Xbalanque stuck his brother's head

◄ **A ball player**
As shown on this pot, the Hero Twins found the padded clothing worn by their father and uncle, and used it in their ball game. It included a wooden or leather yoke around the waist with which to hit the ball.

back on, and the game resumed with another ball. The Hero Twins won the game easily.

CONQUERING DEATH

The lords of Xibalba were angry at their defeat. They caught the twins, burned them in their oven, ground down their bones, and sprinkled the dust in the river. But after six days the twins reappeared, saying that they had put themselves together again, and claiming that they had discovered how to bring the dead back to life. The lords were sceptical, so they challenged the twins to prove what they said. Xbalanque held down Hunahpu, cut out his heart, and then commanded his brother to get up. Hunahpu did so, and the lords of Xibalba were beside themselves with amazement. They were so impressed that some of them insisted the Hero Twins do the same thing to them, so that they could experience what it was like to come back to life. So the Hero Twins held them down in turn and cut out their hearts. But the crafty brothers did not bring the lords back to life again. In this way the Hero Twins conquered death—reducing its power and, consequently, the power of the kingdom of Xibalba. Hunahpu and Xbalanque then returned to the Earth and from there ascended to the sky to become the sun and the moon. Having completed their work of overcoming the all-pervasive power of death, they had ensured that the universe was now ready for the proper creation of human beings to inhabit the Earth.

THE BALL GAME

The Mesoamerican ball game was played between two teams, each comprising two to eleven players. The object of the game was to get a small solid rubber ball across the opponent's goal line, or to succeed in lobbing it through a narrow ring, placed high up on the side wall of the court. The players could use only their knees, elbows, and hips to hit the ball—use of the hands or feet was forbidden. Seen by the Maya as a re-enactment of the struggle between the Hero Twins and the lords of Xibalba, the game also had a religious purpose, and sometimes ended in the ritual sacrifice of the losers.

◄ **Ball court**
This clay model shows the typical shape of a Mayan ball court. The spectators sat on the sides and enjoyed the sight of players fighting for the ball.

THE MAYAN UNDERWORLD

Known as Xibalba (Place of Fear), the Mayan Underworld was the place where everyone—whether they had lived a good and virtuous life or not—went after death. It had nine levels, and was a grim place, ruled by gods who were the bringers of drought, hurricanes, and war. On arrival, the deceased had to cross rivers of blood, and undergo a series of trials with the fearsome lords who lived in Xibalba. If they passed these tests they were allowed to live with the Hero Twins in the sky. The Mayan people hoped that they would be as successful in passing the tests as the Hero Twins, who survived all the ordeals.

◄ Funerary vessel
Among the Maya, funerary customs varied; some high-ranking people were cremated, and their ashes placed in ornate vessels.

THE FIRST PEOPLE

The creators finally succeeded in creating the first four men out of maize dough, and four women were created for them. Heart of Sky blew mist into their eyes, so that they could only see what was close by, and not aspire to be gods. These people flourished, but they longed for light. They asked the gods for fire, and the gods agreed, provided the people made sacrifices in thanks.

► Blood-letting rite
To honor the gods, blood-letting rites were conducted, in which a priest ceremonially cut a worshipper's tongue on a rope of thorns.

◄ Mayan people
The Maya referred to themselves as the "true people," and believed they were mediators between their world and that of the gods.

HERE IS THE NEW CREATION, MADE OF MUD AND EARTH. IT DOESN'T LOOK GOOD.

Popol Vuh

MAYAN RELIGION

The Maya worshipped a pantheon of nature gods, and the priests who presided over their religion were well versed in history (especially the genealogies of the Mayan rulers, which confirmed their power), rituals, and the calculation of the calendar. Their rituals honored groups such as fishermen, hunters, and beekeepers, and the most important ritual is believed to be the festival that marked the Mayan new year.

► An inscription from Palenque
Temple inscriptions at sites like Palenque used the Mayan pictorial glyphic writing to record the history of the rulers, including their conquests and alliances.

▼ Mayan temple
The typical Mayan temple, like this one at Chichen Itza, was set on top of a pyramid with nine levels, mirroring the levels of the Mayan Underworld.

THE MAYAN CALENDAR

The Maya had a number of different ways of counting the days, months, and years, and these calendars were used in their religion to calculate feast days and other important dates. The oldest of the Mayan calendars, dating from at least the 6th century BCE and attributed to the god Itzamna, was a 260-day calendar incorporating cycles of 13 days. This system was usually chosen for working out when to hold religious rituals and feasts. The Maya also had a 365-day calendar that incorporated cycles of 20 days. The two calendars were sometimes combined to form longer cycles.

Mayan calendar stone

AZTEC NATURE GODS

Many Aztec gods controlled the natural forces on which the people depended for their survival. Some of these deities were dreaded beings, ruthless in their dealings with the Earth and its inhabitants; their actions reflected the harsh climate and conditions of Aztec lands, in the region now known as Mexico. Their stories are frequently associated with the custom of human sacrifice—one deity, for example, demanded an offering of human blood before allowing the crops to ripen.

XIPE TOTEC

The name of the god Xipe Totec means "flayed lord," and this gives a clue to his story. He was the god of spring, and whenever there was a famine on Earth, it was said that he skinned himself to show the seed heads how to burst out of their buds. The rituals dedicated to Xipe Totec involved the devotees taking the flayed skins of sacrificial victims and putting these on themselves – the skin would fall off just as Xipe Totec's skin had done, revealing the devotee beneath, symbolically encouraging the plants to sprout in spring. In another sacrificial ritual dedicated to Xipe Totec, victims were tied up and shot with arrows. Their blood was made to drip onto a round stone that represented the Earth; this symbolized the fertilization of the ground.

▲ **Foaming waters**
Whirlpools, waterfalls, and other manifestations of rapidly moving water were especially sacred to Chalchiuhtlicue, who was often shown seated in front of flowing water. Her titles included the "Foaming One."

▶ **Goddess of beauty**
Chalchiuhtlicue was often depicted as a beautiful woman dressed in blue and green and wearing elaborate jewelry; sometimes she also wore a reed headdress.

▲ **Flayed lord**
The god of spring, maize, and fertility, Xipe Totec was usually portrayed as a young man, as if to symbolize the young crops about to mature.

▶ **Aztec farmer**
Maize was a key crop of Mesoamerica, and many pictures and statuettes from the region depict this staple crop being harvested by the people.

CHALCHIUHTLICUE

Chalchiuhtlicue (She of the Jade Skirt) was the Aztec goddess of beauty and the sister of the rain god Tlaloc (*see opposite*). She was seen as the embodiment of the patterns of light shining on moving water. As a water goddess, she was close to her brother, and for a while the two became man and wife. But the presence of two water-related deities in heaven caused many floods and storms on the Earth. So the pair had to part, and the god Quetzalcoatl took Chalchiuhtlicue to the Earth, where she became the presiding goddess of rivers, streams, lakes, and other bodies of water.

◄ Dark deity
Tezcatlipoca was often said to be black in color and to represent the "black sun" as it traveled across the sky in the hours of darkness.

▼ Tlaltechutli
In one version of the Aztec creation myth, Tezcatlipoca defeated the primordial monster, Tlaltechutli, and created the Earth upon its back.

TEZCATLIPOCA

Originally a sun god, Tezcatlipoca (Smoking Mirror) was deposed from his position and ended up as the Aztec god of the Underworld. One of his physical forms was a great wind that blew at night; on other occasions, he took the shape of a black jaguar (*see below*). The deity also sat in the sky as the Great Bear constellation. He was believed to roam the Earth at night in the form of a skeleton, with his heart visible behind his ribs. It was said that the only way to defeat him was to tear his heart out. Tezcatlipoca carried a mirror to see into people's minds, and allowed those who had the skill to see its images to have a glimpse of the future.

TLALOC

The Aztec rain god Tlaloc had four palaces, each one atop a mountain, and in every palace he kept a vast tub of water. One of these brought about the morning rain, one the midday showers, one the evening drizzle, and one fierce storms. The deity kept cloud servants, the Tlaloques, who carried the rain to Earth, where it served a dual purpose; the rain fertilized the ground, and also acted as the manifestation of Tlaloc's anger during a severe storm. Tlaloc also had a beautiful garden that was filled with flourishing plants and lush orchards. It was an idyllic place where the souls of the people who had died from illness went after death; victims of Tlaloc's own power (those who were killed by lightning strikes or by drowning) were also allowed to enter the god's paradise.

► Rain god vessel
Vessels made in the shape of Tlaloc's head are thought to have been used to collect rainwater during sacred rituals performed to honor the god. Many such vessels have been found at the Aztec site of Tenochtitlan, in Mexico City.

◄ Quetzalcoatl
The feathered serpent god Quetzalcoatl came to be identified with Ehecatl, the Aztec god of wind. He became linked with Tlaloc, as the Aztecs believed that winds heralded the coming of the rain.

► Tlaloc's weapon
Tlaloc's thunder was sometimes compared to the sound of a vast tomahawk or axe striking the sky. Consequently, this weapon became closely associated with the deity.

THE JAGUAR

In Aztec religion, the jaguar represented the deity Tezcatlipoca, Quetzalcoatl's rival. After being removed from his position as the sun god by Quetzalcoatl, Tezcatlipoca took the form of a jaguar, and came to be known as Tepeyollotl (Heart of the Mountains). As the Aztec deity of the night, he would roar loudly, a sound people associated with the noise of falling rocks and erupting volcanoes. Tezcatlipoca's destructive power was enormous, and in one myth, after losing his status as the sun god, he destroyed the world in revenge. The jaguar became a symbol of power to the Aztecs, and one group of elite Aztec warriors was even known by the name of the creature.

Tezcatlipoca as the Jaguar

▲ **Museum display of voodoo spirits**
This selection of diverse objects from a display in a museum dedicated to the
voodoo religion includes a human skull and crossbones and several colorful
and elaborately carved wooden representations of various gods or spirits.

THE CARIBBEAN

The indigenous people of the Caribbean region, the Taíno, had a rich mythology of gods and spirits that not only endured, but influenced the beliefs of those who arrived later from Europe and Africa.

The Taíno came to the Caribbean from South America around 5000 BCE. They brought with them beliefs about high gods who presided over a series of creations, as well as beliefs about countless spirits who permeated the world and had the power of shape-changing—a highly relevant concept in a region often drastically altered by hurricanes and storms.

The Taíno believed there were two classes of spirits: *goeiza*, spirits of the living, and *hupia*, spirits of the dead. *Hupia* were said to look like bats and to seduce or kidnap women at night. There were also gods called *cemís*, chief among whom were Yúcahu, "spirit of cassava," and god of the sea, and Atabey, goddess of fertility and fresh water. Some accounts also name Yukiyú, who helped farmers and loved peace, and Juracán, god of storms and hurricanes. The term *cemís* was also used for figures that were imbued with great spiritual power, being inhabited by the gods they represented.

NEW ARRIVALS

The end of the 15th century was the beginning of European influence in the Caribbean, with the arrival of Christopher Columbus in the Bahamas. Later, Europeans brought African slaves to the area, further adding to the cultural mix. Caribbean mythology's best-known myths developed as an amalgam of local

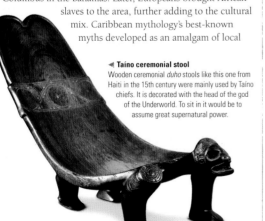

◄ Taíno ceremonial stool
Wooden ceremonial *duho* stools like this one from Haiti in the 15th century were mainly used by Taíno chiefs. It is decorated with the head of the god of the Underworld. To sit in it would be to assume great supernatural power.

► Imported thunder god
Shango, the thunder and lightning god of the Yoruba people of Nigeria, became an important figure in many parts of the Caribbean. He is often represented as he is here by an *oshe*, or double-headed axe.

Taíno, European, and African elements. The most famous example of this mix of cultures is undoubtedly the Haitian belief system called voodoo, also known as Vodou.

Voodoo combines folkloric elements from the indigenous Taíno peoples, African beliefs based on the mythology of peoples such as the Yoruba, Kongo, and Dahomey, and rituals strongly influenced by the Roman Catholicism of the French colonists who first came to the Caribbean in the 17th century. It also features a large number of gods or spirits, known as *loa*, who govern all areas of existence from fertility to death and from elephants to fish. Rituals of the religion are presided over by priestesses as well as priests. The less well-known Santería religion of Cuba displays a similarly rich and complex combination of local and imported beliefs and practices.

A HOST OF SPIRITS

Other parts of the Caribbean developed different blends of these multiple cultures. In Guyana, for example, as well as in many of the island communities of the area, people spoke of a host of malevolent spirits called *jumbees*, spirits that embraced all kinds of beings, including spirits that lived in rivers, malevolent animals, and the spirits of women who died in childbirth. There were also *jumbees* who resembled European creatures like werewolves and vampires. For many people in the region, such spirits were vividly and universally present, exerting a huge influence over their daily lives.

THE FIVE ERAS

The creation story of the Taíno people of the Caribbean island of Hispaniola is unusual in that it describes not only the creation of men and women, but also outlines a series of five historical eras, narrating in brief the history of the people up to the arrival of the European settlers in the 15th century. In addition, there are other myths that describe the activities of the primal humans, as well as how the ocean, fish, moon, trees, and birds came into being.

THE MYTH

The creation of the universe and the people who live in it spanned five eras. At the beginning of the first era, the son of the supreme god Yaya rebelled against his father, and Yaya killed him. The great god placed his son's bones in a huge gourd that he hung up in his house. A few days later, Yaya looked in the gourd and found that the bones had turned into fish swimming in water. Yaya's wife took some of the fish and cooked them, and the pair relished the meal. One day, the gourd broke open—some say it was done by visitors to Yaya's house—and the water poured over the Earth, forming the ocean that surrounds the Caribbean islands.

THE EMERGENCE OF HUMANITY

The second era began when the first people, the Taíno, appeared on Earth. They emerged from one of two caves in Caonao on the island of Hispaniola, and learned to survive by fishing in the sea. But some of those who came out were caught by the sun and transformed into trees because they returned home at dawn. Another man, who was supposed to stand guard at the cave while the others were fishing, was turned into stone by the sun for neglecting his duties. Seeing this, one of the men awoke before dawn, hoping to catch fish before the sun rose, but he was captured by the sun and made into a bird that sings at first light. As time went by, the remaining Taíno left to explore the other islands, and began to cultivate the fertile soil they found there.

A NEW WAY OF LIFE

In the third era, women were created as partners for the men, so that the population could grow, and the people

▲ **Rock drawings**
Taíno petroglyphs (rock carvings), with their strong, graphic outlines, often depict the deities that inhabit the Taíno mythological universe. This image of the Earth goddess Atabey shows her sitting in the position sometimes adopted during childbirth.

became civilized and learned the art of survival. The fourth era saw them spreading across the islands of the Caribbean, founding settlements, and learning how to cultivate cassava, their staple crop. They built villages and developed their eloquent language, living in harmony. For many years all was well, but things changed when the first Europeans arrived in the Caribbean.

The fifth and final era of the Taíno began with the arrival of Christopher Columbus, the European navigator, in 1492. The Taíno saw this event as a disaster, because it led to the destruction of their traditional way of life. The European settlers treated the Taíno cruelly and brought with them new diseases, which led to the extinction of many tribes.

▲ **Taíno symbol**
The outer and inner circles in this seal of one of the Taíno tribes depict the sun and moon respectively.

YAYA AND THE SONS OF ITIBA

Some versions of the story about the creation of the ocean tell how Yaya left the gourd containing the fish unattended one day. It happened that the four sons of Itiba Cahubaba, an Earth mother figure who had died in childbirth, arrived at Yaya's house. When they saw the gourd, they took it down to investigate and ate some of the fish. Suddenly, they heard Yaya returning, and they hurriedly tried to replace the gourd, but it fell to the ground and was smashed, spilling its contents. The four brothers then fled to the home of their grandfather.

THE WATER FROM THE GOURD GUSHED OUT. THIS THEY SAY IS THE ORIGIN OF THE OCEAN.

▲ Fish of the ocean
The fish contained in Yaya's gourd spilled out when it broke. This bounty of the sea became the source of the Taíno's livelihood.

► Taíno gourd
The gourd is both a storage container and a symbol of temptation. Some myths say that the broken gourd became a canoe in which Itiba's sons rowed away.

THE FIRST CREATURES

The Taíno creation story tells how the sun turned various people that came out of a mythical cave into birds, trees, or stone. Birds feature in many Taíno myths; one of the Taíno people is turned into a bird that sings at dawn, and the woodpecker helps make the first women (*see below*). Another myth tells how the hummingbird got its iridescent feathers: a man was once punished for committing incest by being turned into the moon, with its stained face; the hummingbird carried the son of the moon in its beak to show him to his father, so the moon rewarded the bird with its brilliant plumage. Taíno myths also narrate tales of Guayahona, part culture hero and part shaman, who traveled to distant lands in search of the alloy guanin, revered by the Taíno for its golden sheen.

Hummingbird with jewel-like feathers

▲ Cave of origin
The first Taíno emerged from a cave called Ceibajagua. The other Caribbean peoples came out of another cave, and followed different customs.

▲ Guayahona the explorer
The mythical hero Guayahona traveled on many journeys of exploration; on one occasion he persuaded all the women on his island to come away with him.

◄ Caribbean fisherman
Taíno myths often refer to fishing expeditions, since fishing was one of the main occupations of the Taíno, who were also excellent boat builders.

THE CREATION OF WOMEN

The Taíno creation myth explains that the first humans were only men. When returning from fishing one rainy day, the men saw curious creatures falling from the trees. They looked like women but were asexual. Instinctively, the men knew that these creatures were the women they needed, and, having captured them, fastened woodpeckers to their bodies. Thinking them to be trees, the woodpeckers bored openings in them, thus carving out female sexual organs. And so the first women were created.

◄ Woodpecker
The *inriri* or woodpecker, referred to in the myth as the "one who makes holes in the trees," was greatly revered by the Taíno for its role in creating women.

GHEDE

Ghede was an ancient Haitian god of love, sex, and fertility. In Haitian voodoo, Ghede is the god of death, as well as the name for a group of spirits who represent both death and fertility. The concept of the *loa* is essential to voodoo culture. The *loa* are important ancestral spirits who symbolize and influence specific aspects of the natural world. They include the spirit known as Baron, who, according to different voodoo traditions, is either the leader of the spirits or an aspect of Ghede. All these spirits are the focus of a number of Haitian beliefs and rituals concerning the opposite—but linked—themes of death and sexuality.

GHEDE AND SEXUALITY

As a spirit of sexuality, Ghede regards sex as something inevitable, not a matter of good or evil. He has a rapacious sexual appetite, which is mirrored by a healthy craving for food and alcohol, aspects of his character that serve to emphasize the earthy and high-living side of this spirit. Ghede likes to engage in explicit sexual conversation, and holds up for ridicule or embarrassment those people who try to suppress their sexual feelings, or who generally tend to adopt a repressed attitude to sex. He frequently makes erotic jokes and flaunts his sexuality without any inhibition. He is also an embodiment of resurrection and life energy, hence he has potent healing powers, which are believed to be especially effective on children. The sophisticated and stylish Ghede is closely linked to his bumbling, peasant-like younger brother, Azacca, the spirit of agriculture and the patron of farmers, whose ceremonies he often attends.

▲ Followers of Ghede
Ghede is believed to enjoy dancing, and his dance is fast and expressive. During festivals held in Ghede's honor, such as the Day of the Dead, his followers dance in abandon, often swept up into an ecstatic trance.

◄ Black rooster, symbol of Ghede's consort
Ghede is a spirit of death and fertility, and offerings to the god include black roosters, candles, miniature coffins, and sequined bottles containing rum. The black rooster is also one of the symbols of Maman Brigitte, who is Ghede's consort.

► Maman Brigitte's sign
Like Ghede, Maman Brigitte has a strong sexual appetite. In voodoo rituals, designs known as *vevers* are drawn on the earth to invoke the gods. Maman Brigitte's *vever* incorporates a heart and crosses.

BARON SAMEDI

Baron Samedi is the most familiar aspect of the *loa* (ancestral spirit) known as Baron, other incarnations being Baron La Croix and Baron Cimetière. Baron is seen by different traditions as the chief of the Ghede spirits, or as their father, or as the personification of the spirit known as Ghede. He is often portrayed as an elegant figure with a white or skull-like face, black clothes, a white top hat, and dark glasses. He smokes a cigarette in a long holder and carries a cane. Baron Samedi is a "psychopomp," a being who is able to communicate between the worlds of both humans and spirits. He leads the souls of the dead to the Underworld. He is also said to control the zombies—the soulless bodies of the dead —and possesses the power to bring them back to life by restoring their souls.

▲ Baron Samedi
Baron Samedi is portrayed in various ways. Sometimes he wears a large, elaborate hat with the image of a human skull on the front.

▲ Baron Samedi's symbol
Voodoo is a mix of African, Caribbean, and Roman Catholic beliefs, and the cross is prominent in Baron Samedi's *vever*, since he is associated with death.

GHEDE AND DIVINATION

The traditional haunt of Ghede is the crossroads, symbolic of the place where the worlds of the living and dead, of people and spirits, come together. As the spirit who presides over this meeting place, Ghede is believed to have special powers of prophecy and the gift of second sight. People therefore come to the spirit seeking answers to pressing questions, especially those concerning fertility. They make an offering to the spirit and request a priest to ask Ghede questions. The answer comes back in the form of a pattern of drops of rum trickled onto the ground, or in the form of cryptic messages from rolls of a dice or the turning of particular tarot cards. The advice that the spirit gives may often be unpalatable to the supplicants; nevertheless, they believe it to be sound, and give it great respect.

GHEDE SPIRITS

Ghede is also the name for a group of spirits who perform different functions as psychopomp and mediator between the worlds of the living and the dead. They are easily accessible to devotees, and ready with their advice. These spirits have distinct characters and roles. For example, Ghede Nibo takes the form of a young man who died early, perhaps as a result of violence; he is considered to be a guardian of tombs and a protector of people who die young. Ghede Ti Malis is a trickster spirit, whose pranks include tricking people out of food.

► Voodoo flag
Among the objects that are considered essential for voodoo rituals is a sequined flag depicting symbols of Ghede. The unfurling of this flag signals the formal start of the ceremony.

GHEDE

195

▲ **Inca gold plate**

The Incas valued gold as being the sweat of their sun god Inti, but the Spanish conquerors in the 16th century valued it simply as a precious metal and melted down most Incan gold artifacts. This gold plate depicts Inti in all his glory.

SOUTH AMERICA

Although South America produced a number of cultures with different deities and myths, the most enduring civilization was that of the Incas, who were based on the west coast of the continent and in the high Andes.

South America has been home to a succession of highly sophisticated civilizations during the last three millennia. Most of the more advanced cultures were based in the Andes, in the areas now forming parts of Peru, Chile, Bolivia, and Ecuador. Beginning with the Chavin culture (c.850–200 BCE) in northern Peru, there were a number of other empires based in and near Peru, including the Paracas Empire, the Moche culture, and the civilizations of Huari and Tiahuanaco, all between around 600 BCE and about 900 CE.

MYTHICAL THEMES

Although they left substantial physical remains—such as buildings, carvings, pottery, gold jewellery, and textiles—none of these cultures developed a writing system, so little is known in detail about their myths. However, scholars interpret many of the figures in their art as deities, and they are usually described today by their salient features: the Staff God, the Fanged God, the Jaguar God, and so on. Study of later indigenous peoples shows their reverence for ancestor spirits, for deities associated with the local landscape, and for fertility gods.

Local spirits, creator deities, and culture heroes—figures who bring important skills such as farming to the people—are typical of the belief systems of the various peoples of the rest of South America. A further theme that stands out clearly in some of these early cultures is their devotion to the sun. The great gateway at the major archaeological site of Tiahuanaco has a figure that resembles a sun god, and one important Moche temple is believed by experts to be a place where people worshipped the sun.

▶ Silver cob of maize
Skilled Inca metalworkers made this silver model of cobs of corn, which shows how important cultivated maize was to the Incas as a staple food. At a large ceremony during the annual maize harvest in May, young Inca nobles processed through the streets of Cuzco, chanting hymns.

ARRIVAL OF THE INCAS

The Incas, who built up an Andean empire between 1230 and 1532, looked upon Tiahuanaco as one of their places of origin, and, like their forebears, they worshipped the sun. The Incas believed their rulers were descendants of Inti, the sun god. They also had an origin myth based near the city of Cuzco in Peru. A group of ancestors—three brothers and three sisters—emerged from caves near Cuzco and set various precedents for the real Inca rulers, such as wearing gold jewellery, marrying their sisters, and setting up mountaintop shrines.

▲ Deer-headed figure
Animal spirits, as represented by this deer-headed Moche pottery figure, played an important role in traditional South American mythology and religion.

EMPIRE AND GODS

The Incas had a huge empire, stretching all along the western edge of South America from Ecuador to central Chile. Their capital was at Cuzco, but they had other urban centers, such as Machu Picchu. The empire was held together by an advanced bureaucracy and a good road network. Their state religion centered on worship of Inti at a large temple in Cuzco, but the Incas had many other deities, including a creator, Viracocha, a fertility god, Ilyap'a, and a moon goddess, Mama Kilya. Skilled metalworkers, they also gave gold great religious significance. An enduring myth of El Dorado ("the golden man"), well known to the Incas, originated in Colombia, where the initiation ceremony for a new king involved him being covered in gold dust, after which he was taken to the center of a lake and offered more gold to its waters. Such stories gripped the imagination of Spanish conquerors who arrived in the 16th century in search of great riches—and still fascinate people to this day.

INCA BEGINNINGS

In the centuries preceding the Spanish conquest of Peru in the 16th century, the Incas built a vast empire in the Andes mountains of western South America. They had a sophisticated oral culture, and their mythology tells many different tales of their origin, all of which feature an ancestor called Manco Capac who, together with a number of followers, emerges into the world from a cave.

THE MYTH

The Incan creator god, called Con Tiki Viracocha, or simply Viracocha, was one of the most important deities in Incan mythology. In most versions of the creation story, he emerged from the waters of Lake Titicaca to create a race of giants. But he was dissatisfied with these creatures, and so he brought about a great flood called *Unu Pachacuti* that drowned them. Subsequently, he created the first humans out of pebbles that he found beside the lake. He gave these people a variety of languages, costumes, and foods, and then spread them around the world; though some say that Viracocha sent the first humans to a cave to await the appropriate time for emergence. It was believed by some that the cave was at a place called Pacaritambo (Tavern of the Dawn), which is about 16 miles (25km) southwest of modern-day Cuzco. Others believed that the real name of the place was Tambotocco (Tavern of the Windows), because the people had made three ceremonial entrances to the natural cavern.

> ▶ **Manco Capac**
> Like all Incan rulers, Manco Capac was always associated with the sun. Some said he wore a cape of gold during his arrival ceremony in Cuzco.

THE EMERGENCE

Chief among the Andeans was a man called Manco Capac, who dwelt in the cave with his three brothers and three sisters. One of his sisters, Mama Ocllo, was also his wife. Together, they constituted the Incan royal family and became the ancestors of the Incan rulers who followed them. Eventually, a small group of people representing Incan nobility came out of the cave through one of its entrances.

▲ **Cuzco**
The Peruvian city of Cuzco was the Incan capital. Second only to Lake Titicaca, Cuzco and its neighborhood was the most important area in Incan religion, with a number of shrines and sacred sites.

A number of people representing the lower classes of peasants and slaves emerged from the other two entrances to the cave. Then the first Incan settlements were established.

THE PEOPLE AND THE SUN GOD

Some chroniclers of the origin myth told a different version of the story. They said that Manco Capac and the other Incas had been set down by the sun god Inti, on the shores of Lake Titicaca. The deity gave Manco Capac a staff or rod of gold and instructed the people to travel around the region, advising them to plunge the gold rod into the ground whenever they stopped to eat or rest. Inti told them that after traveling for a while, they would arrive at a place where the staff would vanish completely into the ground on being plunged. This would indicate that the soil at that location was deep and fertile, and Inti told Manco Capac to build a grand city at that site. The people followed the sun god's commands and after having wandered for some time, they reached a place where the rod disappeared from view into the ground. The Incas built their capital city of Cuzco not far from this spot, and Manco Capac became the first ruler of the Incan kingdom. Thus began the Incan dynasty.

VIRACOCHA

The Incas believed that after creating humans, Viracocha stayed back to watch over them. The deity disguised himself as a beggar and wandered among the Incas to work miracles, and to teach his people how to live. But most humans did not listen to what the god had told them, and he returned from his trip to Earth in tears. He thought that one day his tears would cause another flood that would destroy all of humanity. This is why masks depicting Viracocha often show tears descending from the god's eyes.

Viracocha gold mask

▼ **Quipu**
The Incas used a device called a quipu, made of lengths of knotted string or leather, to keep records and accounts.

▲ **Machu Picchu**
This mountaintop city is an impressive Incan site. It has a temple with three windows, perhaps recalling the Incan emergence from a three-mouthed cave.

► **Incan pot**
Anthropomorphic pots, brightly glazed and sometimes depicting the heads of deities, were common in Incan pottery.

THE INCAS

Although they did not develop the wheel or a conventional system of writing, the Incas had a sophisticated civilization. Their craftsmen excelled in textiles and pottery, and the Incas were master builders too, constructing stone buildings with walls that fitted together without mortar. The long network of roads built across their Andean territories ensured that the Incas could develop a system of communication to hold the empire together. Their myths acknowledge both their humble beginnings at Lake Titicaca and their aspiration to create a vast empire beneath the rays of the sun god Inti.

PACA MAMA IS MOTHER EARTH, TO WHOM WE ALL MUST RETURN SOME DAY.

DEITIES OF THE SEA AND THE EARTH

In Incan mythology, the sea and the Earth were actually two goddesses. The sea was Mama Cocha (Sea Mother), who was the patron of fishermen and sailors. The Earth was Paca Mama (Earth Mother), who was a very important Incan deity; she was the consort of the sun god Inti, and the people sacrificed llamas in her honor. Some stories in later Incan mythology describe how Paca Mama was married to Pachacamac, the god of fire and rain, and together they created the stars, the sun, the moon, and the world.

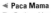

◄ **Paca Mama**
The Earth goddess was seen as a fertility figure and portrayed as a naked woman. A ritualistic sacrifice of her creature, the llama, was made before the Incas first entered Cuzco.

GARCILASO DE LA VEGA

The son of a Spanish conquistador and an Incan princess, Garcilaso de la Vega (1539–1616) spent most of his adult life in Spain, but staunchly defended the culture of his mother's people. In 1609, he published the *Royal Commentaries*, in which he described the Incan culture and way of life; a second volume eight years later told the story of the Spanish conquest of the Incas. His portrayal of Incan life is invaluable because it comes from first-hand knowledge, though his account of the Incan religious beliefs and practices seems to have been distorted by his Christian outlook.

Garcilaso de la Vega

SKY GODS OF THE ANDES

The Incas were known as the people of the sun. Their emperors traced their descent from the sun god Inti, and the deity had pride of place in important temples. But the people also revered a host of other deities of the sky, beings who usually protected the Incas, and ensured that there was enough water for their crops. Occasionally, they also reminded the people of their godly power, with dramatic phenomena such as lightning bolts or eclipses.

INTI

The Incan sun god was called Inti, and was also known as "the leader of the daytime." For the Incas, he was the most important among all their deities. A friendly god, he did not simply look down on the Earth and warm it with his rays, but also actively helped the inhabitants. In one such myth, the Incan ancestors—Manco Capac and Mama Ocllo—were Inti's son and daughter, whom he taught the skills of life and sent to Earth to show the Incas how to live. They then became the ancestors of the Incan dynasty. The Incan rulers built many lavish temples to Inti in Cuzco, the Incan capital, one of which was known as the House of Gold because of its rich decoration. Its main chapel was oriented in such a way that the image of Inti's face caught the light of the rising sun each day. Inti was often depicted as a golden disc with rays of light emanating from it.

▲ **Incan farming**
Incan farmers, who grew a wide range of crops from potatoes to squashes, were especially attached to the thunder god Illapu, and made sacrifices at his altars in the hope of rain.

▲ **Inti motif**
This cotton textile from the early Nazca culture of Peru has a design featuring radiating elements and warm colors that represent the sun god Inti.

▶ **Priestess figure**
Ceremonies in honor of the sun god were performed by specially trained priestesses called *mamaconas* (chosen women), who also acted as concubines of the Incan emperor.

▶ **Intihuantana post**
This structure at Machu Picchu, known as Intihuantana (hitching post of the sun), is thought to have been used for rituals or calendar calculations.

ILLAPU

The Incan thunder god Illapu was a warlike deity whose weapon was the slingshot. One myth describes how he crossed the sky with giant strides, casting a great shadow, which became the Milky Way. He aimed his sling at a pot of water carried by his sister. As he fired, the leather of his sling made a booming noise that was the thunder, and the stone flashed with lightning as it flew through the air. When it hit the pot, rain poured down from the sky. As a bringer of rain, Illapu was widely revered by the Incas. They built temples to the god—usually on mountains to get closer to the sky where Illapu lived—and went there to pray for rain. If the people needed rain desperately, they sometimes made human sacrifices to appease Illapu.

MAMA KILYA

The moon goddess Mama Kilya was the consort and, some say, the sister of Inti. As the sun god's female counterpart, she was seen as the maternal ancestor of the Incan rulers, and presided over the night. During a lunar eclipse, the Incas thought that a monster was taking a bite out of Mama Kilya, and considered this omen to portend disaster—they waved weapons at the sky and made loud noises to frighten the monster away. Mama Kilya was also the goddess of women, guarding them during their monthly cycle, protecting female fertility, and enforcing marriage vows.

▲ **Moon goddess**
The Incas believed that the goddess Mama Kilya watched over them at night, and her large face and big eyes could be seen clearly on the night of a full moon.

▲ **Silver artefact**
Gold was Inti's metal, and silver was Mama Kilya's. Silver objects were made in her honor, and her shrine at Cuzco's main temple was richly decorated with silver.

CHUICHU

The Incas believed that the rainbow was a two-headed, dragon-like deity called Chuichu. They realized there was a connection between the rainbow and the sun, though they did not quite understand how its multicoloured effect was produced. They considered the rainbow to be a gift or message from the sun god Inti, indicating the presence of the benevolent deity Chuichu. Because he linked the world of the gods in the sky with the Earth, Chuichu was thought of as a kind of heavenly messenger or courier, who helped the deities of both the sun and the rain in bringing their life-giving gifts to the Earth. Some people regarded the rainbow god as an even more magical presence that linked the three fundamental parts of the Incan cosmos—the sky, the Earth's surface, and the underground realm.

STAR DEITIES

The Incas considered the stars to be benevolent deities, looking down on them at night just as Mama Kilya did. Unlike some cultures in other parts of the world, who saw the stars as rather randomly scattered across the sky, the Incas identified different star groups or constellations, just as astronomers and astrologers do today. But their groupings of stars had specifically Incan names and identities: they thought of Lyra as the Llama, Scorpio as the Cat, and the Pleiades as the Little Mothers or the Storehouse. Some of these constellations were revered by specific sections of Incan society. For example, the Storehouse was widely worshipped by farmers and growers, because it was said to protect and nurture stocks of seed.

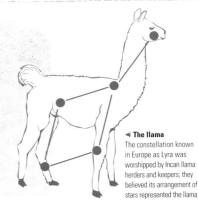

◄ **The llama**
The constellation known in Europe as Lyra was worshipped by Incan llama herders and keepers; they believed its arrangement of stars represented the llama.

OCEANIA

▲ **Aboriginal cave art**
Rock painting has a long history in Australia. Aborigines paint pictures of their
ancestors and early families directly onto rock to form a close link between them
and the land. This example is in Kakadu National Park in the Northern Territory.

AUSTRALIA

The myths of the indigenous people of Australia are diverse and yet share many similarities. They explain and reinforce the bond between the people and the land, which is said to have been brought into being at the very beginning of time.

When the Europeans arrived in Australia at the end of the 18th century, they found a continent inhabited by around 400 different Aboriginal tribes. Each of these tribal groups was small—sometimes just a handful of families, sometimes as many as 50—and each had found a niche in which Australia's sometimes extremely harsh landscape could sustain life. The Aborigines lived by hunting and gathering, and had done so for millennia—no one is sure when people originally came to Australia, though they may have arrived from Indonesia around 50,000 years ago. Although the incoming Europeans saw the indigenous people as "primitive" because they had not developed skills such as metalworking or pottery production, they were in fact very well adapted to living on their land.

▲ **Kangaroo spirit**
This Aboriginal artwork shows a number of ancestor figures, including a prominent kangaroo spirit. Such images reflect the key position of stories of origins and their importance for the identity of the people.

MYTHS OF ORIGIN

Each of Australia's Aboriginal tribes has its own language and its own myths, and for them these stories explain the origins and the very existence of the Aboriginal people. For the Aborigines, the historical, European account of their arrival on the continent many thousands of years ago is largely irrelevant. Instead, their existence in Australia is accounted for by their myths, which describe each tribe's intimate association with the land where it lives and their ancestors' roles in giving form to the land. Unfortunately, because not all of Australia's tribes have survived, some of these myths have been lost. But those that are still known remain central to Aboriginal beliefs, and are constantly retold.

ANCESTRAL JOURNEYS

Although these sets of Aboriginal myths are all different, they share many similarities. They focus on ancestral beings —often animal spirits—who in the beginning made journeys across the country, bringing the land and all its geographical

features into being, bringing to life all the plants, animals, and other living things that inhabit it, and giving life to all the spirits of the place: even to the spirits of people and beings who will be born in the future.

This ancient process of bringing all aspects of the world to life is known as the Dreaming, or Dreamtime, a name that reflects the idea that the ancestor spirits awoke from a long sleep in order to carry out this process of animation, and then subsided into an eternal sleep when they had completed their great task.

STORIES OF THE DREAMTIME

The ancient events of the Dreaming or Dreamtime still exist on a level that can be experienced today. By retelling stories of the Dreamtime, and by carrying out the correct rituals, Aborigines can relive the creative process and achieve a kind of communion with the spirits. In this sense, the Dreamtime is always present. Dreamtime stories consist of journeys across the land, which is criss-crossed with ancient pathways that represent the narratives of different tribes and explain the existence of a variety of natural features, from rocks and mountains to creeks and water holes. Many such sites have profound spiritual meaning, as do the many myths themselves, which are dramatically brought to life in tribal rituals and in artistic depictions.

▶ **Bark painting depicting a Wandjina**
In the Kimberley region of Western Australia, the Wandjina are ancestral creator spirits who also bring life-giving rain. Paintings of such beings are said to embody them and are deeply revered.

THE RAINBOW SNAKE

Known by many names, the Rainbow Snake is an almost universal spirit in the Aboriginal mythology of Australia. He has many roles to play, and in some cultures, even plays a part in the creation of humanity. Two themes stand out in the myths about the Rainbow Snake. One is his ability to bring forth water—which gives life, but can turn into an overwhelming flood that is capable of wiping out entire tribes. The other is his function as a bridge, linking the Earth and the sky, and giving humans access to the wisdom of the spirit world.

ESCAPE FROM THE SNAKE'S BELLY

In western Arnhem Land, the wooded area on the coast of the Northern Territory, the Rainbow Snake is called Ngalyod, and is sometimes portrayed with a pair of slender horns and the tail of a crocodile. Ngalyod was feared for eating humans and known for his foul temper, and in one particular myth, devoured a child who had annoyed him by crying. A popular tale about Ngalyod links him with the creation of humanity. One day, the snake was hungry and ate three birds, one of which was a pewee. As snakes do, he swallowed his prey whole. Once inside the serpent's belly, the birds tried to escape, beginning to peck a hole through Ngalyod's abdomen. The three finally emerged as the first humans, and soon afterwards, killed the Rainbow Snake to set up home on Earth.

◄ **Ngalyod**
The Rainbow Snake is a favorite subject of the artists of Arnhem Land, where he is revered as the presiding spirit of the rainy season, and is also associated with fertility, abundance, and life-giving powers.

▲ **Ngalyod and Yingarna**
In the creation myth of western Arnhem Land, Ngalyod is the son of the primal Dreaming mother, Yingarna, and helps her look after her other children.

◄ **Aboriginal bark painting**
The Aborigines painted images of their myths with natural pigments on bark. Depictions of an individual's spirit land were often painted on the coffin when the person died.

THE INUNDATION

The Djauan people of Arnhem Land tell how a fisherman found the black bones of a fish that other men had eaten. He recognized the bones as those of a rare fish that he had been looking for, and became both angry and sad. The fisherman sang a song to Kurrichalpongo, the black rock snake, and it came down from the sky in a great curving bow of many colors (the Rainbow Snake). The snake made a hole in a billabong (a lake), releasing a great flood over the land that swept away all the neighboring tribes, leaving behind only the Djauan. After this, the snake laid some eggs, which, when they hatched, carved out rivers, hills, and other features of the landscape.

▲ **People and the snake**
The Rainbow Snake was a teacher of shamans and the bringer of water, but according to certain myths, he was also the creator of the first man and woman.

▲ **Aboriginal healers**
Shamans were assisted by the spirits that they contacted when they were engaged in shamanic healing rituals. Here, a healer performs a traditional bloodletting ceremony using an ox horn.

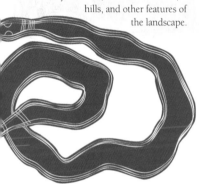

▲ **Black rock snake**
Because of the creature's power to cause floods, the Djauan traditionally ask the black rock snake's permission before taking water from a billabong, or before fishing.

THE END OF THE RAINBOW

The shamans of Aboriginal Australia have always been regarded with respect for their power to heal the sick and to see the future. It was believed that the shamans received their knowledge from the spirits, and different myths describe how they gained this knowledge. These stories usually involvd the shamans traveling to the heavens, sometimes flying through the sky. One version of the myth describe how the shamans journeyed to the sky by traveling up the body of the Rainbow Snake. The voyage up the rainbow took the shamans from the land of the living to the realm of the spirits and ancestors at the end of the Rainbow Snake's body. Here, they dwelled with the spirits for a period of time, receiving instruction in the arts of healing and divination.

TAIPAN

The snake known as Taipan is often identified with the Rainbow Snake. He had awesome power over life and death, and could even control the rain and the thunder. Taipan had a son whom he loved deeply, but one day, his son fell in love with the daughter of Wala, the blue-tongued lizard, and the pair eloped. Wala was angry that his daughter had taken a husband without asking his permission, and so pursued the couple, killing Taipan's son. Distraught over his son's death, Taipan sent most of his family to live in the dark depths of the Earth, and two of his sisters to heaven, where they took some of their dead nephew's blood and added its color to the rainbow.

▲ **Blue-tongued lizard**
The myth describes how the blue-tongued lizard Wala carried the heart and blood of Taipan's son to the grieving Taipan, to show the latter what the lizard had done in his fury.

THE PRIMAL SISTERS

A widespread Aboriginal myth from Australia describes a pair of ancestral sisters, often known as the Wawilak or Wagilag Sisters, who travel across Arnhem Land. They have a traumatic encounter with the Rainbow Snake, seen as a conflict between the male and female entities, which culminates in the snake swallowing the women. The sisters survive, however, and finally escape the snake's stomach to coexist with their arch rival, reinforcing the idea that both male and female forces are needed for creation to be balanced.

THE MYTH

One day, two women walked out of the ocean and stepped onto the shore of Arnhem Land, in Australia's Northern Territory. They were sisters and the elder one was carrying a baby, while the other one was pregnant. The sisters walked inland looking for animals to eat. Both carried spears and were proficient in their use. The sisters were creators, and as they traveled, they gave names and shapes to the landscapes through which they walked—essentially bringing them into existence. They made steady progress until the pregnant sister began to feel apprehensive about her impending delivery. So the sisters set up camp and lit a fire by a water hole at a place called Mirrirmina.

▲ The sisters
The Rainbow Snake encircles the two women, along with their children, in the centerpiece of this painting depicting the myth about the primal sisters.

THE RAINBOW SNAKE'S CREATURES

The elder sister went to hunt for food, while the younger sister lay still and eventually gave birth. But something strange happened when the elder sister came back and began to prepare a meal. All the animals that she had caught and killed leapt out of the cooking pot, ran off, and jumped into the water hole. The sisters did not know that the pool was home to the Rainbow Snake. He owned all the animals in the area, and would not let the sisters eat them. After this had happened a few times, the elder sister went to the pool to investigate. The Rainbow Snake heard her coming and was at last roused from his sleep. He reared up and attacked the two women who had invaded his land, and he swallowed both the sisters and their children.

THE SISTERS RETURN

The Rainbow Snake made a lot of noise doing this; his commotion roused all the other snakes, who asked him what was going on. At first he lied, saying that he had caught and eaten a kangaroo, but they did not believe him. He finally admitted to eating the sisters. Immediately, a mighty wind blew and a monsoon lashed its way across the landscape. The rain and wind were so powerful that the Rainbow Snake was forced to vomit up the sisters and their children onto an ant hill, where they were returned to life.

◀ Ant hill
When the Rainbow Snake vomited the sisters onto the ant hill, the painful and repeated bites of the ants brought the women and their children quickly back to life.

THE SISTERS

The story of the two sisters—often known as the Wawilak Sisters—is told in different versions by the many Aboriginal tribes. However, the common theme in every version of the story is the depiction of a confrontation between opponents of opposite sexes. The primal sisters represent female wisdom—they are praised as accomplished hunters and they have the power to give form to the land. When the Rainbow Snake swallows them, he gains some of their wisdom in the process. Since that time, it has always been the male members of the tribe who look after the traditions of tribal wisdom and lore, and hand them down from one generation to the next.

▶ **Tribal representations**
The sisters are often depicted in carvings used during rituals. The younger sister (on the right) wears a girdle across her chest to strengthen her breasts since she has just given birth.

KUNAPIPI

Certain versions of the story depict the Earth Mother Kunapipi as the mother of the Wawilak sisters. She is also sometimes considered to be an eternal "Old Woman" figure, and the female counterpart to the male Rainbow Snake. Other myths describe her as the creator of men, women, and the animals of the world. Kunapipi asked her followers to paint themselves to show allegiance to specific families or groups. She is also believed by some to have been an ancient wanderer who traveled with a group of primal heroes and heroines. Her wise and creative character represents the feminine side of spirituality.

▲ **Galah parrot**
The Galah parrots painted themselves in a ritual as per Kunapipi's instructions.

▲ **Crocodile**
Another of the ancient family groups that worshipped Kunapipi were the crocodiles, who painted themselves green.

ABORIGINAL DEITIES

There are thousands of deities in Aboriginal mythology, and the common feature among them is that they are thought to be closely connected to the land they cross and bring into existence; this is clearly illustrated in the myths of the Wawilak sisters. Many of the deities are shape-changers, who may take the form of an animal, but can, at the same time, be the ancestors of a human tribe or family. Most are specific to certain regions and rooted in the land, but some, such as the Rainbow Snake, are known all over Australia.

◀ **Wandjina**
The Wandjina are spirits that control fertility and the natural elements. They are depicted with white stripes on their bodies, representing falling rain.

▼ **Sun deities**
According to one myth, the sun is a torch carried across the sky each day by the solar goddess Gnowee, who is looking for her lost son.

RITUALS AND CELEBRATIONS

Aboriginal rituals are performed on many occasions, from the celebration of a birth to the burial of the dead. Other ceremonies—attended by the whole tribe—can retell in song and dance the stories of the spirits of Dreamtime. A few rituals are thought to have been first performed by the primal sisters to keep the Rainbow Snake at bay. The rituals show how all of creation is linked together by the ancestors.

Painting of an Aboriginal ceremony

THE BRAM-BRAM-BULT

A number of Aboriginal myths center around pairs of brothers. One such story describes the adventures of two ancestors, Yuree and Wanjel, who are also known as the Bram-Bram-Bult. Their myth not only explains how the brothers name and bring to life the different features of the Australian landscape, but also narrates their encounters with deadly rivals, including an echidna spirit called Wembulin who the brothers fight and kill to avenge their nephew's death.

THE MYTH

There was once a great spirit called Doan, a powerful hunter who had taken the form of a small gliding possum. One day, he began hunting a mighty kangaroo called Purra. The chase went on for many miles, but the kangaroo continued to elude Doan. The possum had almost caught up with Purra when he entered the territory of an echidna spirit called Wembulin, who was resting with his two daughters. Wembulin attacked Doan, and although at first the possum managed to escape, he was eventually caught and killed. Wembulin and his daughters ate Doan and set off in pursuit of the kangaroo.

THE BROTHERS' REVENGE

Doan's two maternal uncles, Yuree and Wanjel, were brave warriors who had won renown for their many adventures. They were very fond of their nephew, and when Doan went missing they set off to look for him. As they searched they found a colony of ants carrying strands of a possum's hair and bits of its flesh to their nest, and the brothers began to suspect that their nephew had been killed. Soon they came to the place where Wembulin had attacked Doan, where they found the

> ▶ **Carved figure**
> Australian Aboriginal art is rich in carved figures. According to the Bram-Bram-Bult myth, Yuree carved a figure resembling Wanjel out of wood, bringing his brother back to life.

remains of his body and signs of a tremendous struggle all over the ground. The two brothers started off in pursuit of the echidna to avenge their nephew's death. Being highly accomplished trackers they soon found his trail and followed it tenaciously, finding Wembulin and his family on the third day. The brothers launched a surprise attack and killed the echidna; they then took his two daughters as their wives.

THE WORK OF CREATION

On the journey home Yuree and Wanjel began to regret marrying the echidna sisters. They saw that the pair were angry at their father's death and seemed likely to take revenge. So the brothers killed their wives and set off into the countryside. As they traveled, they brought the world around them into existence, by naming all the plants, rocks, trees, and rivers of the region, gradually transforming a chaotic void into a vibrant landscape.

As time went by, Yuree and Wanjel completed the task of creation and undertook a series of adventures that culminated in Wanjel's death. However, the resourceful Yuree revived him and the two brothers began a long journey from which they never returned. Some accounts say that they live on as Castor and Pollux, the two bright stars of the constellation of Gemini.

▲ **Killing Wembulin**
After tracking Wembulin for three days, the two brothers found the echidna sleeping. They crept up on him silently and killed him.

AUSTRALIA

210

KEY CHARACTERS

Like most characters in the Aboriginal stories of Dreamtime, some in the myth of the Bram-Bram-Bult take the form of animals, though they are seen as eternal spirits. Some of these spirits are the ancestors of the people who told the story, and are therefore assigned supernatural roles. Thus, although no ordinary possum can kill a kangaroo, Doan could chase Purra because he is playing out an incident in the lives of the ancestors. However, in spite of the power and energy of Doan and Wembulin, the story's true heroes are Yuree and Wanjel, who are admired for their bravery and resourcefulness.

▲ Purra
In the Bram-Bram-Bult, the mighty Purra is the prey of a hunter. However, in many other Australian myths, the kangaroo is a hero and an ancestor spirit.

▲ Doan
A creature of remarkable strength for his size, Doan's speed in the hunt is perhaps inspired by a gliding possum's ability to move effortlessly through the air.

THE SOUTHERN CROSS

The night sky plays an important role in Aboriginal myths, including the story of the Bram-Bram-Bult. During one of their exploits, the brothers stopped a ferocious emu called Tchingal from attacking a man named Bunya—they transformed the man into a possum and killed the emu with their spears. The constellation of the Southern Cross, often associated with the brothers, is believed to represent the emu, the possum, and the spears used to kill Tchingal.

➤ Southern Cross
The Aboriginal people of the northwest coast saw the four "pointer" stars of the Southern Cross as symbolizing the origin of fire, a very vital resource.

> WE ARE ALL VISITORS TO THIS TIME, THIS PLACE... OUR PURPOSE HERE IS TO OBSERVE, TO LEARN, TO GROW, TO LOVE AND THEN WE RETURN HOME.
>
> Australian Aboriginal proverb

THE DEATH OF WANJEL

At the end of the story of the Bram-Bram-Bult, Wanjel was bitten by a poisonous snake called Gertuk. Yuree tried hard to save him, but the snake's venom killed his brother. So Yuree took a tree trunk and carved it into a figure resembling Wanjel, and then magically gave it life. After reviving Wanjel, Yuree taught him to walk and talk, and the two brothers continued on their travels. They finally reached the end of the country and made their home in a cave. After their death, the Bram-Bram-Bult ascended to the sky, where many believe they continue to live on as a pair of stars.

◄ Gertuk
Venomous snakes such as the one that bit Wanjel are found all over Australia. In certain versions of the myth, the snake called Gertuk was actually a mopoke, a small spotted owl of Australia.

SIBLING PAIRS

Pairs of siblings, especially brothers, are quite common in the Aboriginal myths of Australia. These range from close, devoted brothers like Yuree and Wanjel, to contrasting brothers with opposite characters, who are often in conflict with each other. One such myth describes how a flood is unleashed when two brothers fight over the ownership of water. One of the brothers prudently stores all the water he finds in a leather bag, while the other does not. When the second brother is thirsty, he upsets his brother's bag, making the water spill out and causing a great flood.

➤ Aboriginal bark painting
Sibling pairs are commonly portrayed on Aboriginal bark paintings. One such pair is the Warti-kutjara (the Iguana Men), who rescue a woman from an attack, and later ascend to the sky.

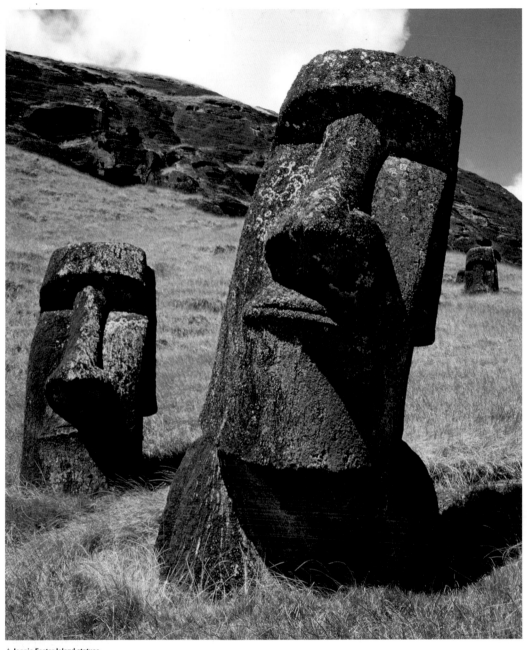

▲ **Iconic Easter Island statues**
There are around 600 large stone heads on Easter Island, some of them almost
65ft (20m) high. Many stand on stone burial platforms known as *ahu*. The heads
probably represent ancestors, although their exact significance is not known.

POLYNESIA

Living on a group of islands thinly spread over an enormous area, the peoples of Polynesia have countless gods and myths, many of which eloquently show their awareness of their beautiful but dangerous marine environment.

The many small Pacific islands that make up Polynesia are mainly spread around the vast triangle defined by Easter Island, Hawaii, and New Zealand. Many archeologists also include in the group the Melanesian islands to the east—the band extending roughly from the Caroline Islands in the northwest to Vanuatu in the southeast—because they share many cultural similarities. The most likely reason for these similarities is that groups of settlers from the Philippines and eastern Indonesia passed through Melanesia on their way to the islands of Polynesia. These migrations probably took place over hundreds of years some time before 1000 BCE.

EARLY VOYAGES

Amazingly, people originally reached these tiny, remote islands by sailing simple dug-out canoes—and, later, plank-built vessels—that were stabilized with outriggers. Although these early navigators developed efficient paddles and sails, they still had to travel the open ocean without compasses or any other navigational aids. To work out which direction they were going in they must have relied instead mainly on the positions of the stars, on wave patterns, and on the prevailing winds. But little is known for sure about how they navigated or whether, once they had reached an island after a voyage of hundreds of kilometers, they were able to return to their homelands again.

▲ **Clan ancestor figure**
This wooden female ancestor figure is one of a number covering the wall of a Maori clan meeting house built in Manutuke on New Zealand's North Island in 1842.

◄ **Supreme Hawaiian deity**
This 19th-century wooden statue represents the supreme Hawaiian creator called Tu or Ku. This powerful god was also a god of war, weather, and plant and animal fertility.

Unsurprisingly, the mythology of these Pacific island peoples contains many stories of voyages. Polynesian heroes traveled not only across the ocean but also to the sun, to the sky, and to the Underworld, where they found fire and brought it back for the people to use. Other traveling deities include gods of fishing, such as Ndauthina of Fiji. His mother tied burning reeds on his head when he was a child and ever after he traveled across the coral reefs, spreading his light across the sea.

ABANDONED HERO

The culture hero and trickster Maui is widely known across Polynesia, where he is also associated with the sea. He was said to have been abandoned as a baby, when his mother threw him into the ocean. Closely linked to the water for the rest of his life, he went fishing and caught land instead of fish. Maui did this using his magical weapon, which was made from the jawbone of an ancestor goddess. He levered up the land with the point of the bone, but when his brothers saw what he had done they kicked up all the land and threw it around the sea, bringing the islands of Polynesia into existence.

STORIES OF THE FLOOD

Maui was in his element in the water, but Polynesian myths also reveal the great dangers of the sea. Hawaii, for example, has a flood myth in which a goddess rose up from the depths to create a giant tsunami, or tidal wave. The resulting flood caused great destruction, but the hero Nu'u built himself a boat in which to escape. Melanesian islands have a similar story in which a hero called Qat escaped a flood in his boat. As is so often the case, the myths of the Pacific island peoples show both their great respect for the dangers of their environment and their ability to cope with them.

TANGAROA

One of the most prominent deities of the Pacific islands is Tangaroa (also known as Ta'aroa or Tagaroa). He is considered to be a sea god in some places, but in Tahiti and among the other island communities, including Samoa, Tonga, and Tuvalu, Tangaroa is known as the creator of the cosmos and all its inhabitants. Some people believe that he was the son of the primal deities Rangi and Papa, but another version of the myth says that he created the universe after tearing apart the two halves of a great shell when emerging from it.

THE MYTH

Long before the world was made, and before even the gods came to control the universe, nothing existed except an endless void, floating within which was a great shell. This was called Rumia, and was shaped like an egg. There was darkness everywhere and nothing could be seen, not even the solitary floating shell. But inside the shell, something was stirring. It was Tangaroa, the creator. He had no father or mother, and no other gods lived with him in the shell. He had brought himself to life and was biding his time before bringing the world into being.

THE SKY AND THE EARTH

At last, Tangaroa began to move. Pushing against the inside of the shell, he heaved until the walls of the shell broke in two. Upon emerging, Tangaroa shouted, "Is there anyone there?" But there was no reply—all around him was only darkness and silence. Subsequently, Tangaroa set about the task of creation. First he took one half of the broken shell and lifted it up to make the great arch of the sky. Next he took the other half and laid it below, to make the ground. Then he looked

> ► **The sea god**
> Since Tangaroa created the other gods from his own body, he is frequently depicted giving birth to the gods who crawl over his body.

around and saw that nothing else but his body was left to be used for the task of creation. So Tangaroa took his own flesh and made the soil on the ground. The god made use of his backbone to create a mountain range and from his inner organs he made the clouds in the sky. Tangaroa even used the nails of his fingers and toes to give shells and scales to the creatures in the sea.

POPULATING THE EARTH

Then Tangaroa called forth the other gods from within him. They began to emerge, and one in particular—the craftsman god Tu—helped Tangaroa continue the process of creation. The pair worked together to make the trees and animals that populated the Earth. Then they made the first humans, who were called Til and Hina, and persuaded them to approach one another to procreate.

Tangaroa saw that everything he had created had a shell, just as he had had one in the beginning. The sky was the shell that contained the sun, the moon, and the stars. The Earth too was a shell; it was an enormous container for all the rocks, rivers, and lakes, and for the plants that grew on its surface and the animals that walked on it. Even human beings had their shells; the wombs of women were the shells from which new life was born.

◄ **The seal deity**
An Easter Island myth relates how the god Tangaroa landed on the island in the form of a seal with a human face and voice.

TANGAROA IN NEW ZEALAND

In New Zealand, Tangaroa is the Maori god of the sea and the son of the primal deities Papa (the goddess of the Earth) and Rangi (the god of the sky). At the beginning of time, Papa and Rangi held each other tight, locking their children within their embrace, but Tangaroa and some of his siblings wrenched them apart to initiate the process of creation. This angered his brother Tawhirimatea, the wind god, who unleashed fierce storms on them. Terrified, some of Tangaroa's descendants hid in the forest. Tangaroa quarreled with his brother Tane, the god of forests, for having given shelter to the runaway creatures. He attacked Tane's land with his tides and swept away all the creatures into his watery realm.

▲ **Yam**
Certain nights of the lunar month were named after Tangaroa. It was believed that the yams planted on these "Tangaroa nights" would produce the best roots.

► **Maori canoe**
The people of the forest made offerings to Tangaroa before setting out in their canoes, since they were entering the realm of Tane's mortal enemy.

◄ **Pele**
The goddess of the volcano, Pele was believed to have created the entire Hawaiian archipelago, but her scorching lava also made her a deity of destruction, who would erupt whenever someone broke a taboo.

▲ **Kukailimoku**
The consort of Hina, and a form of the god Ku (also know as Tu), Kukailimoku was the god of war, woodlands, and crops. He was widely worshipped by craftsmen in Hawaii.

► **Papatuanuku**
Mother Earth, or Papatuanuku, was the female half of the primal couple. When she raised her arm during her long embrace with her husband, Rangi, she gave her children their first glimpse of sunlight.

POLYNESIAN DEITIES

Tangaroa is one of the oldest Polynesian deities, and in some myths, the primary god. Many of the Polynesian deities were worshipped as sky gods, whose forces were unleashed in the form of storms or hurricanes, as in the case of the wind god Tawhirimatea. According to some myths, Tangaroa's son Maui slowed down the sun by lassoing it, and forced it to shine for longer periods in summer. The goddess Hina controlled the tides, and in some versions, was also the goddess of the west wind. There were many powerful Earth deities too, such as the volcano goddess Pele, who was dominant in Hawaii. Other deities included the mother goddess, known variously as Papatuanuku, or Papa, who was present at the beginning of creation.

OTHER POLYNESIAN CREATION MYTHS

Several creation stories told in the Pacific islands feature Maui, who created the islands of Polynesia by fishing them up from the bottom of the sea using a great fish-hook. Some creation myths center on a primal goddess in the Underworld who plucked the first gods and humans from her own body. Others describe a series of sexual unions, beginning with the coupling of light and dark, which engendered everything in the cosmos. Still other stories describe how the islands were formed from the discarded wood chips of the carpenter son of the sky god Tagaloa. However, most myths regard Tangaroa as the creator deity and patron of sailors.

▲ **Rongorongo tablets**
The mysterious hieroglyphic inscriptions on the wooden tablets discovered at Easter Island may record an as yet unknown creation myth.

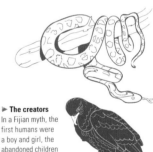

► **The creators**
In a Fijian myth, the first humans were a boy and girl, the abandoned children of the hawk Turukawa. The snake god Degei brought them up and they came together to create the human race.

O TANGAROA IN THE IMMENSITY OF SPACE, CLEAR AWAY THE CLOUDS BY DAY.

Dennis Kawaharada, *1992 Voyage: Sail to Rarotonga, 1992*

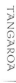

THE ORIGIN OF DEATH

The Maori story of the origin of death involves their forest god Tane. He is one of the sons of the primal deities Rangi and Papa, who had only male children. Tane brings death into the world by breaking a taboo, when, after making a wife for himself out of sand and clay, he goes on to marry his own daughter, the beautiful Hine-titama (Dawn Maiden). It is a sad story, because in many ways Tane, a god who plants the first trees, is a friend of humanity, and yet it is he who becomes the bringer of death.

THE MYTH

Tane's story starts at the beginning of time when there were few gods and no people in the world. Tane spent his time tending to his forests. He faced a great deal of difficulty at first due to improper planting of trees, but eventually they began to flourish. When the trees started growing successfully, Tane no longer had enough to do and became lonely. He wanted a wife, but did not know where to look, because all the children of Rangi and Papa, the primal couple, were male. He first turned to his mother but she rejected him; then he took a number of partners, but their offspring turned out to be reptiles, stones, and streams. This did not please Tane at all, and he wondered how he could find a partner who would satisfy him.

▲ **Hine-nui-te-po.**
The Queen of the Underworld was the goddess of death and of the night, and brought death to all humans, no matter how hard they tried to avoid it.

and, while talking to the local people, happened to mention that she did not know the name of her father. They told her that she was, in fact, Tane's daughter. This revelation shocked and ashamed her so much that she fled to the gloomiest place in the universe—the Underworld, which was also known as the kingdom of Po, or darkness. After some time, Tane realized that his young wife was missing, so he began to look for her everywhere and finally heard her singing. It was a very melancholic song, and its words were "Are you Tane, my father?" Tane realized that Hine-titama had come to know the truth. He knew that her voice was coming from the Underworld, but he could not enter the dark realm—he was prevented from doing so by Hine-titama herself.

MAKING A WIFE

Finally, Tane went to a beach, mixed together some mud and sand, and shaped the mixture into a woman. He stood by her and breathed life into her, and gave her a name—Hine-hau-one (Earth-formed Maiden). After the two lay together, Hine-hau-one gave birth to a daughter called Hine-titama (Dawn Maiden). Hine-titama did not know who her father was, and when she grew up, Tane made her his wife as well. One day, she went to a village

THE COMING OF DEATH

Soon Hine-titama called out to Tane. She told him to stay in the world of light above the ground and be a good father to her children, and to let her remain in the Underworld. She said she would reach out and drag her children down to the dark realm when their time came. From that point on, all humans and animals have had to die. So it was that death came into the world, and the Dawn Maiden from then on became Hine-nui-te-po, the Great Goddess of Darkness.

TANE

As the forest god, Tane gave humanity the gifts of wood and plant fiber, enabling people to make many useful things. But when he planted the first trees, things did not go smoothly. Tane saw the trees as human in form, with their branches as "legs" and their roots as "hair." So he planted them upside-down, with their roots waving in the air, and they did not grow. Then he remembered his stance from when he and his brother, Tangaroa, pushed Rangi and Papa apart at the time of creation, and planted the trees the right way, so that they could take root. Among Tane's other gifts to humanity were light, in the form of the sun and the moon.

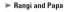

MAUI IN THE UNDERWORLD

The trickster Maui was a mortal but he did not want to die, and so he decided to trick Hine-nui-te-po, the goddess of death. Maui's mother had told him that if a person could crawl through the body of the goddess, then that person would not die. Moreover, the goddess would die herself, and death would be banished for good. One day, Maui came across Hine-nui-te-po when she was asleep. Delighted, he climbed inside the goddess's body, and this made all his friends burst out laughing. One creature, the fantail bird, laughed so much that the sound woke Hine-nui-te-po, and the enraged goddess crushed Maui inside her before he could escape through her mouth. As a result, Maui died and the goddess of death continued her reign.

◀ **Gateway to the Underworld**
The Maori myths describe the process of dying as "creeping into the womb of Sleeping Mother Death," so the gateway to the Underworld is seen as the entrance to Hine-nui-te-po's body, the dark interior of the Earth.

▶ **Maui**
Maui was a great trickster-hero. One Maori myth tells how he hauled up a massive fish from the ocean floor. The fish later became the North Island of New Zealand, which is roughly fish-shaped.

LET THE WATERS BE SEPARATED, LET THE HEAVENS BE FORMED, LET THE EARTH BE.

Maori creation chant

MYTHS OF THE STARS

The Maori gave names and human attributes to the stars and linked them with their deities. For instance, the alignment of the stars of the Matariki (Tiny Eyes), Tautoru (Orion's belt), and Takurua (Sirius) at the end of the year was such that to the Maori they represented the signpost of the goddess of death, rising from the Underworld. Constellations like the Matariki, also known as the Pleiades, were believed to watch over the Earth, and were always seen as a harbinger of a time of plenty.

◀ **The Matariki**
Some myths claim that this star cluster comprises Matariki and her six daughters, who assist the sun on its journey southward.

INDEX

France 71, 72, 80
Freud, Sigmund 43
Freyja 59, 60, 62, 87
Freyr 59, 60
Frigg 60, 63
Fu Xi 131
Funzi 161

G

Ga-gorib 171
Gaia 14, 15, 16, 18, 30, 31, 33
Galahad, Sir 80, 81
Galatea 33
Gamab 171
Ganesh 115
Ganges, River 118, 119
Ganymede 20
Garcilaso de la Vega 199
Garuda 114, 117
Gauna 171
Gawain, Sir 71, 81, 159
Gayomart 102, 103
Geats 68
Geb 144, 147, 150
geese 99
Genghis Khan 99
Geoffrey of Monmouth 71
Germany 57, 72, 80
Gertuk 211
Geryon 36
Gesar Khan 108–9
Ghede 194–5
Ghede Nibo 195
Ghede Ti Malis 195
giants
    Greek 16, 19
    Norse 61
    Northern European 58, 61
Gigantomachia 16
Gilgamesh 93, 96–7
Ginnungagap 58
Glaucus 27
Glittering World 178
Glooscap 159
Gnowee 209
goats 117
Golden Age 23
Golden Fleece 50, 51
Gorgons 40
Graces, Three 21

Gradlon Meur 77
Grail, Holy 71, 80, 81
Greek myths 9, 13–51
Green Knight 71
Grendel 68, 69
Grid 61
Gronw Pebyr 78
Gu 153
Guan Yin 133
Guayahona 193
Gucumatz 184, 185
Guinevere, Queen 71, 80, 81
Gunab 171
Guyana 191
Gwydion 78

H

Hachiman 107, 139
Hadad 111
Hades 16, 17, 18, 21, 32, 34–5, 40
Haiti 191, 194–5
Han Hsiang Tzun 133
Hanuman 63, 126
Harmonia, Queen of Thebes 28
Harmonia (daughter of Aphrodite) 32
Harpies 50
Hathor 87, 143, 144, 150
Haurvatat 103
Hawaii 213, 215
hawks 215
Hayk 158
Heart of Sky 184, 185, 189
Hebe 18, 21
Hecate 35
Hector 44, 45, 159
Hel 34, 61
Helen of Troy 44, 45
Helios 14, 48, 49
hens 155
Hephaestus 17, 18, 22, 25, 30, 31, 32, 33, 40, 53
Hera 16, 18, 21, 25, 28, 29, 33, 44, 45
Heracles 13, 21, 23, 36–7, 50, 51, 107
Hermes 19, 21, 24, 28, 33, 35, 40, 45, 46, 53
Hermod 61

Hero Twins 184–6, 189
heroes 158–9
Hesperides 15, 36
Hestia 16, 18, 52
Hina 214, 215
Hinduism 115–27, 137
Hine-hau-one 216
Hine-nui-te-po 216, 217
Hine-titama 216
Hippolyta 36
Hippolytus 27
hippopotamuses 148
Hiruko 136
Hispaniola 192
Hittites 93, 101
Hlakanyana 173
Ho Hsian Ku 133
Höd 60, 63
Hoenir 59
Holy Grail 71, 80, 81
Homer 27, 33, 44, 45, 46–9
horses
    Celtic myths 79
    Greek myths 27
    Norse myths 59
    Pegasus 41
    Rakhsh 105
    Tibetan myths 108, 109
    Trojan horse 44
Horus 143, 147, 148–9, 150
Howler-Monkey Gods 185
Hrothgar, King of Denmark 68
Huangdi (Yellow Emperor) 131
Huari 197
Humbaba 96, 97
Hun Hunahpu 184, 185
Hunahpu 184–6
Hundred-Handed Giants 14, 15, 16, 33
hunter-gatherers 171
Hydra 36, 37
Hylas 50
Hyperion 14, 15, 49

I

Iapetus 17, 19
Iatiku 181
Ibn al-Kalbi 111
Iceland 58

Idun 61
Iguana Men 211
Ilankaka 162, 163
Iliad 33, 44, 45
Illapu 200
Ilma 64
Ilmarinen 64, 65, 66
Ilya 88
Ilyap'a 197
Immortals, Eight 133
Inanna 87, 93, 96, 97
Inari 139
Incas 9, 197, 198–201
Indonesia 213
Indra 101, 106, 115, 116, 127
Ino 51
Inti 8, 197, 198, 199, 200, 201
Io 20
Ireland 71, 74–5
Isfandiyar, Prince 105
Ishtar 87, 93, 96
Isis 144, 147, 148–9, 150
Islam 101, 110
Ismene 42
Ithaca 48
Itiba Cahubaba 193
Itonde 163
Itzamna 185
Izanagi 136, 137, 138, 139
Izanami 35, 136, 137, 138, 139

J

jackals 143, 151
Jade Emperor 131, 132–3, 134, 135
Jaguar God 197
jaguars 185, 189
Janaka, King 124
Japanese myths 129, 136–9
Jason 13, 50–51
Jiu Tian Xuannü 131
Jocasta 42, 43
Jormungand 61
Joru 108, 109
Jotunheim 58
Joukahainen 64
Joyce, James 49
jumbees 191

Juno 52, 54
Jupiter 13, 52, 73

K

Kagutsuchi 136, 139
Kaikeyi 124
Kalevala 57, 64–7
Kali 106
Kalki 123
Kama 86
kami 137, 139
kangaroos 205, 211
Karnak 145
Kazantzakis, Nikos 49
Khepri 143, 147
Khoikhoi people 171
Khshathra Vairya 103
Kikuyu people 166, 169
Killer of Enemies 179
Kingu 94, 95
Kintu 159
Kitab al-Asnam 111
Knights of the Round Table 71, 80, 81
Kojiki 139
Kom people 155
Kongo people 191
Kotcimanyako 181
Kranyatz 89
Krishna 115, 123
Ku 213
Kukailimoku 215
Kullervo 66, 67
Kumbhakarna 127
Kunapipi 209
Kundry 81
Kurent 89
Kurkar 108, 109
Kurma 123
Kurrichalpongo 207
Kusa-nada-pime 138
Kwammang-a 172

L

labyrinths 39
Lachesis 15

ACKNOWLEDGMENTS

The publisher would like to thank the following for their kind permission to reproduce their photographs:

(Key: a-above; b-below/bottom; c-center; f-far; l-left; r-right; t-top)

1 Alamy Images: Deco (c). 7 The Bridgeman Art Library: Musee de l'Homme, Paris, France (tr). 8 Dorling Kindersley: Judith Miller Image Archive (tl). 10 The Bridgeman Art Library: Museum of Fine Arts, Boston, Massachusetts, USA/Gift in honour of Edward W. Forbes from his friends (l). 12 The Art Archive: Museo della Civilta Romana Rome/Gianni Dagli Orti. 13 4Corners: SIME/Johanna Huber (tr). The Trustees of the British Museum (b). 15 Alamy Images: Interfoto Pressebildagentur (br). Photo SCALA, Florence: (l, tr). 16 akg-images: Erich Lessing (b). 17 The Bridgeman Art Library: Whitworth Art Gallery, The University of Manchester, UK (b). 18 Photo SCALA, Florence: BPK, Berlin (b). 19 The Bridgeman Art Library: Kunsthistorisches Museum, Vienna, Austria (t); Musee Massey, Tarbes, France/Lauros/Giraudon (r). 20 RMN: Hervé Lewandowski (tr). 21 The Bridgeman Art Library: Kunsthistorisches Museum, Vienna, Austria (b). Photo SCALA, Florence: Courtesy of the Ministero Beni e Att. Culturali (r). 22 Ancient Art & Architecture Collection: (b). The Bridgeman Art Library: Prado, Madrid, Spain/Index (r). 23 The Bridgeman Art Library: Galleria Palatina, Palazzo Pitti, Florence, Italy (t); Greek Museo Capitolino, Rome, Italy (c). 24 akg-images: Erich Lessing (br). iStockphoto.com: Volkan Ersoy (t). 25 The Bridgeman Art Library: Staatliche Museen, Berlin, Germany (b). Dorling Kindersley: Peter Wilson (t). 27 The Bridgeman Art Library: Musee du Petit Palais, Avignon, France/Peter Willi (t). 28 akg-images: Rabatti Dominige (t). The Bridgeman Art Library: Musee des Arts Decoratifs, Saumur, France/Lauros/Giraudon (b). 29 akg-images: (cr). 30 The Trustees of the British Museum: (br). Dorling Kindersley: Nick Nicholls/The British Museum (bl). 31 Corbis: Summerfield Press (c). 33 akg-images: Erich Lessing (bl). Corbis: Mimmo Jodice (c). Getty Images: The Bridgeman Art Library (tl). 34 The Bridgeman Art Library: Museo Regional de Oaxaca, Mexico/Giraudon (tr). 35 Alamy Images: The London Art Archive (cl). The Bridgeman Art Library: Private Collection/The Fine Art Society, London, UK (c). 36 The Trustees of the British Museum: (tr). 37 akg-images: (cr). The Bridgeman Art Library: Musee des Beaux-Arts, Angers, France/Lauros/Giraudon (c). 38 akg-images: Erich Lessing (br). The Bridgeman Art Library: The Dayton Art Institute, Dayton, Ohio, USA/Museum purchase with funds provided by the James F. Dicke Family in memory of Timothy M. Webster (t). 39 The Bridgeman Art Library: Archaeological Museum of Heraklion, Crete, Greece/Lauros/Giraudon (c). 40 akg-images: Peter Connolly (c). 41 The Bridgeman Art Library: Museumslandschaft Hessen Kassel/Ute Brunzel (c). Corbis: Christie's Images (cl). 42 The Bridgeman Art Library: Prado, Madrid, Spain/Index (l). 43 The Bridgeman Art Library: Christie's Images (c). Corbis: Bettmann (br). 44 Ancient Art & Architecture Collection: (bl). 45 akg-images:

Erich Lessing (tc). Ancient Art & Architecture Collection: C. M. Dixon (br). 47 The Bridgeman Art Library: Leeds Museums and Galleries (City Art Gallery) UK (cr). 48 The Bridgeman Art Library: Johnny van Haeften Gallery, London, UK (c). 49 PENGUIN and the Penguin logo are trademarks of Penguin Books Ltd: (br). The Art Archive: Civiche Racc d'Arte Pavia Italy/Alfredo Dagli Orti (cl); Museo Capitolino Rome/Alfredo Dagli Orti (bc). 50 Corbis: The Art Archive (bl). 51 The Bridgeman Art Library: Louvre, Paris, France (cb). 52 The Bridgeman Art Library: Louvre, Paris, France (bc). Corbis: Larry Lee Photography (tr). 53 RMN: Jean-Gilles Berizzi (c). 54 The Art Archive: Musée Archéologique Naples/Alfredo Dagli Orti (c). 55 The Bridgeman Art Library: Private Collection/Johnny Van Haeften Ltd., London (tl). Werner Forman Archive: Museo Capitolino , Rome (br). 56 The Bridgeman Art Library: Royal Library, Copenhagen, Denmark. 57 Getty Images: Robert Gibb (bl). Werner Forman Archive: Statens Historiska Museum, Stockholm (tr). 58 TopFoto.co.uk: (t). 59 Dorling Kindersley: Alan Hills/The British Museum (c). Werner Forman Archive: Statens Historiska Museet, Stockholm (b). 60 TopFoto.co.uk: The Granger Collection (c). 61 akg-images: (c). The Bridgeman Art Library: Private Collection/The Stapleton Collection (r). 62 akg-images: (r). Werner Forman Archive: Statens Historiska Museum, Stockholm (l). 63 Alamy Images: The London Art Archive (c). 64 Alamy Images: Esa Hiltula (cr). 66 akg-images: (cr, tr). 67 akg-images: (tr). Getty Images: AFP (br). 69 akg-images: British Library (br). The Trustees of the British Museum: (bl). Dorling Kindersley: The British Museum (c). 70 The Bridgeman Art Library: Bradford Art Galleries and Museums, West Yorkshire, UK. 71 akg-images: Erich Lessing (b). TopFoto.co.uk: EE Images/HIP (c). 72 Werner Forman Archive: National Museum, Copenhagen. 73 Corbis: Weatherstock (bl). The Art Archive: Musée des Antiquités St Germain en Laye/Gianni Dagli Orti (t). TopFoto. co.uk: C. M. Dixon/HIP (br). 74 Mary Evans Picture Library: (bl). 75 The Stapleton Collection: (bc, cl). 76 akg-images: (c). 77 Alamy Images: Christian Darkin (b). 78 Alamy Images: Ivy Close Images (c). 79 Alamy Images: The Photolibrary Wales (c). 80 The Bridgeman Art Library: Private Collection/Christopher Wood Gallery, London, UK. 81 akg-images: (bl). The Bridgeman Art Library: Birmingham Museums and Art Gallery (cr); Bradford Art Galleries and Museums, UK (tl). 82 The Bridgeman Art Library: Nationalmuseum, Stockholm, Sweden. 83 Alamy Images: isifa Image Service s.r.o. (c). The Bridgeman Art Library: Private Collection/Archives Charmet (b). 84 The Bridgeman Art Library: Private Collection/Archives Charmet (l). 85 akg-images: (b). The Bridgeman Art Library: Bibliotheque des Arts Decoratifs, Paris, France/Archives Charmet (br). 86 Mary Evans Picture Library: (tr). The Art Archive: Musée du Louvre Paris/Gianni Dagli Orti (bl). 87 The Art Archive: Private Collection/Eileen Tweedy (tr). 89 Alamy Images: Pat Behnke (br). Corbis: KazumasaTakahashi/amanaimages (t). Getty Images: Tim Rand (bl). 90 Corbis: Araldo de Luca. 92 Ancient

Art & Architecture Collection: 93 Corbis: Nik Wheeler (t). Dorling Kindersley: Alan Hills and Barbara Winter/The British Museum (b). 94 The Art Archive: Musée du Louvre Paris/Gianni Dagli Orti (c). 95 akg-images: isifa Image Service s.r.o (bc). Corbis: Nik Wheeler (cl). 96 RMN: René-Gabriel Ojéda (tr). 97 akg-images: (c). Alamy Images: The London Art Archive (bc). Corbis: Nik Wheeler (bl). 98 The Bridgeman Art Library: Musee de l'Homme, Paris, France (bl). 99 The Bridgeman Art Library: Private Collection/Roger Perrin (cr). Corbis: A & J Verkaik (bl). 100 The Art Archive: Musée Condé Chantilly/Gianni Dagli Orti. 101 The Art Archive: Musée du Louvre Paris/Gianni Dagli Orti (t). Werner Forman Archive: Museo Nazionale Romano, Rome (b). 102 Werner Forman Archive: Euan Wingfield (r). 103 akg-images: Erich Lessing (t). Corbis: James Chen (c); Kazuyoshi Nomachi (bc). 105 The Art Archive: Bodleian Library Oxford (br); Musée Condé Chantilly/Gianni Dagli Orti (bl); British Library (c). 106 Ancient Art & Architecture Collection: B. Wilson (cr). Mary Evans Picture Library: (cl). 107 Werner Forman Archive: Musee Royal de L'Afrique Centrale, Tervuren, Belgium (tl). 108 Robert Harding Picture Library: Jochen Schlenker (cl). 109 Alamy Images: Craig Lovell/Eagle Visions Photography (r, br). 110 RMN: Christian Larrieu (tr). 111 Getty Images: Willard Clay (bl). Werner Forman Archive: Nick Saunders (cl). 112 Corbis: Araldo de Luca. 114 The Art Archive: Rijksmuseum voor Volkenkunde Leiden (Leyden)/Dagli Orti. 115 Werner Forman Archive: (b); Theresa McCullough Collection (t). 117 Alamy Images: ArkReligion. com (tr). Corbis: Hans Georg Roth (bl). Courtesy of The Schøyen Collection, Oslo and London: (br). 118 The Trustees of the British Museum: (tl). Dreamstime.com: Drbouz (bc). 119 Dorling Kindersley: National Museum, New Delhi/Andy Crawford (br). Dreamstime.com: Paul Prescott (c). 120 The Bridgeman Art Library: Victoria & Albert Museum, London, UK. 121 The Bridgeman Art Library: Victoria & Albert Museum, London, UK. 122 akg-images: Ullstein Bild (c). The Bridgeman Art Library: Victoria & Albert Museum, London, UK (bl). 123 The Bridgeman Art Library: Bibliotheque Nationale, Paris, France/Archives Charmet (b). Dorling Kindersley: Derek Hall (tl). 124 Dorling Kindersley: National Museum, New Delhi (bl). 125 Corbis: Luca Tettoni (br). Dorling Kindersley: Crafts Museum, New Delhi/Akhil Bakshi (tl). 126 www. dinodia.com: (bc). 127 Alamy Images: Interfoto Pressebildagentur (tr). The Bridgeman Art Library: Private Collection/Archives Charmet (cl). Corbis: Ajay Verma/Reuters (br). 128 China Tourism Photo Library: (tl). 129 China Tourism Photo Library: (b, t). 130 Mary Evans Picture Library: (bl). 131 China Tourism Photo Library: (t). Corbis: Earl & Nazima Kowall (tr). 132 Ancient Art & Architecture Collection: Uniphoto (tr). 133 China Tourism Photo Library: (br, tl). 135 Ancient Art & Architecture Collection: Uniphoto (br, cl, cr). 136 Corbis: Peter Harholdt (cr). 137 Corbis: Asian Art & Archaeology, Inc. (cr); Demetrio Carrasco/JAI (t). 138 © The Trustees

of the Chester Beatty Library, Dublin. (tr). 139 Alamy Images: Japan Art Collection (br); JTB Photo Communications, Inc. (bl). 140 Ancient Art & Architecture Collection. 142 Werner Forman Archive. 143 Ancient Art & Architecture Collection: (b). Corbis: Sandro Vannini (t). 144 Mary Evans Picture Library: (c). 145 Getty Images: Richard Nowitz (cr). Werner Forman Archive: (b); Egyptian Museum, Cairo (cl). 146 The Bridgeman Art Library: British Museum. 147 The Bridgeman Art Library: British Museum (c). 148 Ancient Art & Architecture Collection: P. Syder (t). Werner Forman Archive: Egyptian Museum, Cairo (b). 149 Ancient Art & Architecture Collection: (cl, br). 150 Dorling Kindersley: John Hepver/The British Museum (br). 151 Ancient Art & Architecture Collection: (tc, bc). Werner Forman Archive: (clb). 152 Werner Forman Archive: Museum fur Volkerkunde, Berlin. 153 Werner Forman Archive: British Museum, London (b); Private Collection, New York (t). 154 Alamy Images: Suzy Bennett (b). Werner Forman Archive: Entwistle Gallery, London (tr). 155 Werner Forman Archive: (bl). 156 The Art Archive: Antenna Gallery Dakar Senegal/Gianni Dagli Orti (tl). 158 Corbis: Frédéric Soltan (t). 159 akg-images: British Library (tl). The Art Archive: Royal Palace Caserta Italy/Gianni Dagli Orti (br). 160 Dorling Kindersley: Judith Miller Image Archive. 161 akg-images: Erich Lessing (b). Werner Forman Archive: Entwistle Gallery, London (cr). 162 Corbis: Anthony Bannister/Gallo Images (br). Werner Forman Archive: (tr). 164 akg-images: Erich Lessing (c). Dorling Kindersley: Pitt Rivers Museum, University of Oxford (bl). 165 Alamy Images: Interfoto Pressebildagentur (tr). Corbis: Peter Adams (br). Dorling Kindersley: David Garner/Exeter City Museums and Art Gallery (cl). Werner Forman Archive: Kasmin Collection (tl). 166 The Bridgeman Art Library: British Museum. 167 Corbis: Michele Burgess (c). Dorling Kindersley: Powell-Cotton Museum, Kent (b). 168 Alamy Images: Images of Africa Photobank (b). Robert Estall Photo Agency (t). 169 Alamy Images: Frantisek Staud (bl). Images of Africa Photobank (c). 170 Getty Images: Volkmar Wentzel (t). 171 Ancient Art & Architecture Collection: Dorling Kindersley: Pitt Rivers Museum, University of Oxford (c). 172 Alamy Images: Ariadne Van Zandbergen (cr); Timothy O'Keefe (bl). 174 Werner Forman Archive: Pigorini Museum of Prehistory and Ethnography, Rome. 176 Werner Forman Archive: Haffenreffer Museum of Anthropology, Brown University, Rhode Island, USA. 177 Getty Images: Melissa Farlow (b). Werner Forman Archive: Sheldon Jackson Museum, Sitka, Alaska (c). 178 Corbis: James Sparshatt (b). 179 Corbis: Geoffrey Clements (b). Werner Forman Archive: Schimmel Collection, New York (br). 180 Werner Forman Archive: Glenbow Museum, Calgary, Alberta,USA (c). 181 Science Photo Library: Science Source (b). Werner Forman Archive: Field Museum of Natural History, Chicago (c). 182 Werner Forman Archive. 183 Photo SCALA, Florence: (b). Werner Forman Archive: Liverpool Museum (c). 184 Alamy Images: Mary Evans Picture Library (cb). 185 The

Bridgeman Art Library: Museo Arqueologico, Mexico City, Mexico (c). Werner Forman Archive: David Bernstein, New York (cl). 186 The Bridgeman Art Library: Worcester Art Museum, Massachusetts, USA (br). Werner Forman Archive: Dallas Museum of Art (c). 187 Alamy Images: Deborah Waters (br). Ancient Art & Architecture Collection: Dr. S. Coyne (cr). 188 Alamy Images: imagebroker (tl). The Bridgeman Art Library: Musee de l'Homme, Paris, France (bl). 189 Ancient Art & Architecture Collection: (br). Werner Forman Archive: British Museum, London (tl). 190 Corbis: Robert Holmes. 191 The Bridgeman Art Library: Musee de l'Homme, Paris, France (b). Werner Forman Archive: (cr). 192 Corbis: Stephanie Maze (cr). 193 Alamy Images: Banana Pancake (bl). Corbis: Tom Walker (ca). 194 Corbis: Les Stone/Zuma (cr). 195 Alamy Images: Mary Evans Picture Library (tr). TopFoto.co.uk: Tony Savino/The Image Works (br). 196 Alamy Images: Deco. 197 Werner Forman Archive: (b). 198 Alamy Images: Mireille Vautier (tr); North Wind Picture Archives (b). 199 Ancient Art & Architecture Collection: (c). Dorling Kindersley: Sean Hunter (t). Wikipedia: (br). 200 The Art Archive: Alfredo Dagli Orti (bc). Werner Forman Archive: David Bernstein, New York (cr). 201 Ancient Art & Architecture Collection: (c). Corbis: Kazuyoshi Nomachi (tr). 202 The Trustees of the British Museum. 204 Ancient Art & Architecture Collection: 205 Ancient Art & Architecture Collection: (t). Werner Forman Archive: (c). 206 Alamy Images: Penny Tweedie (bc). The Bridgeman Art Library: Corbally Stourton Contemporary Art, Australia (t). 207 Corbis: Michael & Patricia Fogden (b). Getty Images: Hulton Archive (tr). 208 RMN: Hervé Lewandowski (r). 209 Alamy Images: Horizon International Images Limited (br). Werner Forman Archive: (tr). 210 Corbis: Penny Tweedie (br). 211 Corbis: Takashi Katahira (tr). Werner Forman Archive: (br, tl). 212 Corbis: Ric Ergenbright. 213 Ancient Art & Architecture Collection: (bl). Werner Forman Archive: (c). 214 The Bridgeman Art Library: British Museum, London, UK/Peter Willi (tr). 215 Werner Forman Archive: British Museum, London (clb). 217 Werner Forman Archive: Museum fur Volkerkunde, Berlin (br). Otago Museum, Dunedin (tr).

Jacket images: Front and Back: iStockphoto.com: Bülent Gültek (background). Front: Alamy Images: Interfoto Pressebildagentur (cr); Christine Osborne Pictures tc; David Sanger Photography br/Harbuz. Corbis: Randy Faris ftr. Getty Images: Richard Ross fbr; Randy Wells tr. iStockphoto.com: AF-studio (top band). TopFoto.co.uk: 2006 Alinari tl. Back: Alamy Images: bygonetimes tl; Mary Evans Picture Library tc; David Sanger Photography tr. iStockphoto. com: AF-studio (top band).

All other images © Dorling Kindersley For further information see: www.dkimages.com

DK would like to thank Sarah Tomley; Camilla Hallinan; Richard Horsford; Elizabeth O'Neil; Alicia Ingty; Chuck Wills; Caroline Hunt for proofreading; and Hilary Bird for the index.